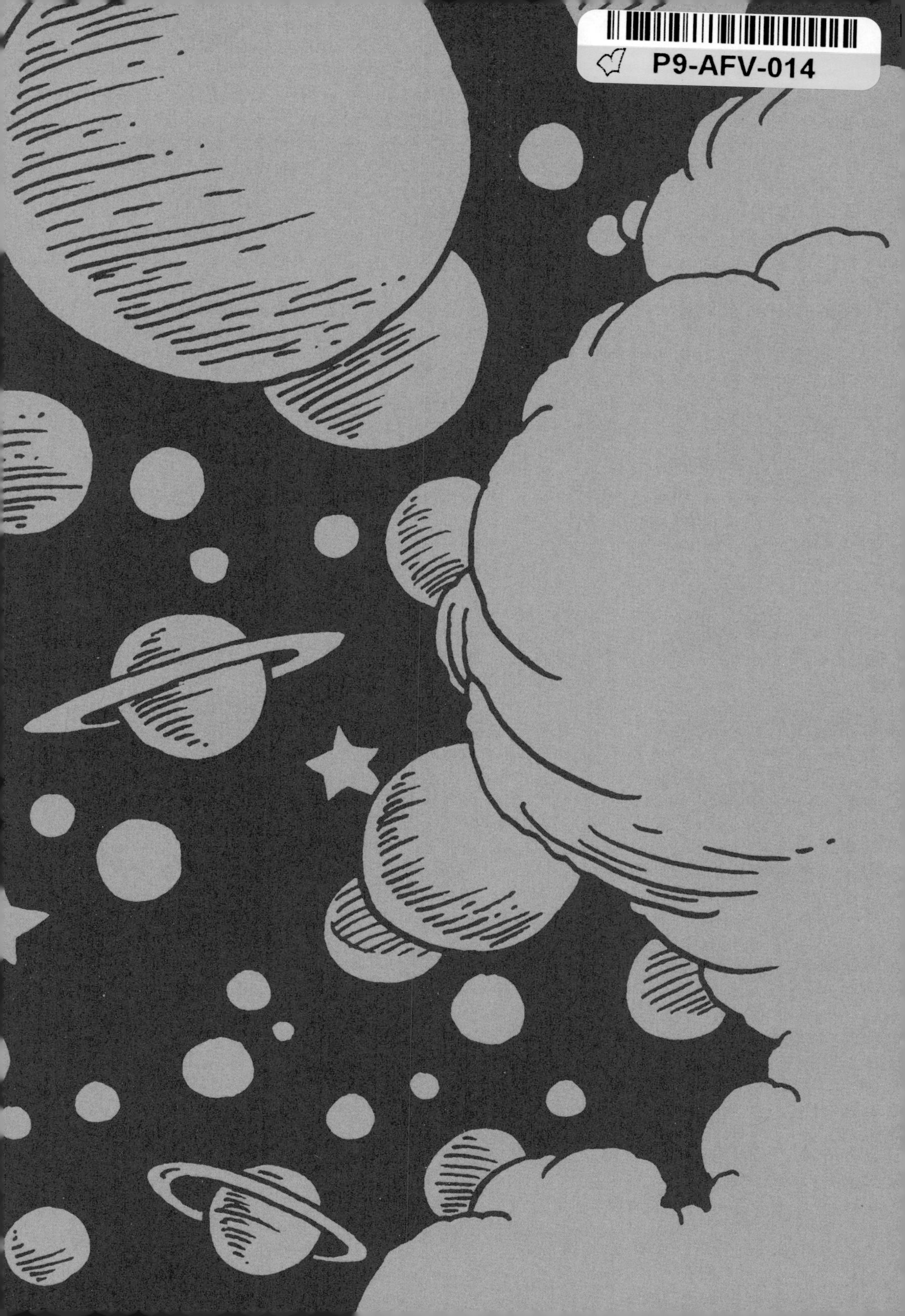

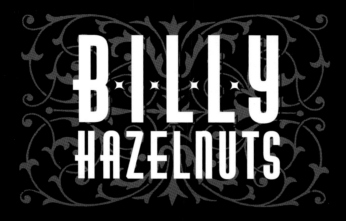

BILLY HAZELNUTS

AND THE

CRAZY BIRD

Tony Millionaire

FANTAGRAPHICS BOOKS
7563 Lake City Way
Seattle, WA 98115

Editorial Liaison:
GARY GROTH

Book Design:
JACOB COVEY

Associate Publisher:
ERIC REYNOLDS

Publishers:
GARY GROTH &
KIM THOMPSON

 For a free full-color catalogue of comics and cartooning, including more books by MR. MILLIONAIRE, call 1-800-657-1100. Our many books may be viewed and also purchased on our worldwide web site at www.fantagraphics.com.

First Fantagraphics Books edition: April 2010.

ISBN 978-1-56097-917-3

Printed in Singapore.

Go soon to www.tonymillionaire.com.

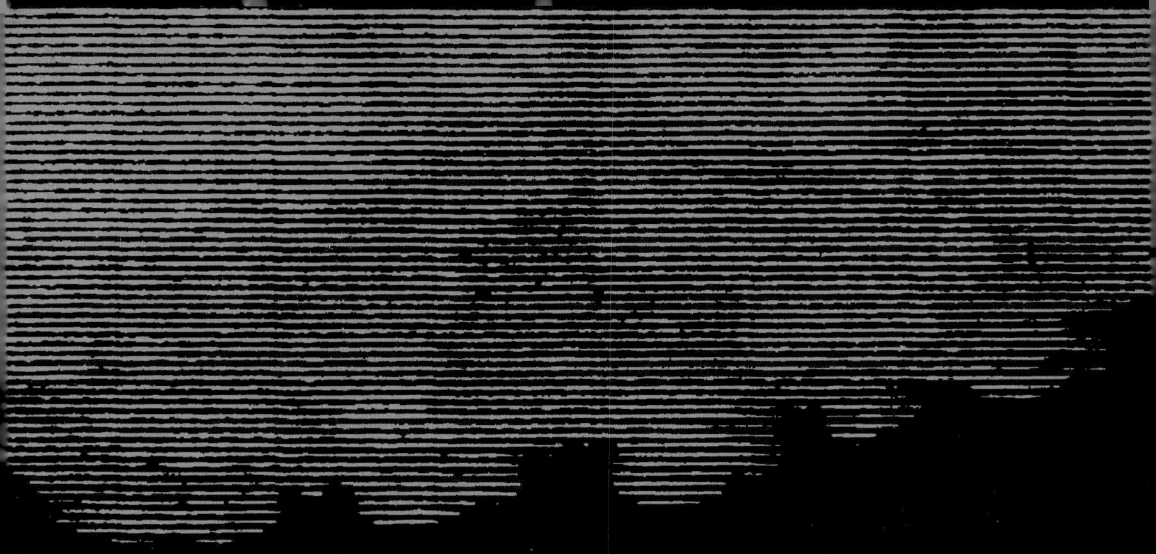

For

PHOEBE

and

PEARL

Chapter One

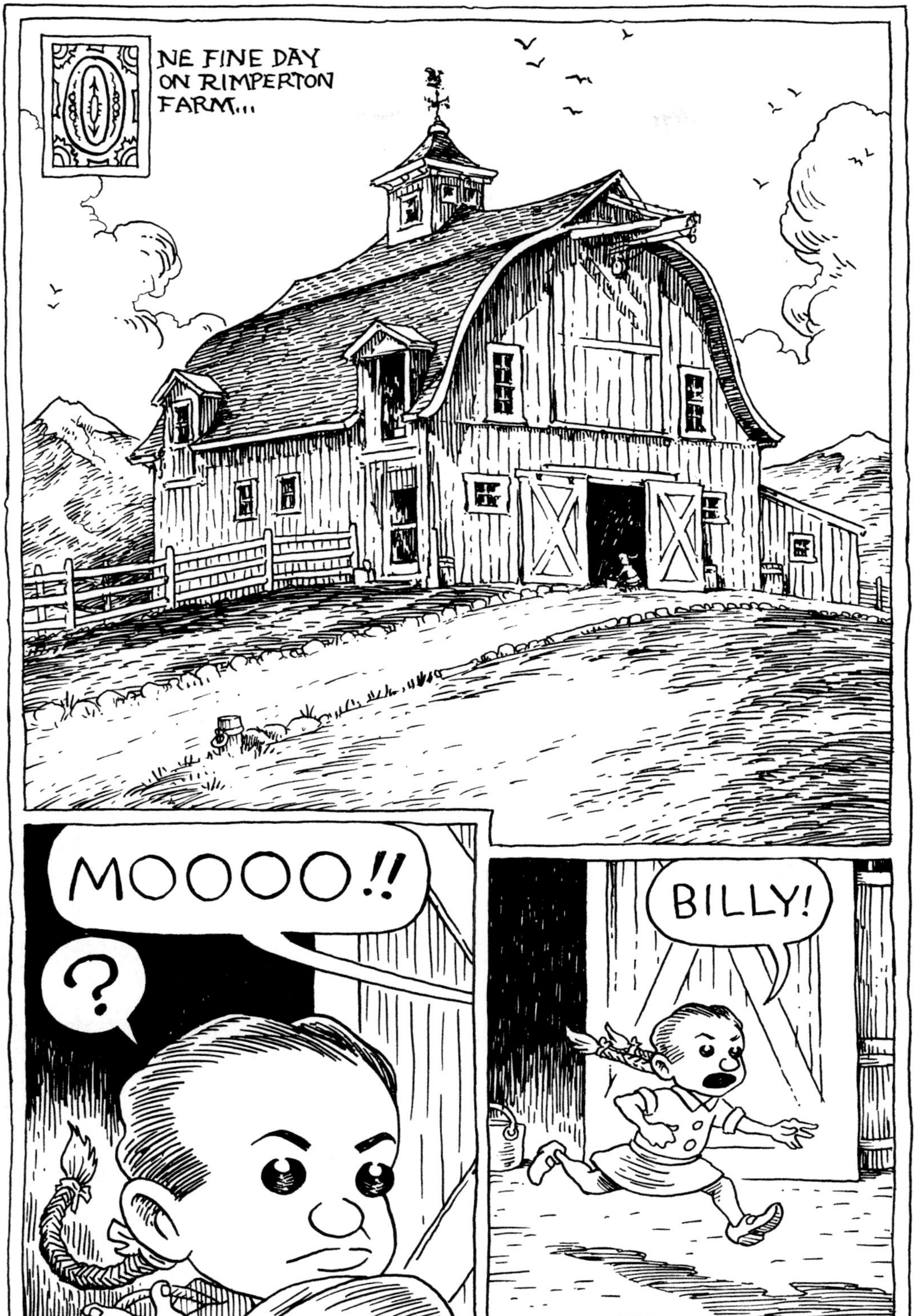
ONE FINE DAY ON RIMPERTON FARM...
MOOOO!!
?
BILLY!

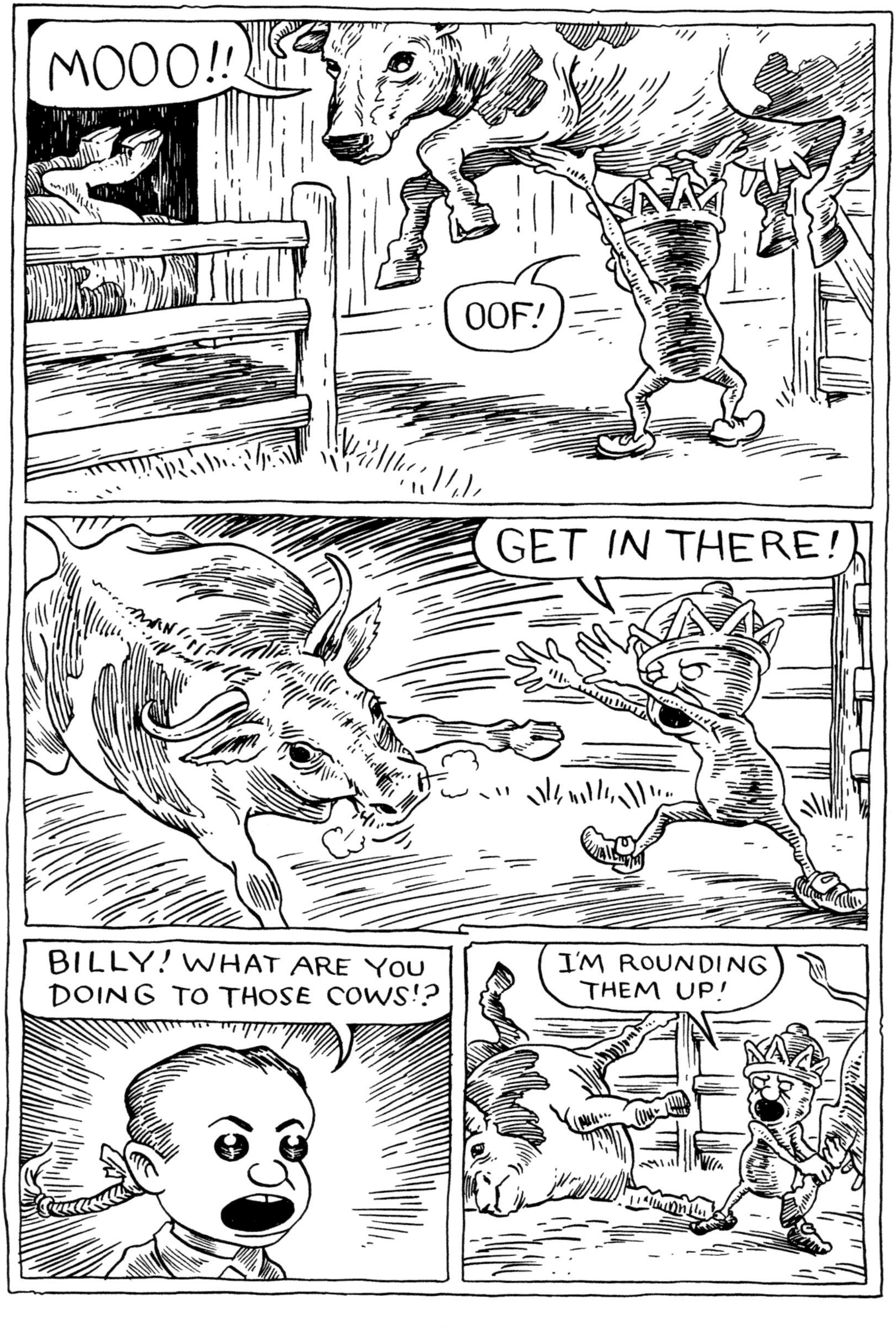
MOOO!!
OOF!
GET IN THERE!
BILLY! WHAT ARE YOU DOING TO THOSE COWS!?
I'M ROUNDING THEM UP!

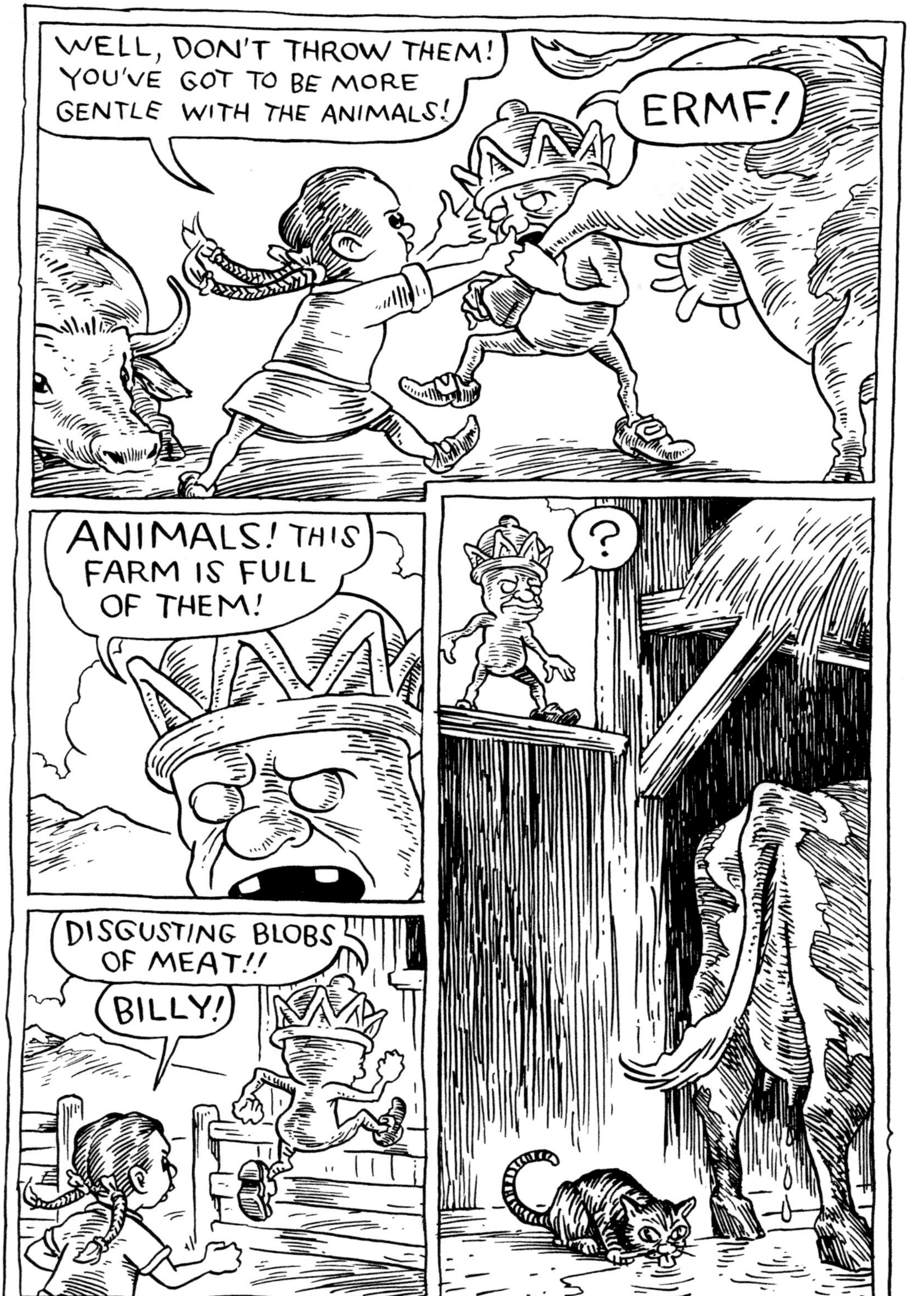
WELL, DON'T THROW THEM! YOU'VE GOT TO BE MORE GENTLE WITH THE ANIMALS!
ERMF!
ANIMALS! THIS FARM IS FULL OF THEM!
DISGUSTING BLOBS OF MEAT!!
BILLY!
?

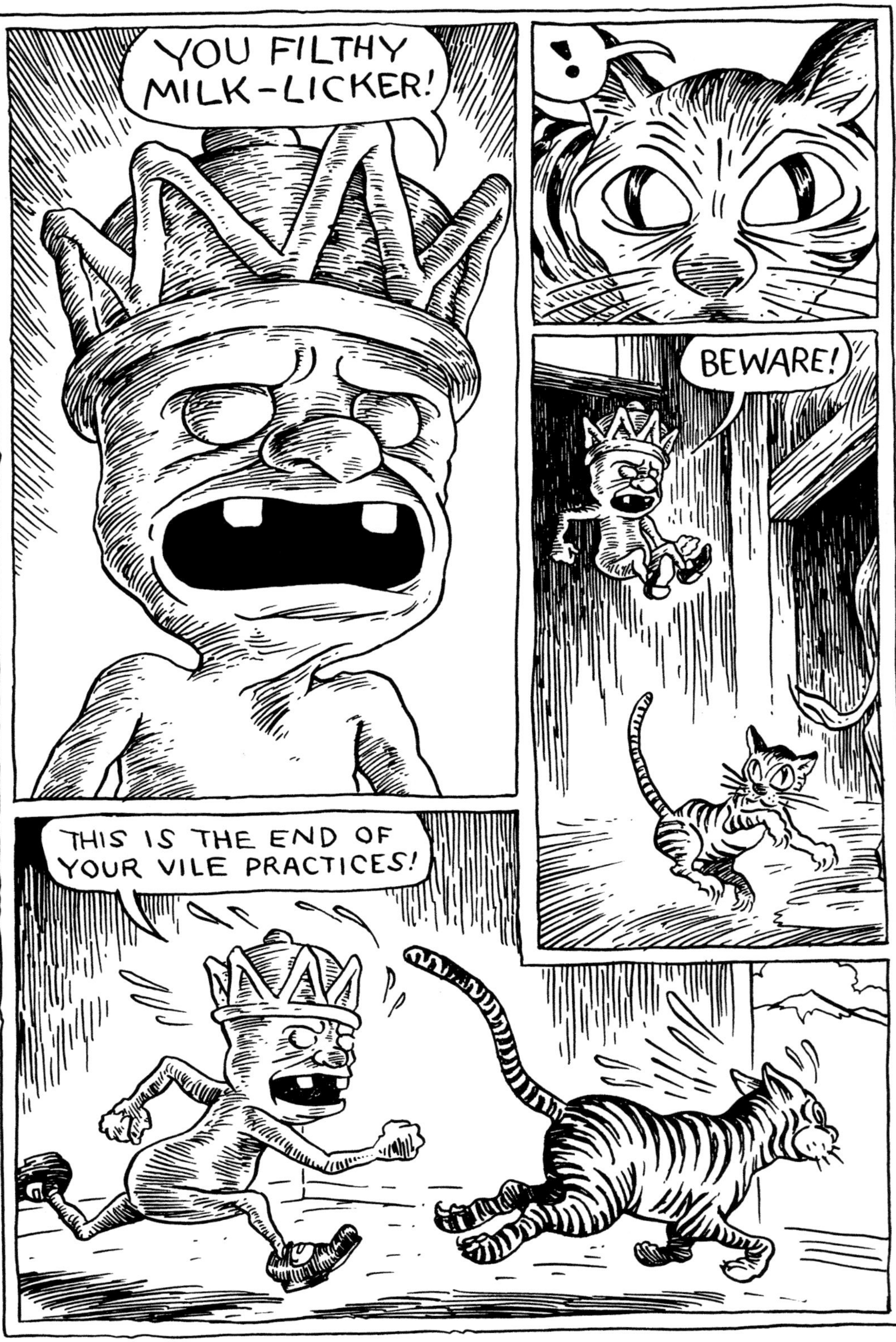
YOU FILTHY MILK-LICKER!
!
BEWARE!
THIS IS THE END OF YOUR VILE PRACTICES!

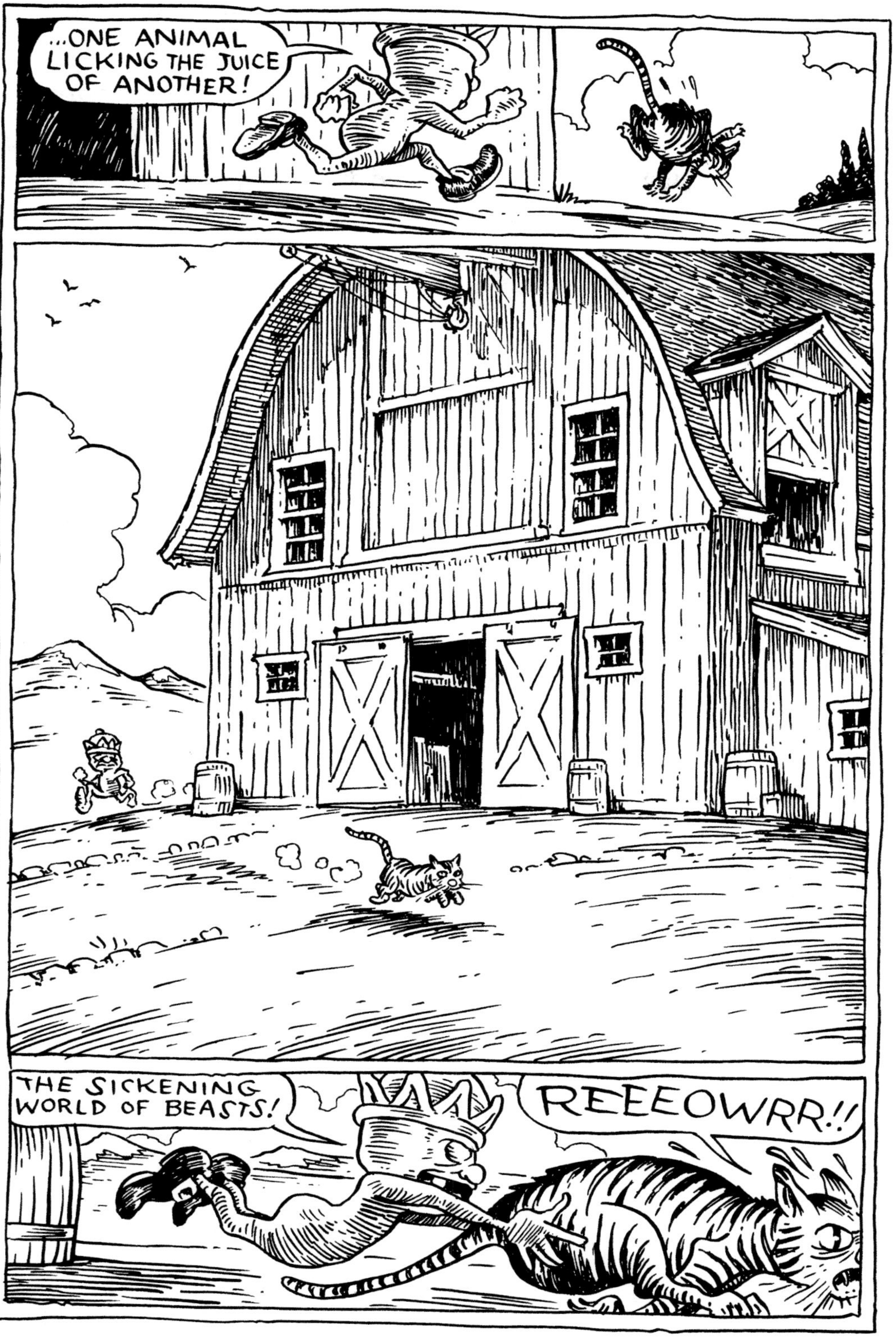
...ONE ANIMAL LICKING THE JUICE OF ANOTHER!
THE SICKENING WORLD OF BEASTS!
REEEOWRR!!

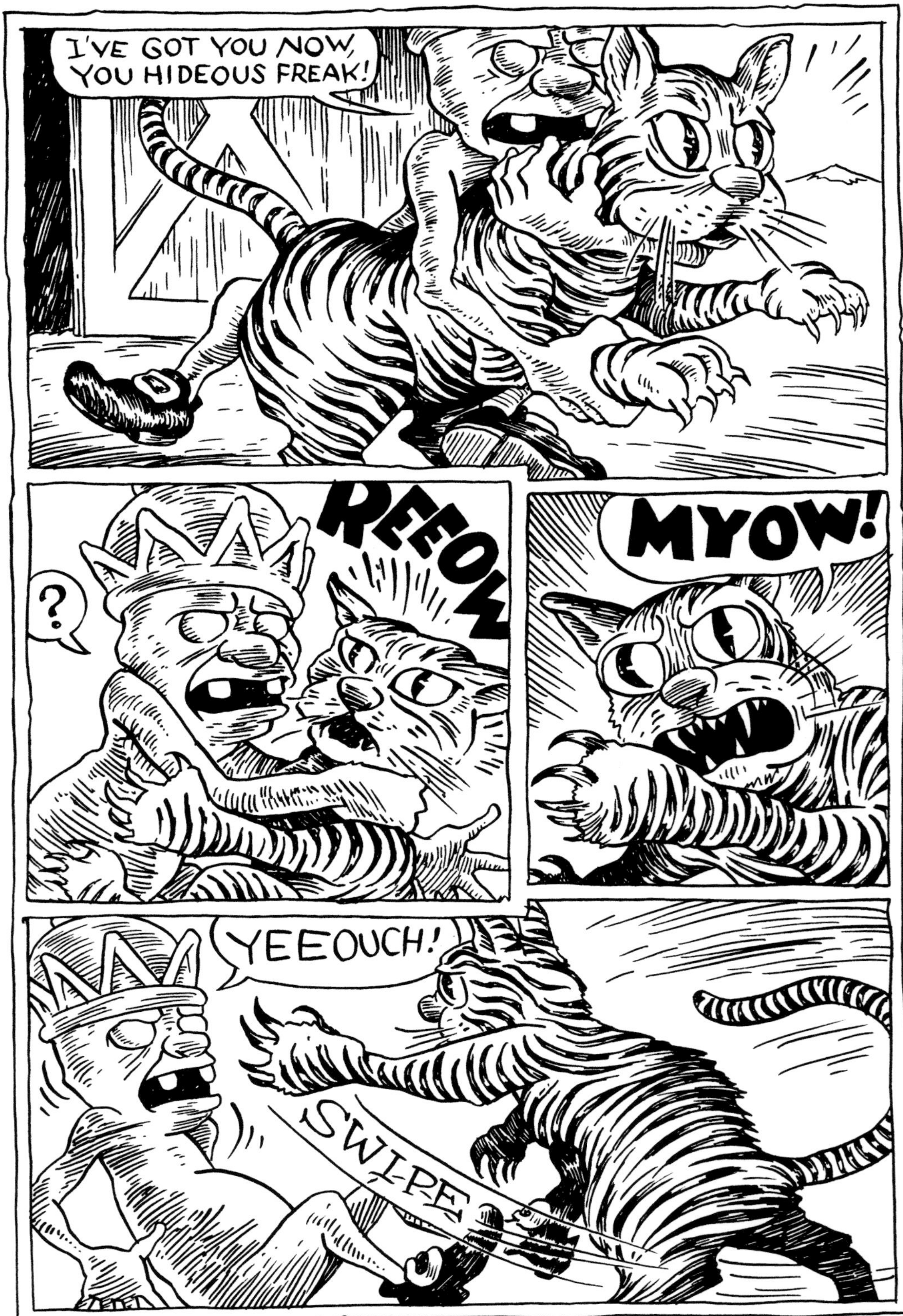
I'VE GOT YOU NOW, YOU HIDEOUS FREAK!
?
REEOW
MYOW!
YEEOUCH!
SWIPE

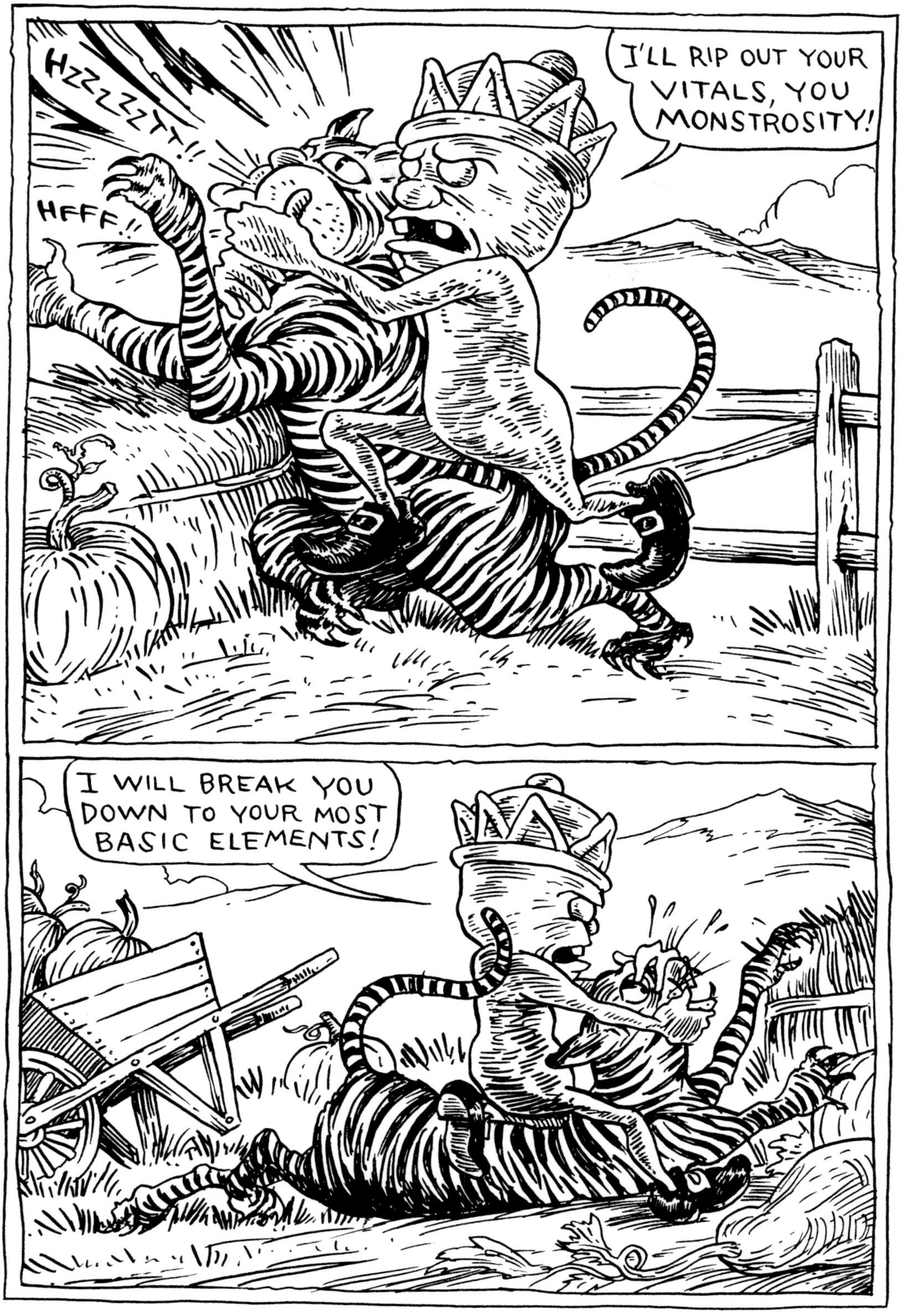
HZZZZZZZT!
HFFF!
I'LL RIP OUT YOUR VITALS, YOU MONSTROSITY!
I WILL BREAK YOU DOWN TO YOUR MOST BASIC ELEMENTS!

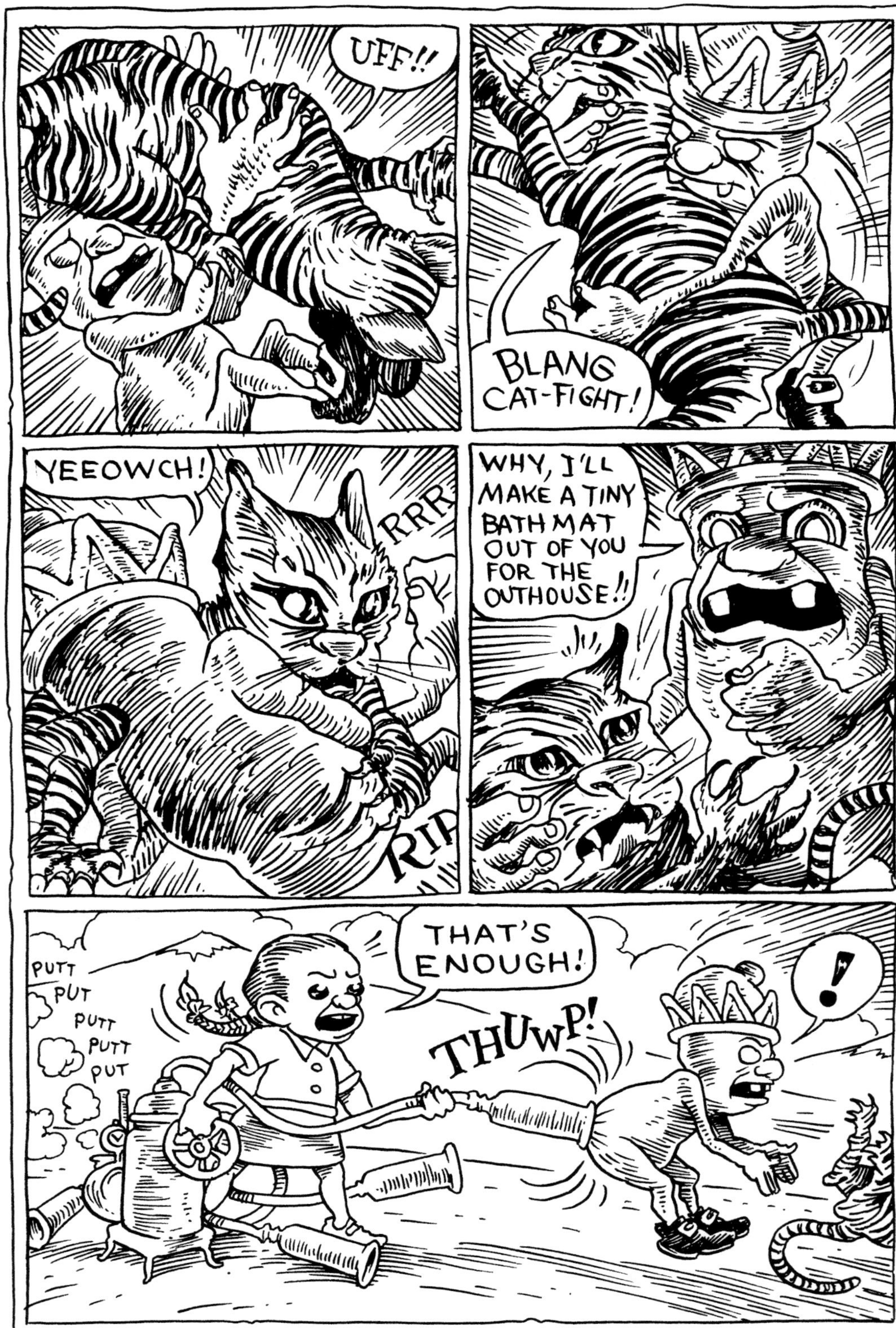
UFF!!
BLANG CAT-FIGHT!
YEEOWCH!
RRR
RIP
WHY, I'LL MAKE A TINY BATH MAT OUT OF YOU FOR THE OUTHOUSE!!
PUTT PUT PUTT PUTT PUT
THAT'S ENOUGH!
THWP!
!

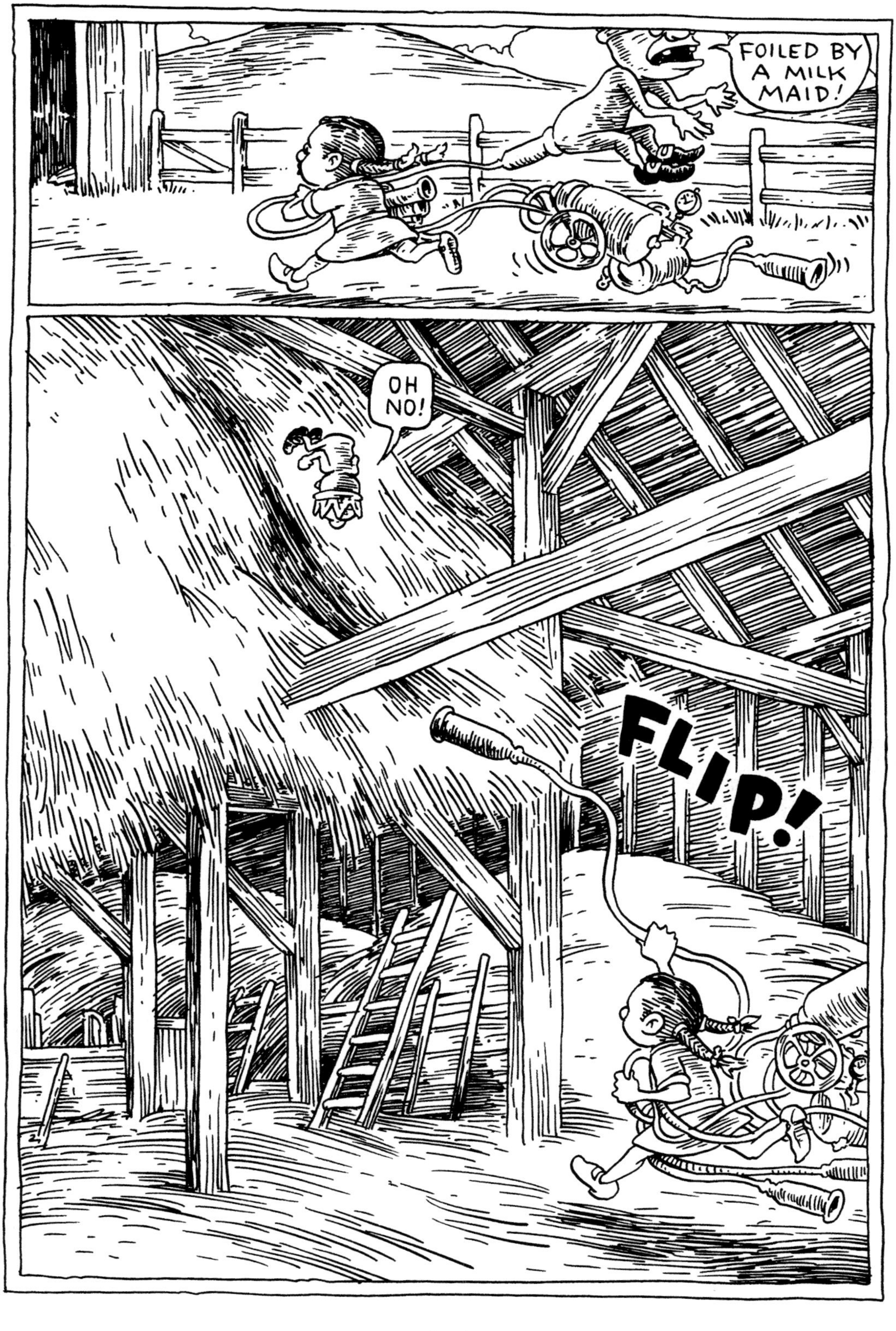
FOILED BY A MILK MAID!
OH NO!
FLIP!

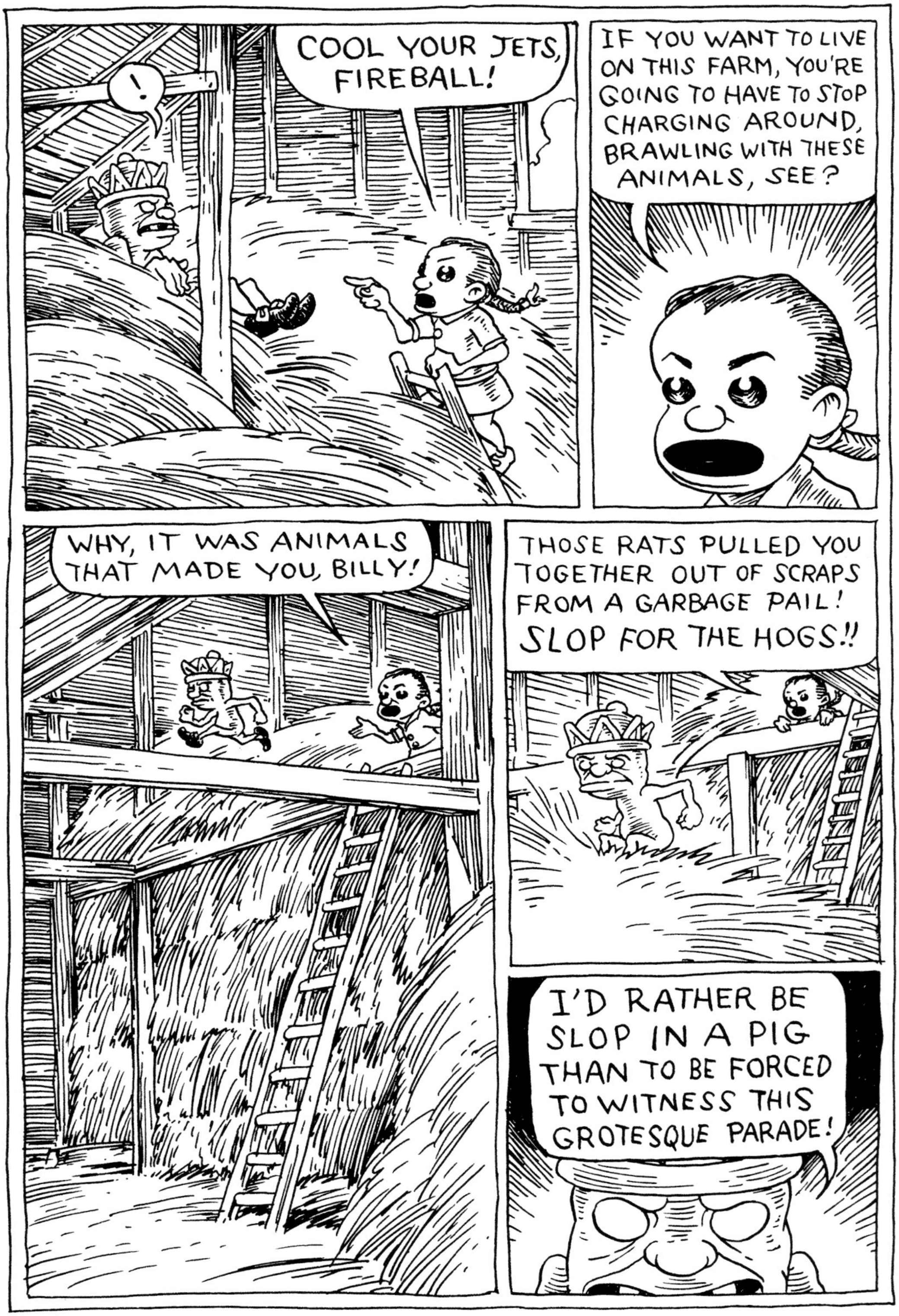
!
COOL YOUR JETS, FIREBALL!
IF YOU WANT TO LIVE ON THIS FARM, YOU'RE GOING TO HAVE TO STOP CHARGING AROUND, BRAWLING WITH THESE ANIMALS, SEE?
WHY, IT WAS ANIMALS THAT MADE YOU, BILLY!
THOSE RATS PULLED YOU TOGETHER OUT OF SCRAPS FROM A GARBAGE PAIL! SLOP FOR THE HOGS!!
I'D RATHER BE SLOP IN A PIG THAN TO BE FORCED TO WITNESS THIS GROTESQUE PARADE!

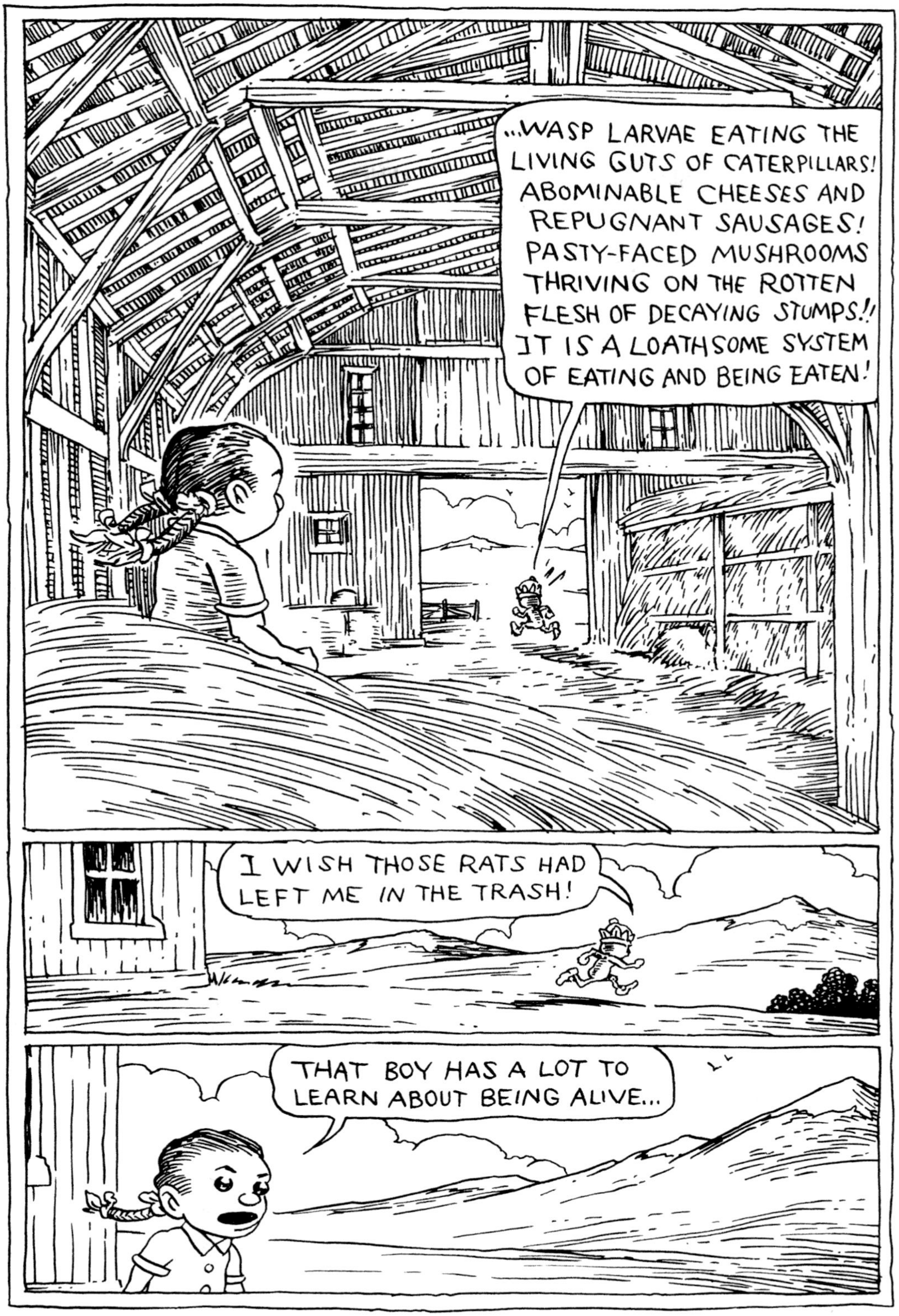
...WASP LARVAE EATING THE LIVING GUTS OF CATERPILLARS! ABOMINABLE CHEESES AND REPUGNANT SAUSAGES! PASTY-FACED MUSHROOMS THRIVING ON THE ROTTEN FLESH OF DECAYING STUMPS!! IT IS A LOATHSOME SYSTEM OF EATING AND BEING EATEN!
I WISH THOSE RATS HAD LEFT ME IN THE TRASH!
THAT BOY HAS A LOT TO LEARN ABOUT BEING ALIVE...

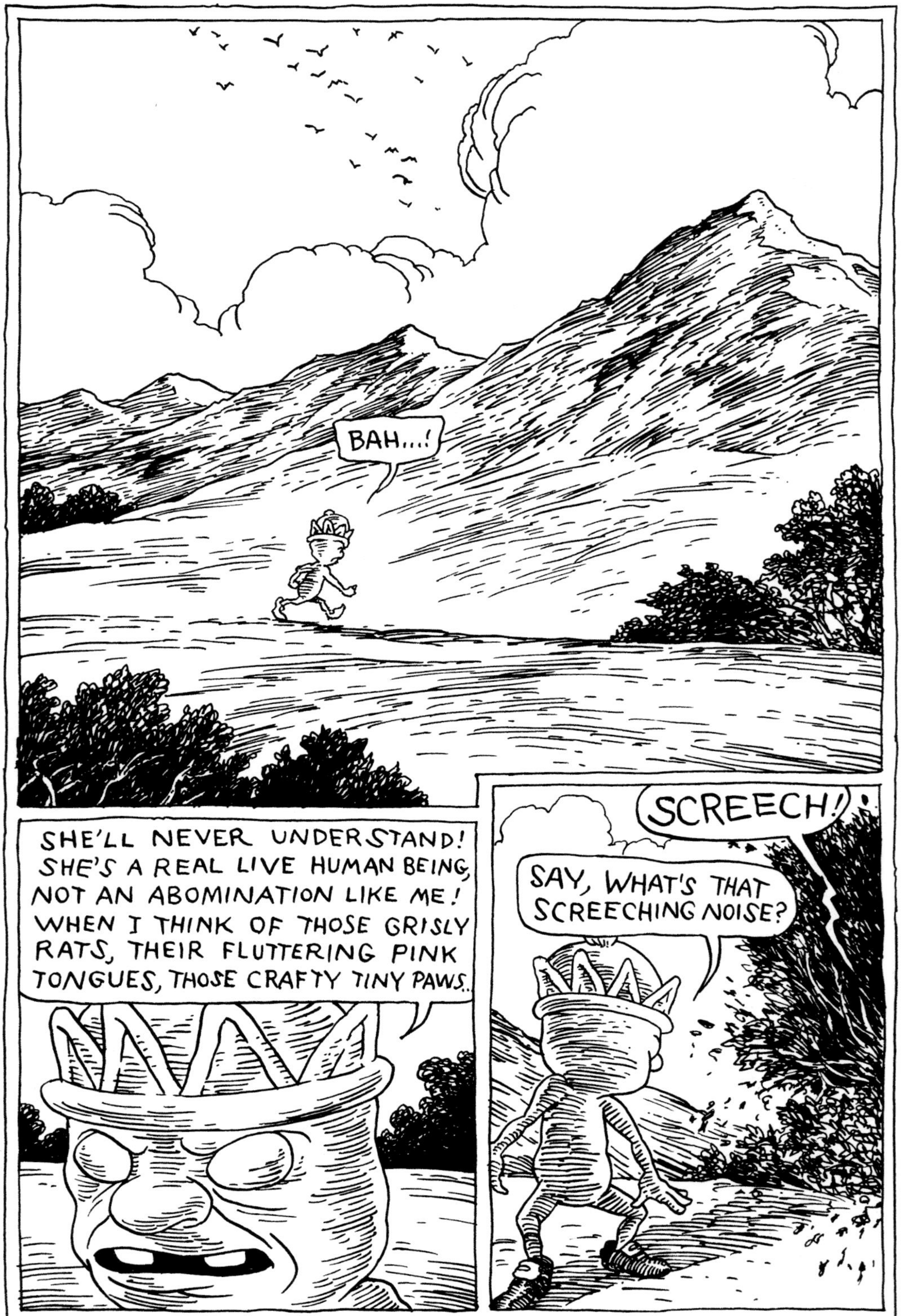

BAH...!
SHE'LL NEVER UNDERSTAND! SHE'S A REAL LIVE HUMAN BEING, NOT AN ABOMINATION LIKE ME! WHEN I THINK OF THOSE GRISLY RATS, THEIR FLUTTERING PINK TONGUES, THOSE CRAFTY TINY PAWS..
SCREECH!
SAY, WHAT'S THAT SCREECHING NOISE?

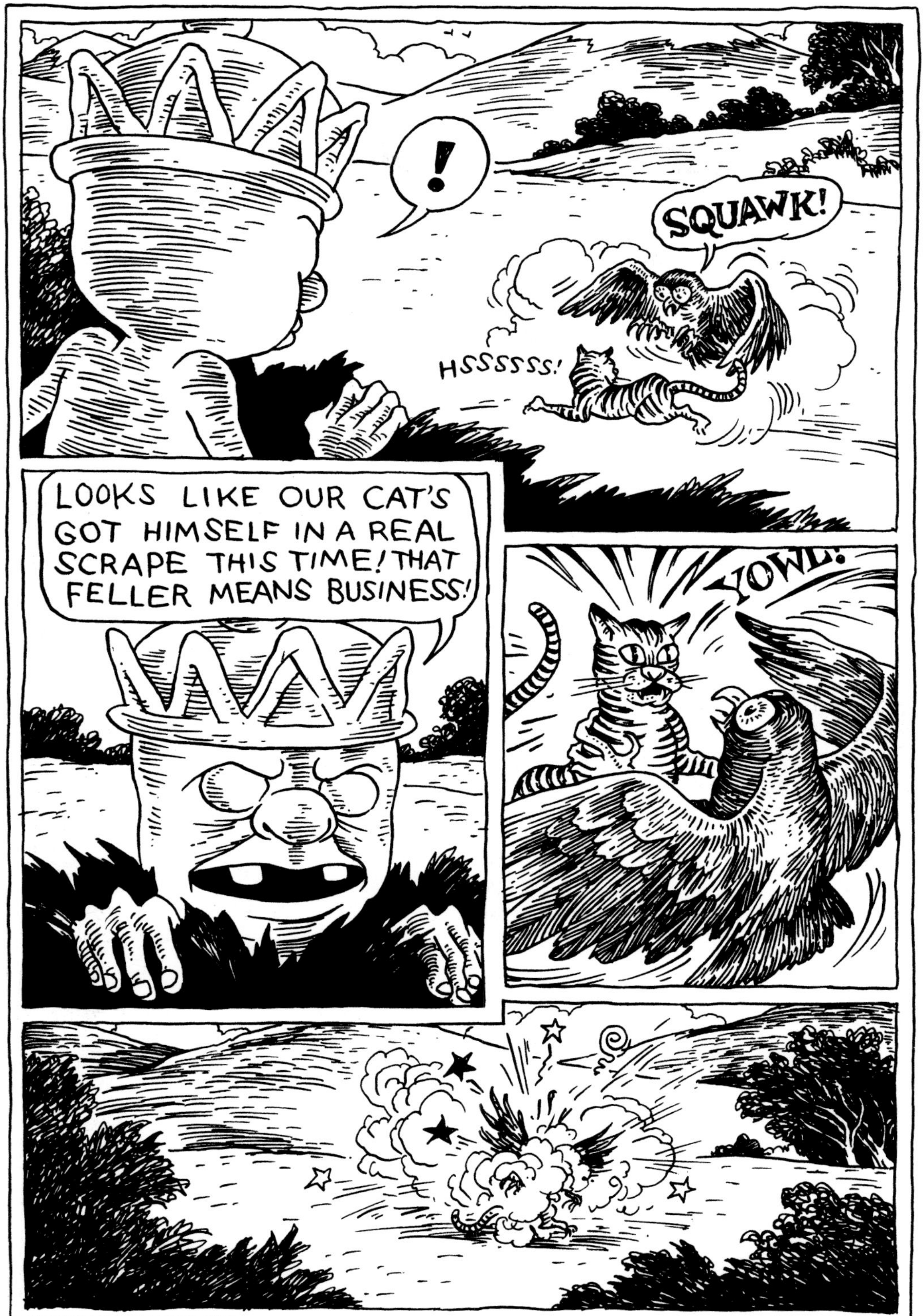
!
SQUAWK!
HSSSSSS!
LOOKS LIKE OUR CAT'S GOT HIMSELF IN A REAL SCRAPE THIS TIME! THAT FELLER MEANS BUSINESS!
YOWL!

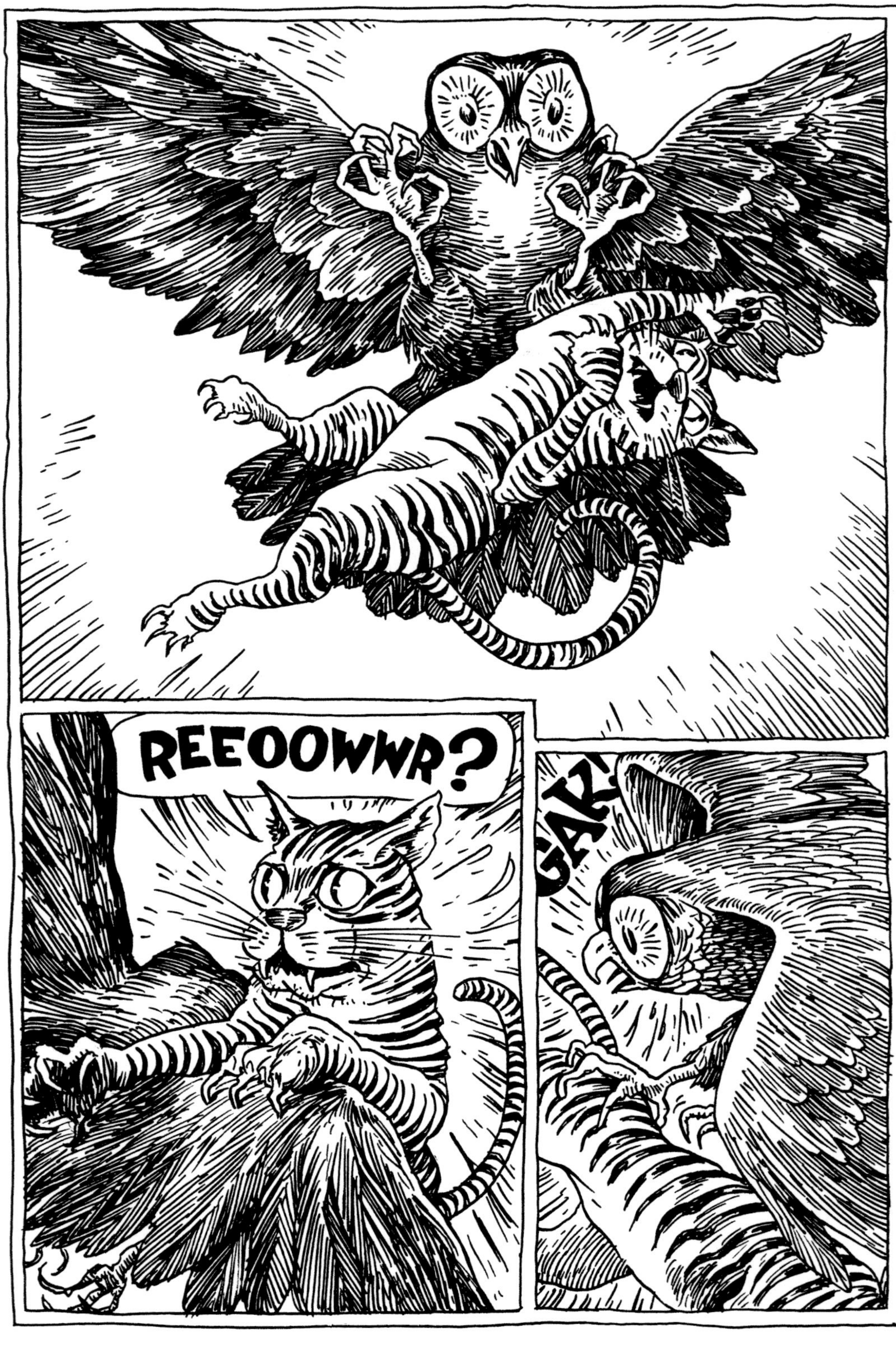
REEOOWWR?
GAK!

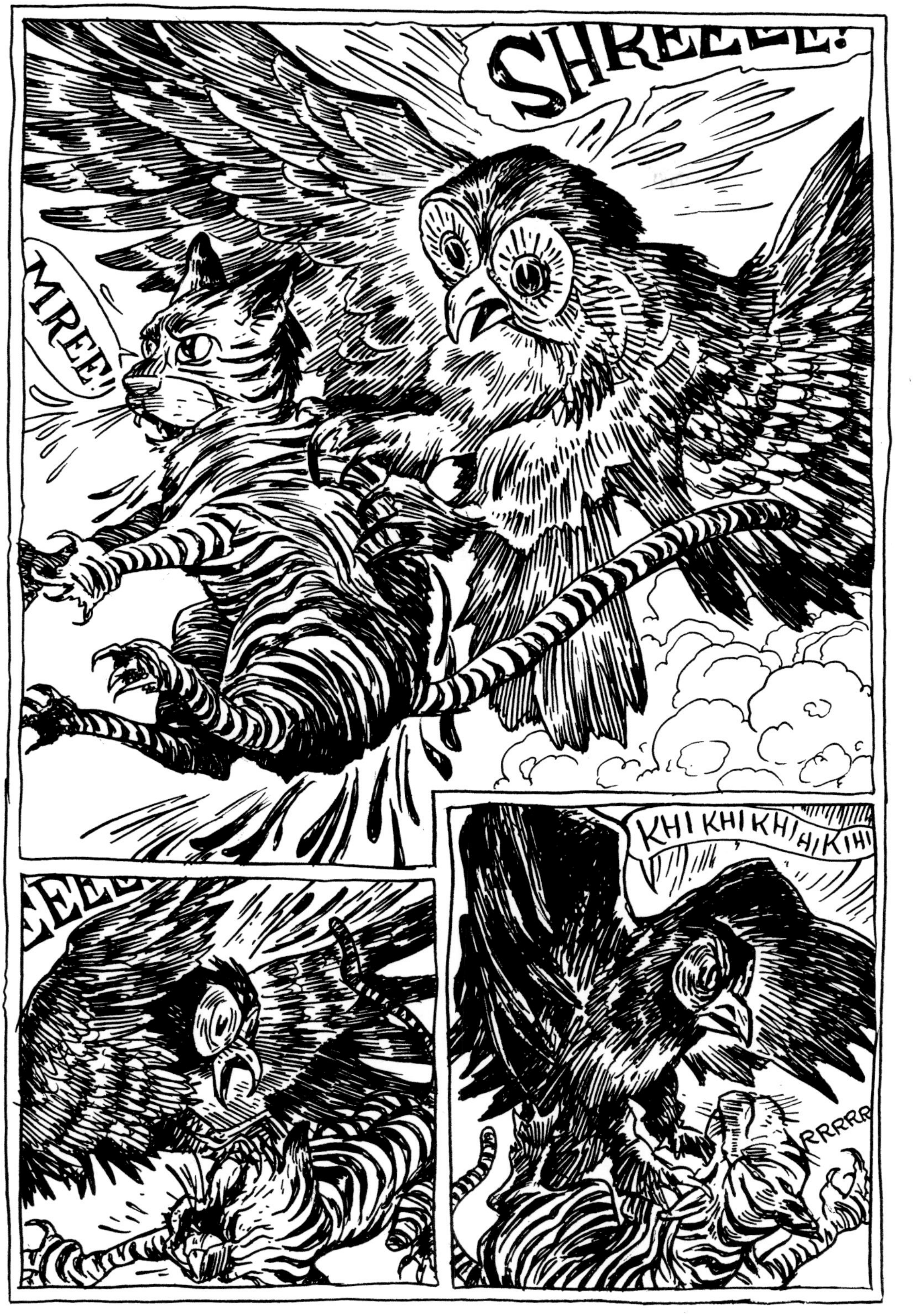
SHREEEE!
MREE!
EEEE
KHI KHI KHI HI KIHI
RRRRR

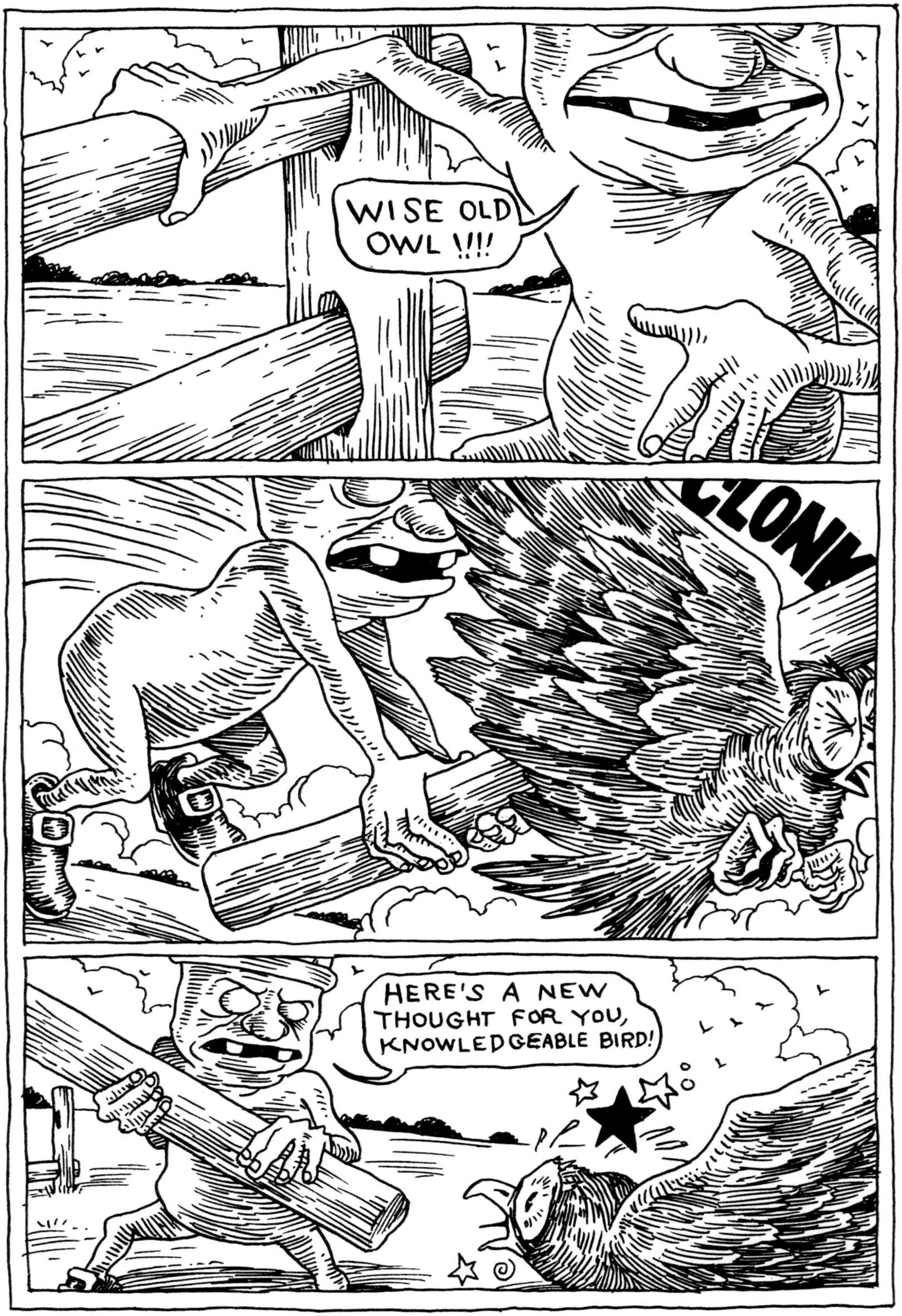
WISE OLD OWL !!!!
CLONK
HERE'S A NEW THOUGHT FOR YOU, KNOWLEDGEABLE BIRD!

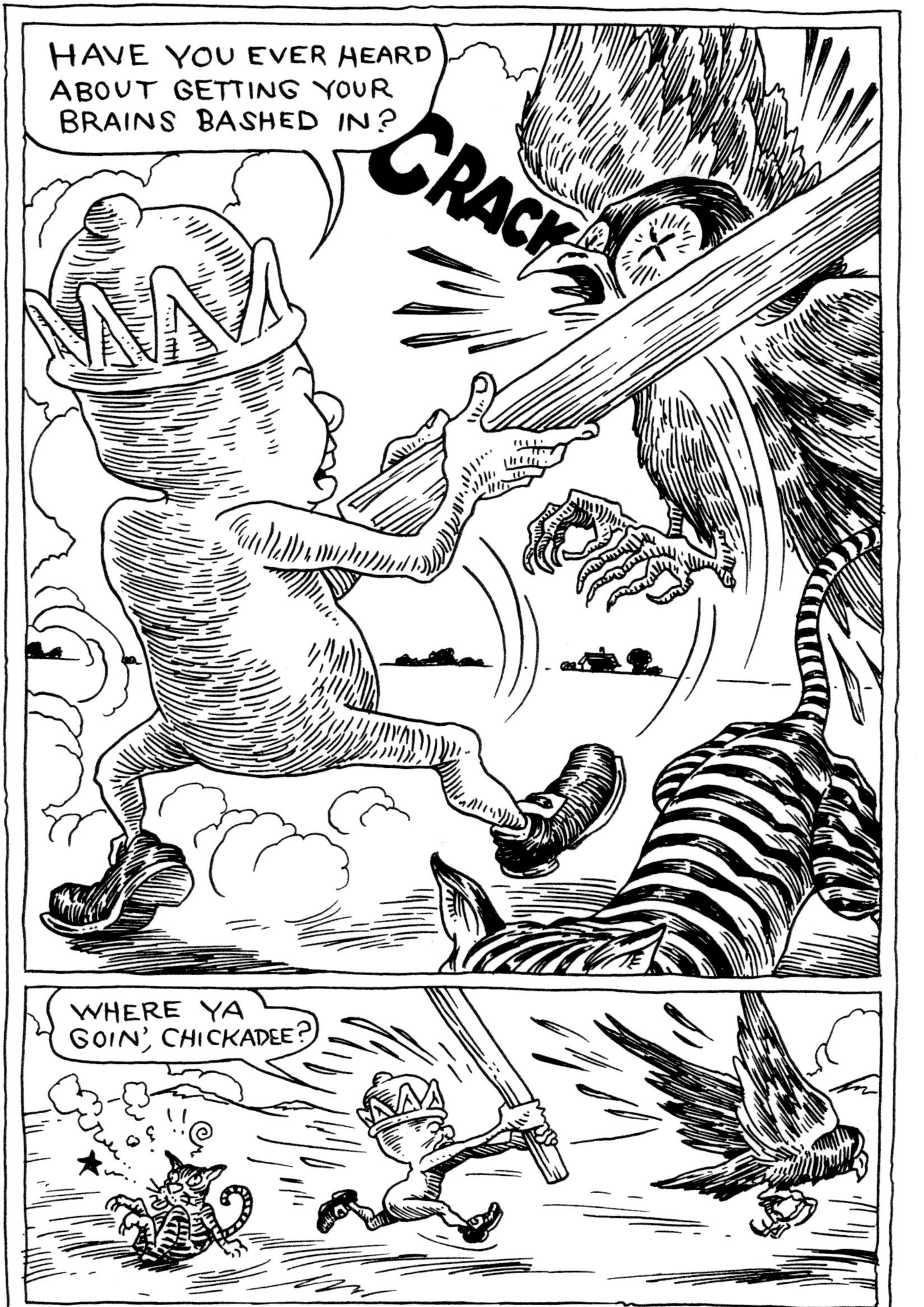
HAVE YOU EVER HEARD ABOUT GETTING YOUR BRAINS BASHED IN?
CRACK
WHERE YA GOIN', CHICKADEE?

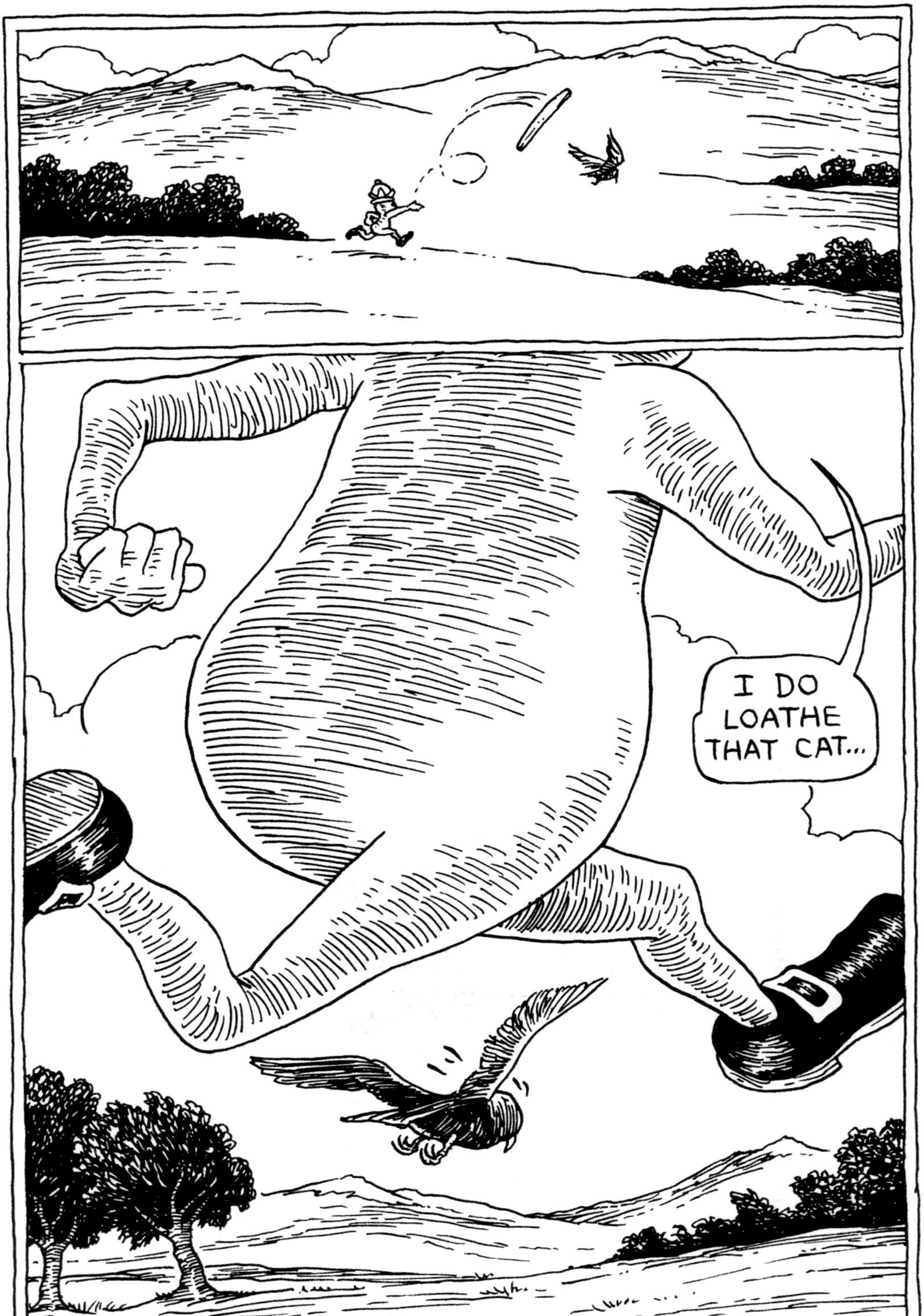
I DO
LOATHE
THAT CAT...

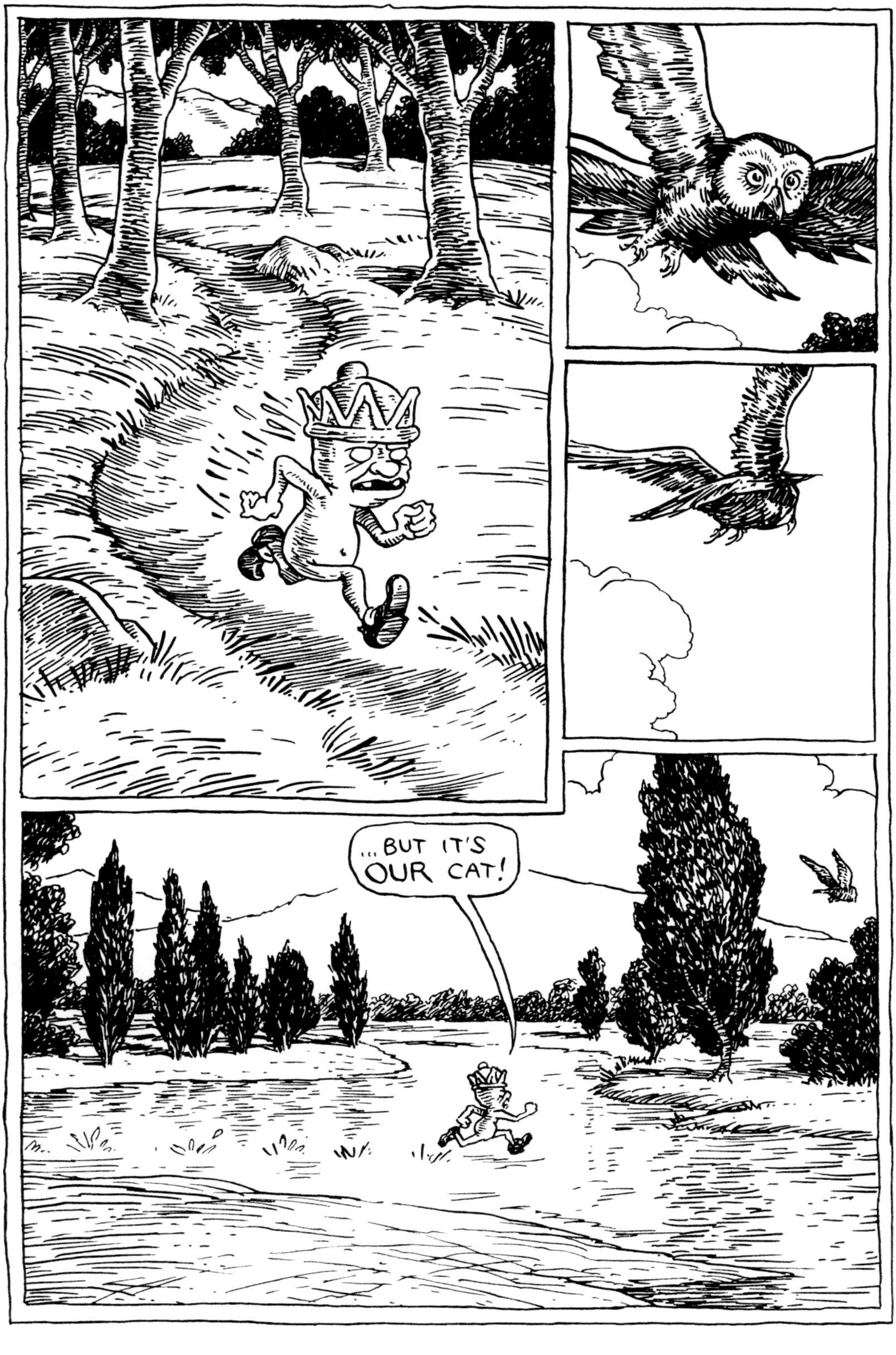
...BUT IT'S OUR CAT!

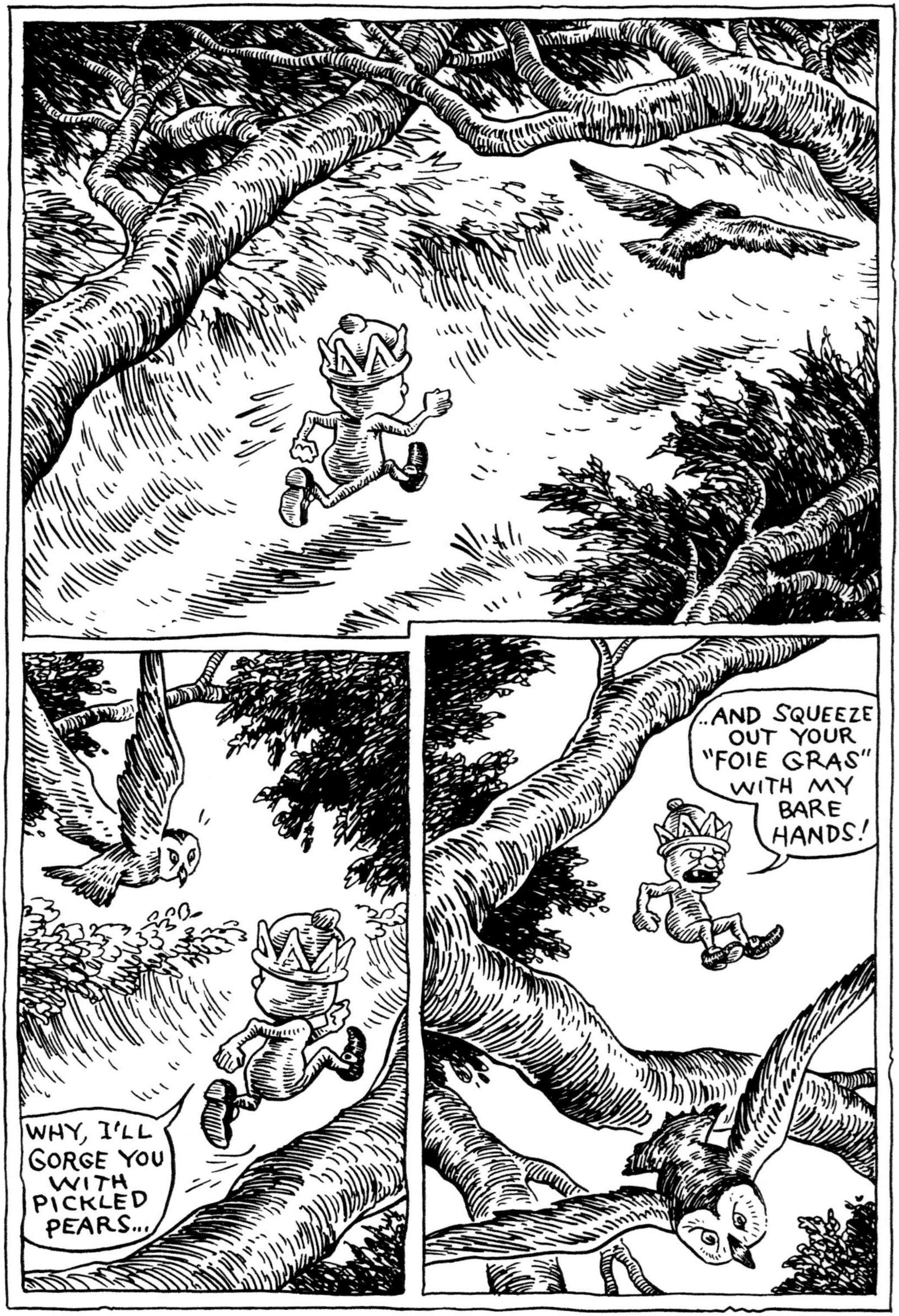
WHY, I'LL GORGE YOU WITH PICKLED PEARS...
..AND SQUEEZE OUT YOUR "FOIE GRAS" WITH MY BARE HANDS!

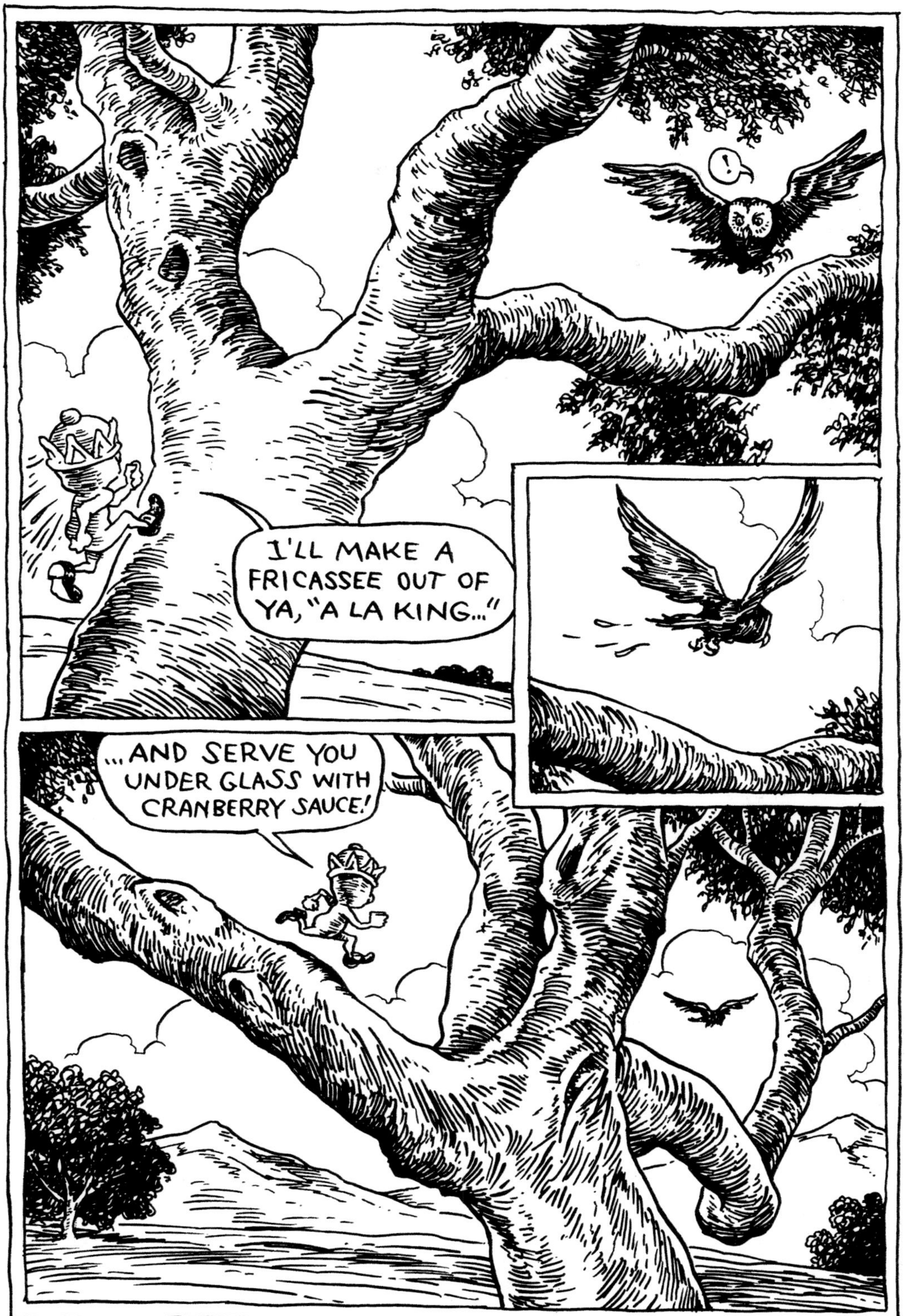
!
I'LL MAKE A FRICASSEE OUT OF YA, "A LA KING..."
...AND SERVE YOU UNDER GLASS WITH CRANBERRY SAUCE!

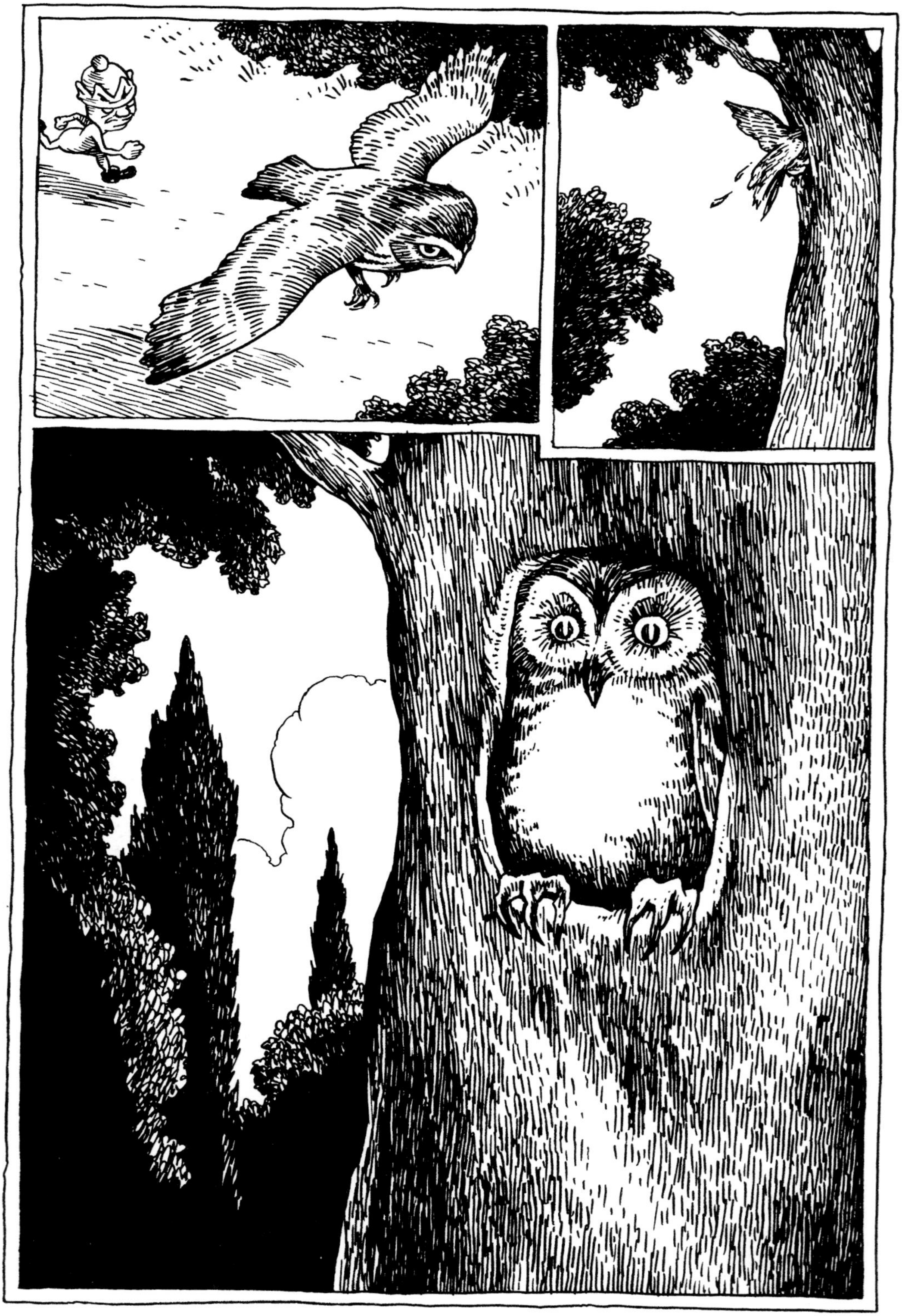

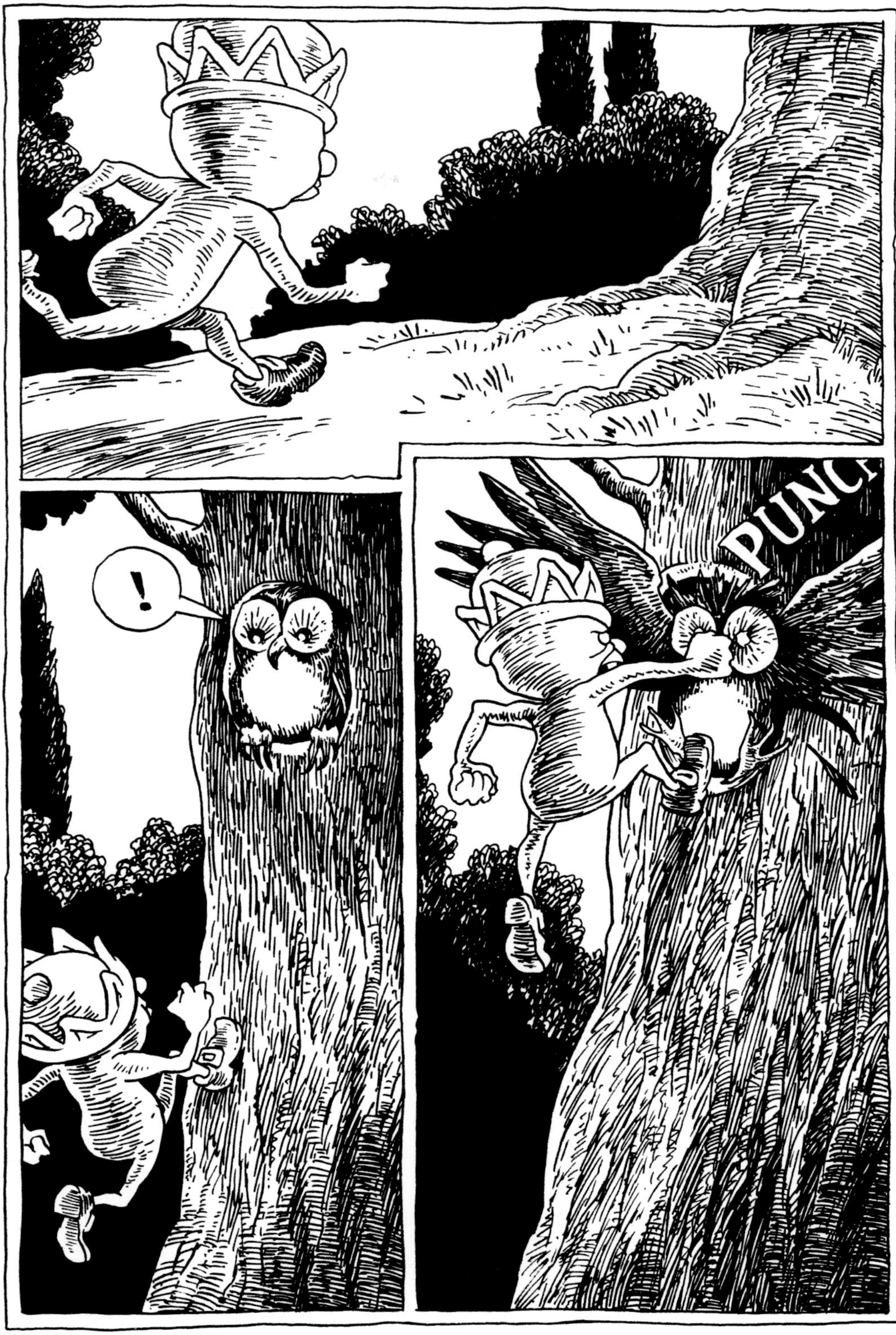
!
PUNC

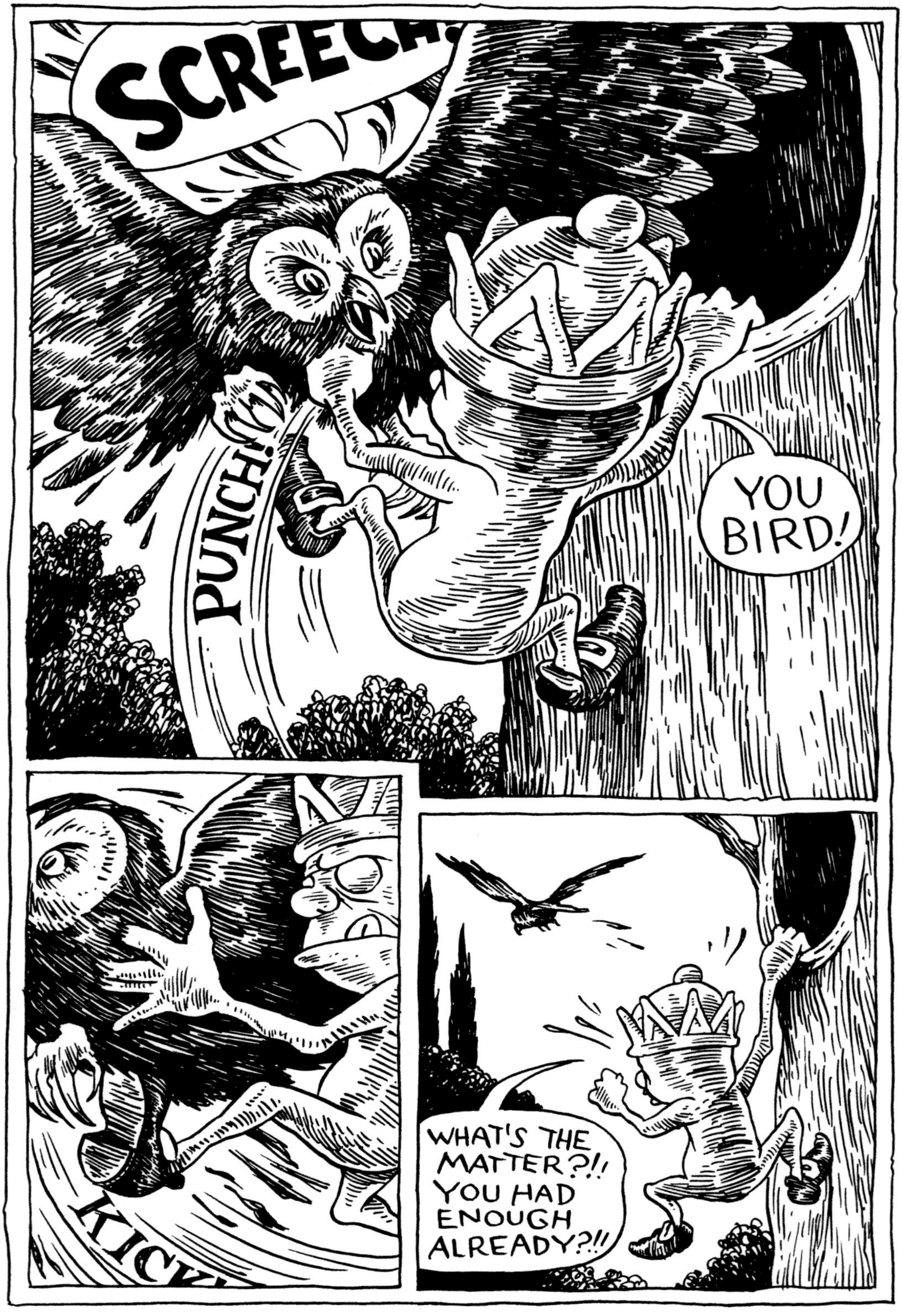
SCREECH!
PUNCH!
YOU BIRD!
KICK
WHAT'S THE MATTER?!! YOU HAD ENOUGH ALREADY?!!

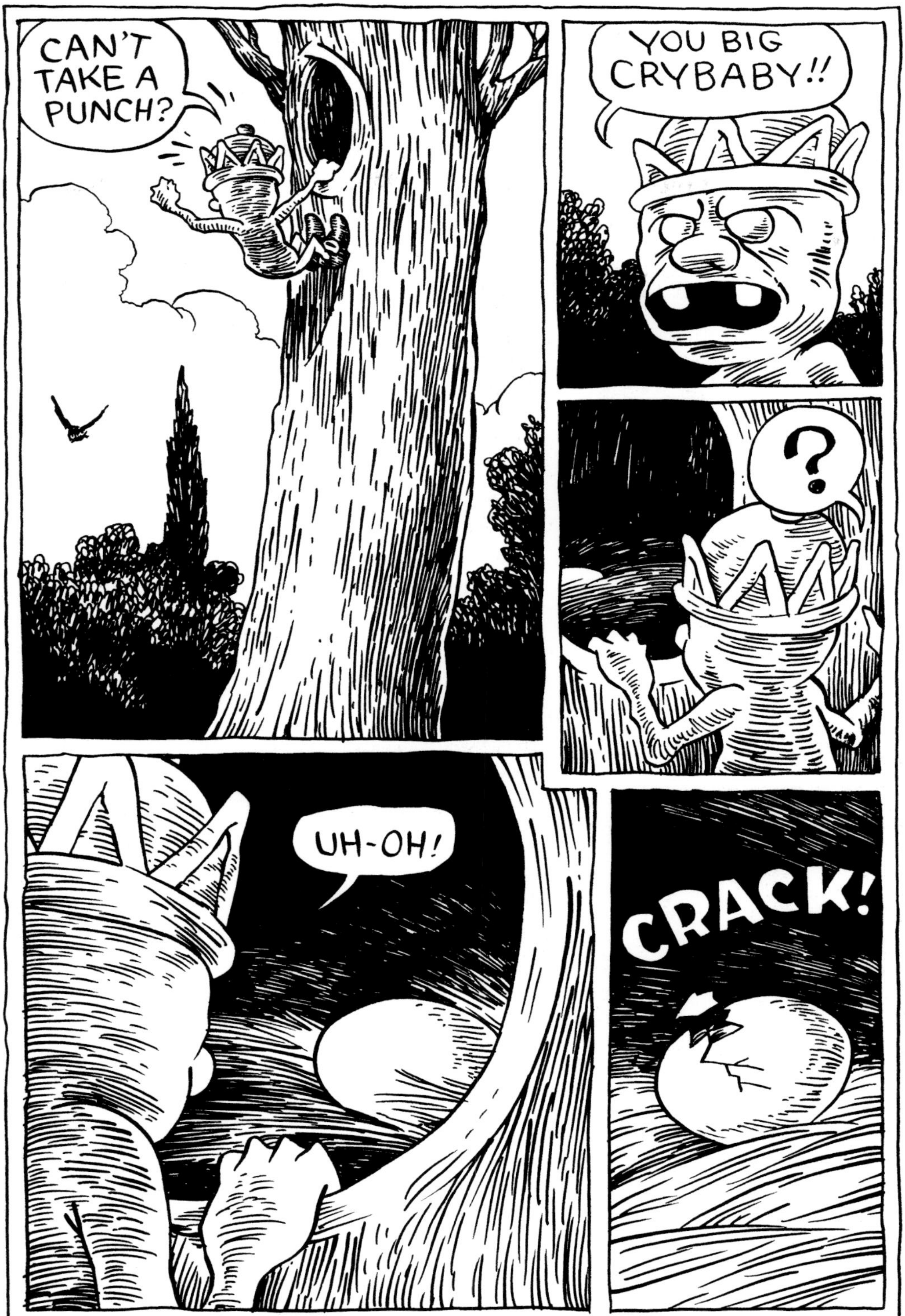
CAN'T TAKE A PUNCH?
YOU BIG CRYBABY!!
?
UH-OH!
CRACK!

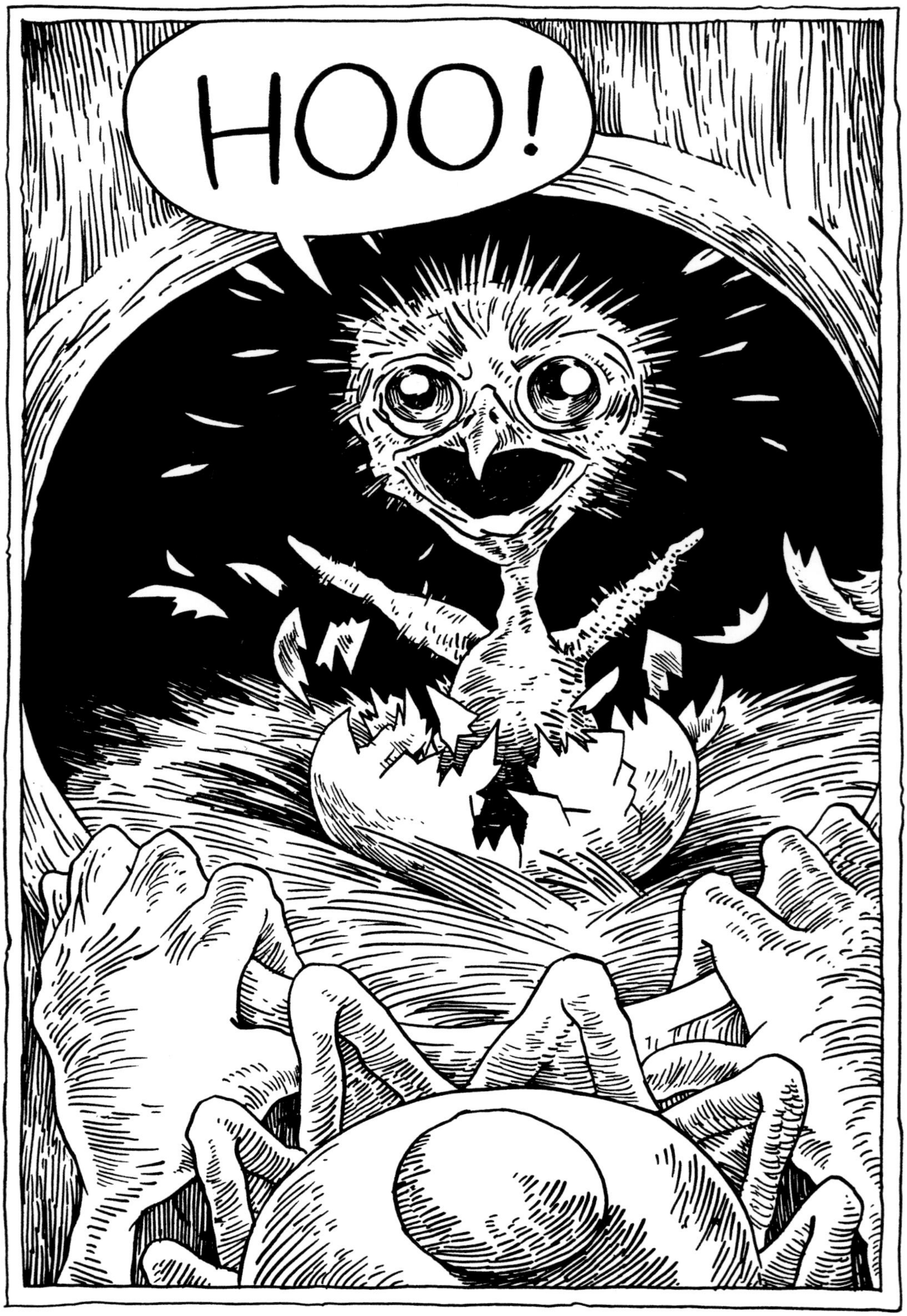
HOO!

❦ Chapter Two ❧

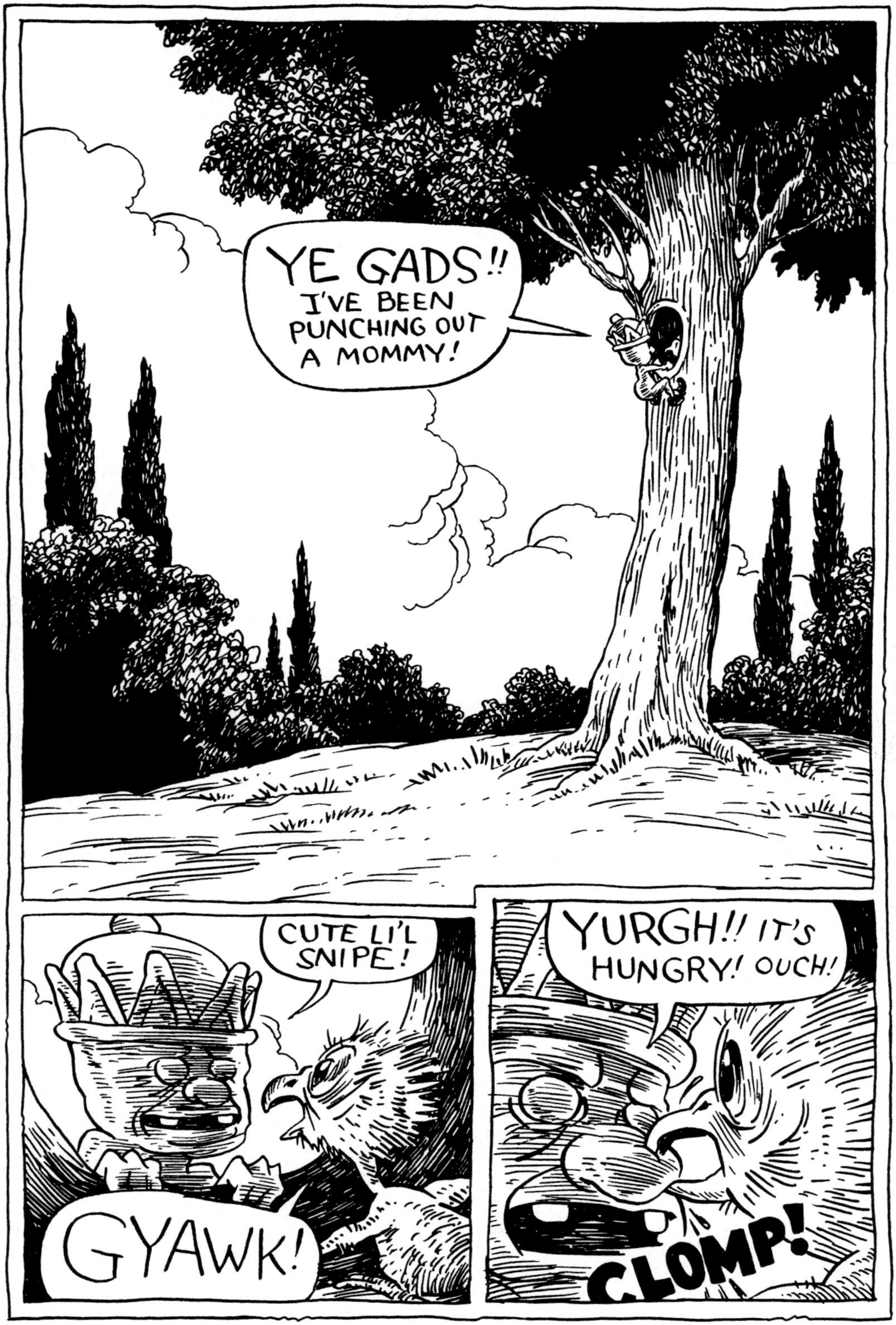
YE GADS!! I'VE BEEN PUNCHING OUT A MOMMY!
CUTE LI'L SNIPE!
GYAWK!
YURGH!! IT'S HUNGRY! OUCH!
CLOMP!

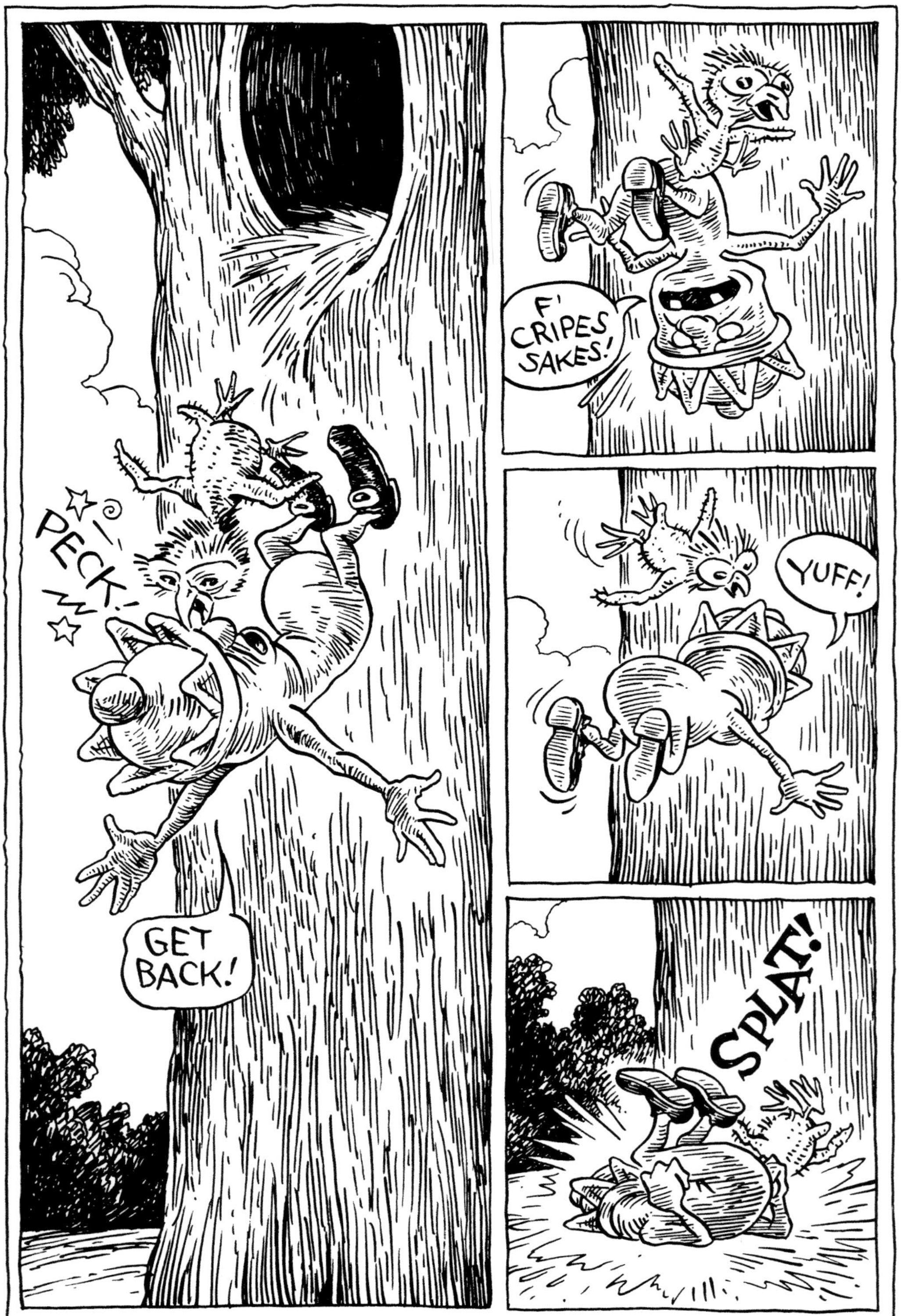
PECK!
GET BACK!
F' CRIPES SAKES!
YUFF!
SPLAT!

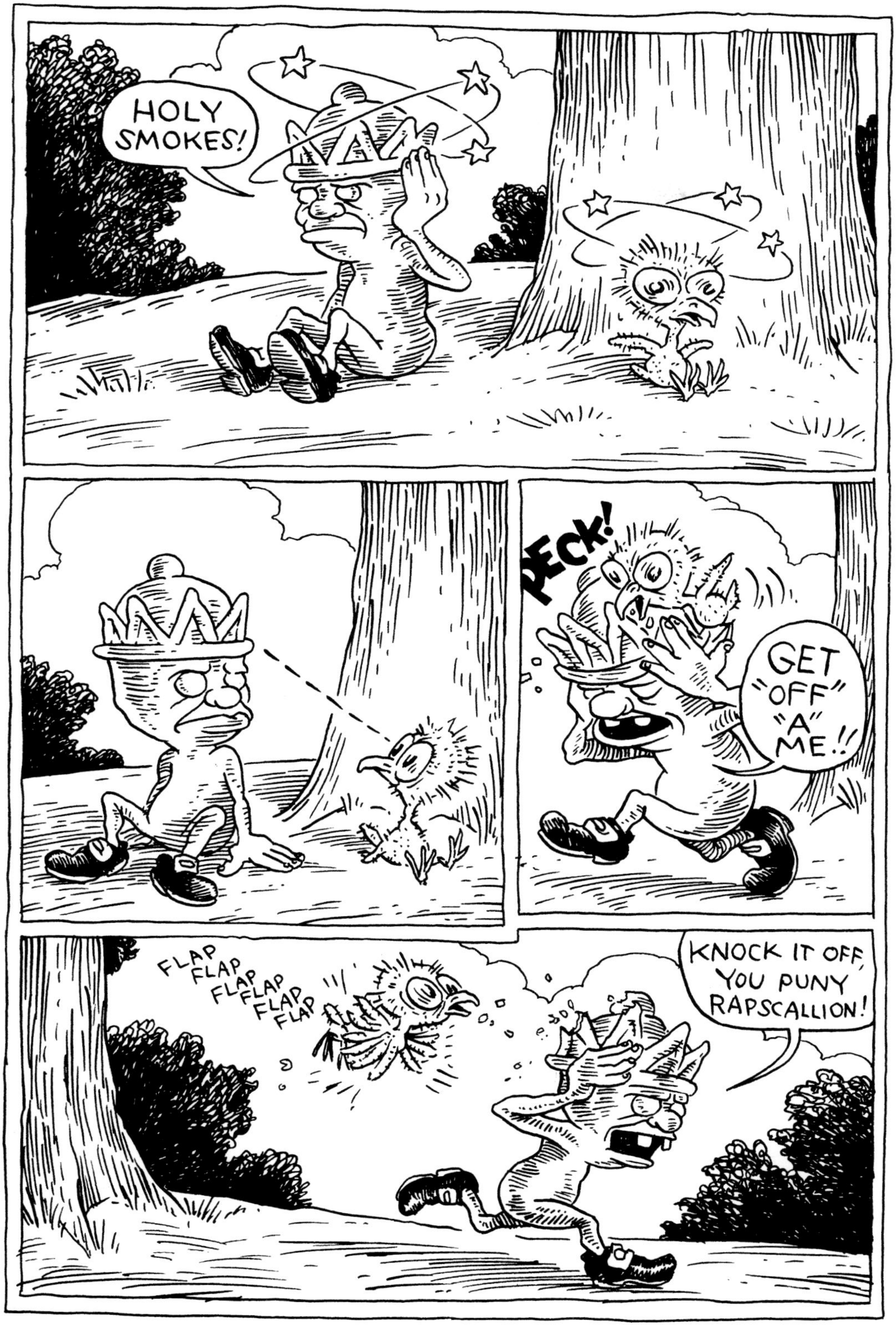
HOLY SMOKES!
PECK!
GET "OFF" "A" ME!!
FLAP FLAP FLAP FLAP FLAP FLAP
KNOCK IT OFF, YOU PUNY RAPSCALLION!

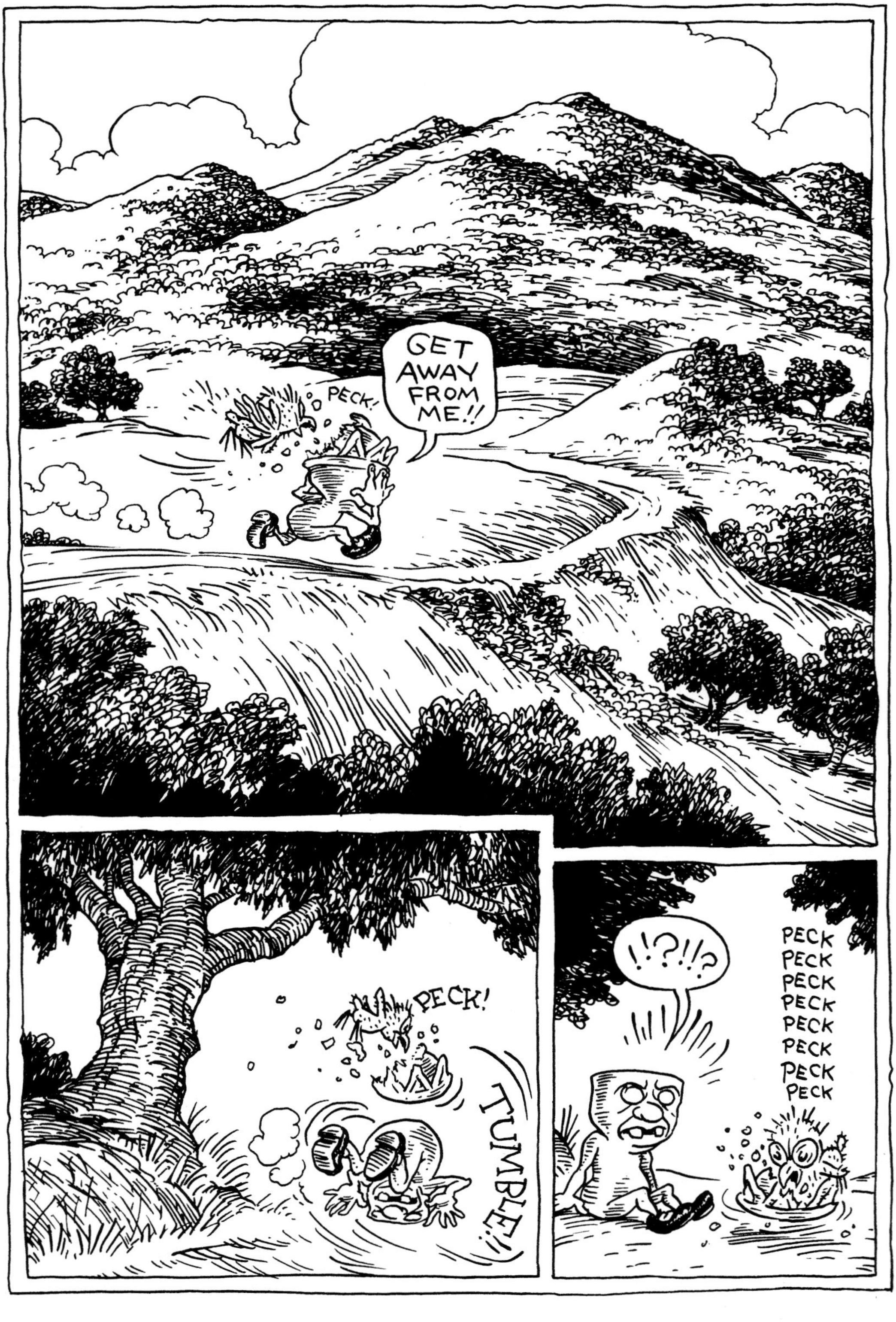

PECK!
GET AWAY FROM ME!!
PECK!
TUMBLE!!
!!?!!?
PECK
PECK
PECK
PECK
PECK
PECK
PECK
PECK

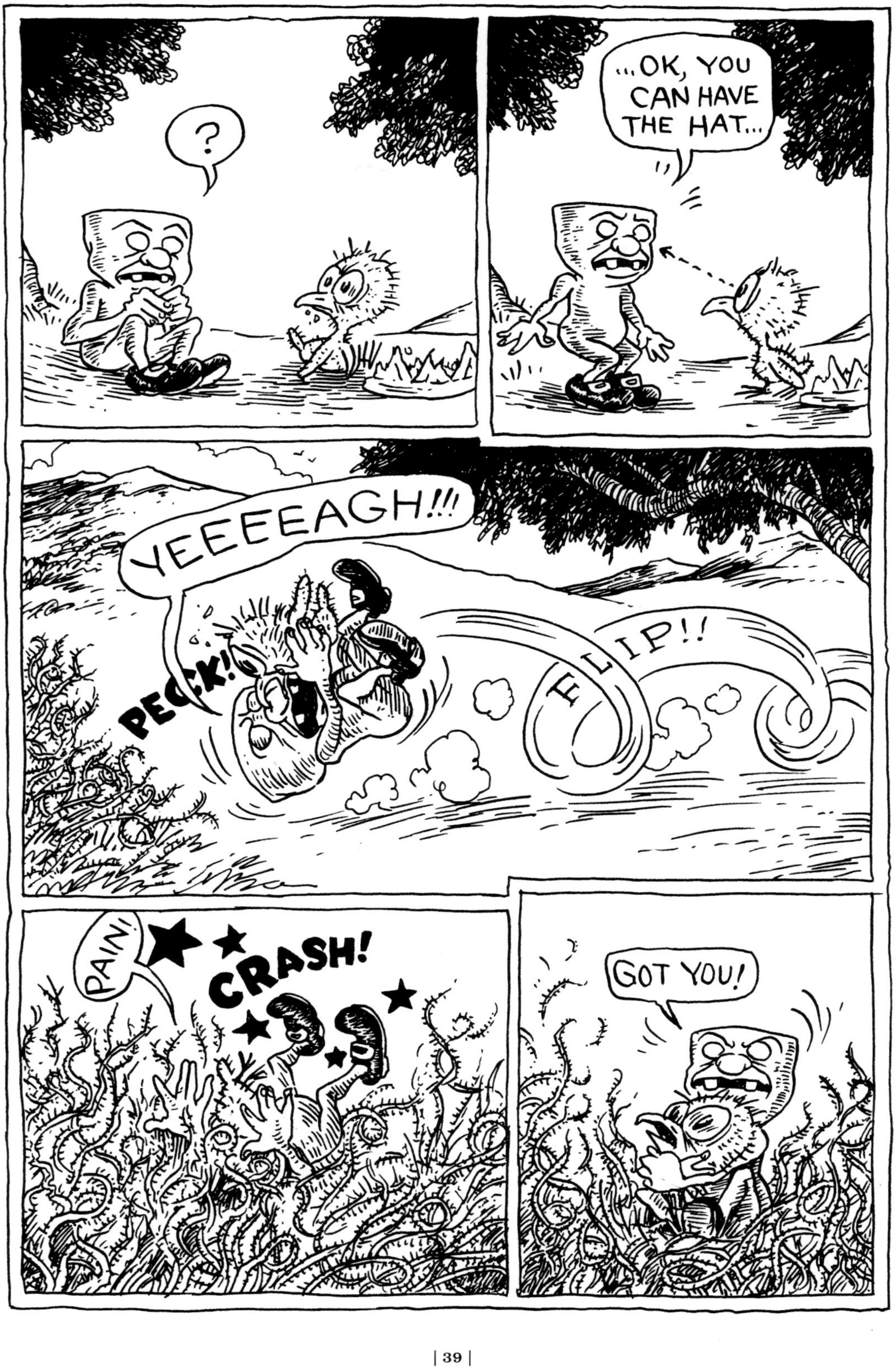
?
...OK, YOU CAN HAVE THE HAT...
YEEEEEAGH!!!
PECK!
FLIP!!
PAIN!
CRASH!
GOT YOU!

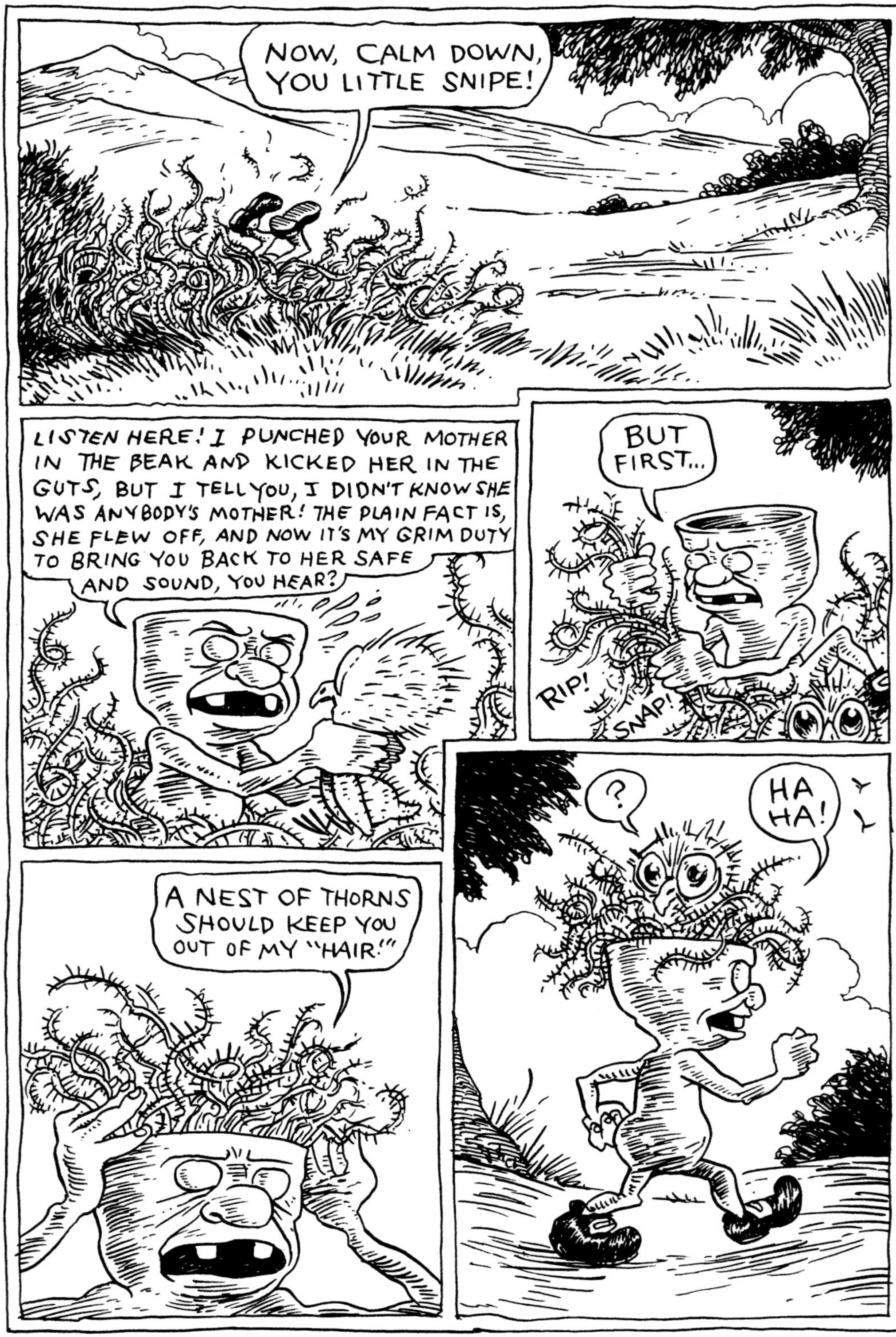
NOW, CALM DOWN, YOU LITTLE SNIPE!
LISTEN HERE! I PUNCHED YOUR MOTHER IN THE BEAK AND KICKED HER IN THE GUTS, BUT I TELL YOU, I DIDN'T KNOW SHE WAS ANYBODY'S MOTHER! THE PLAIN FACT IS, SHE FLEW OFF, AND NOW IT'S MY GRIM DUTY TO BRING YOU BACK TO HER SAFE AND SOUND, YOU HEAR?
BUT FIRST...
RIP!
SNAP!
A NEST OF THORNS SHOULD KEEP YOU OUT OF MY "HAIR!"
?
HA HA!

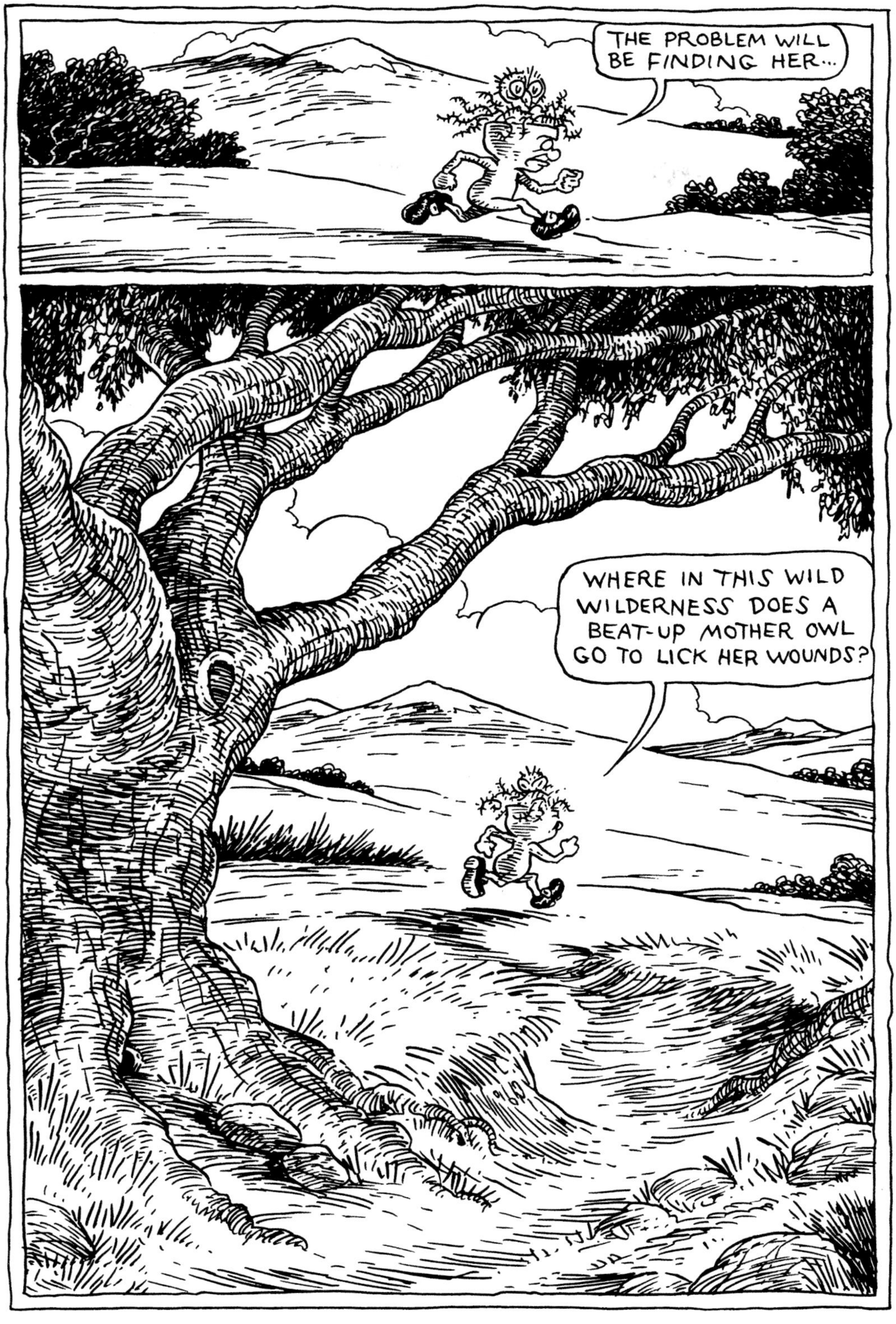
THE PROBLEM WILL BE FINDING HER...
WHERE IN THIS WILD WILDERNESS DOES A BEAT-UP MOTHER OWL GO TO LICK HER WOUNDS?

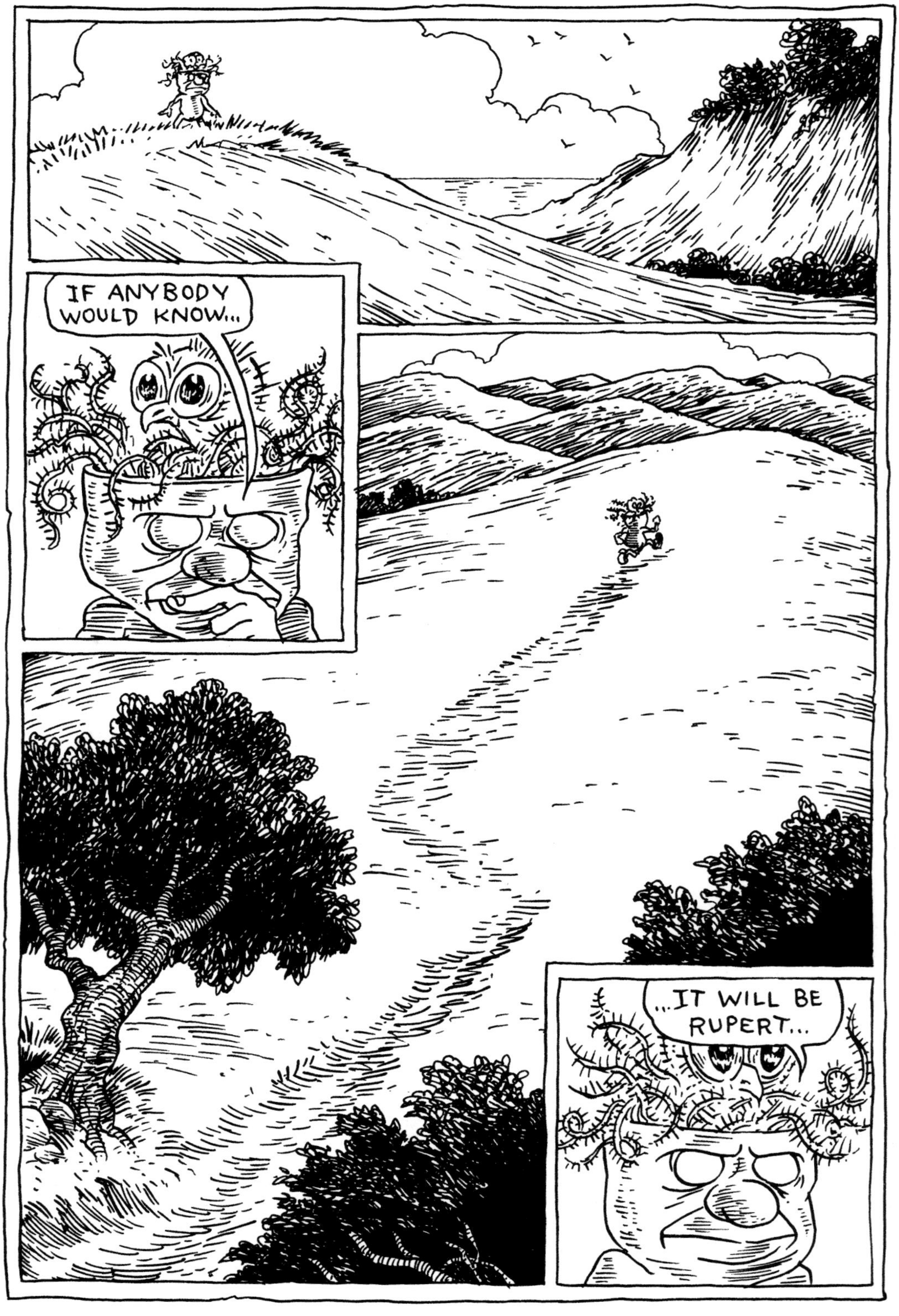
IF ANYBODY WOULD KNOW...
...IT WILL BE RUPERT...

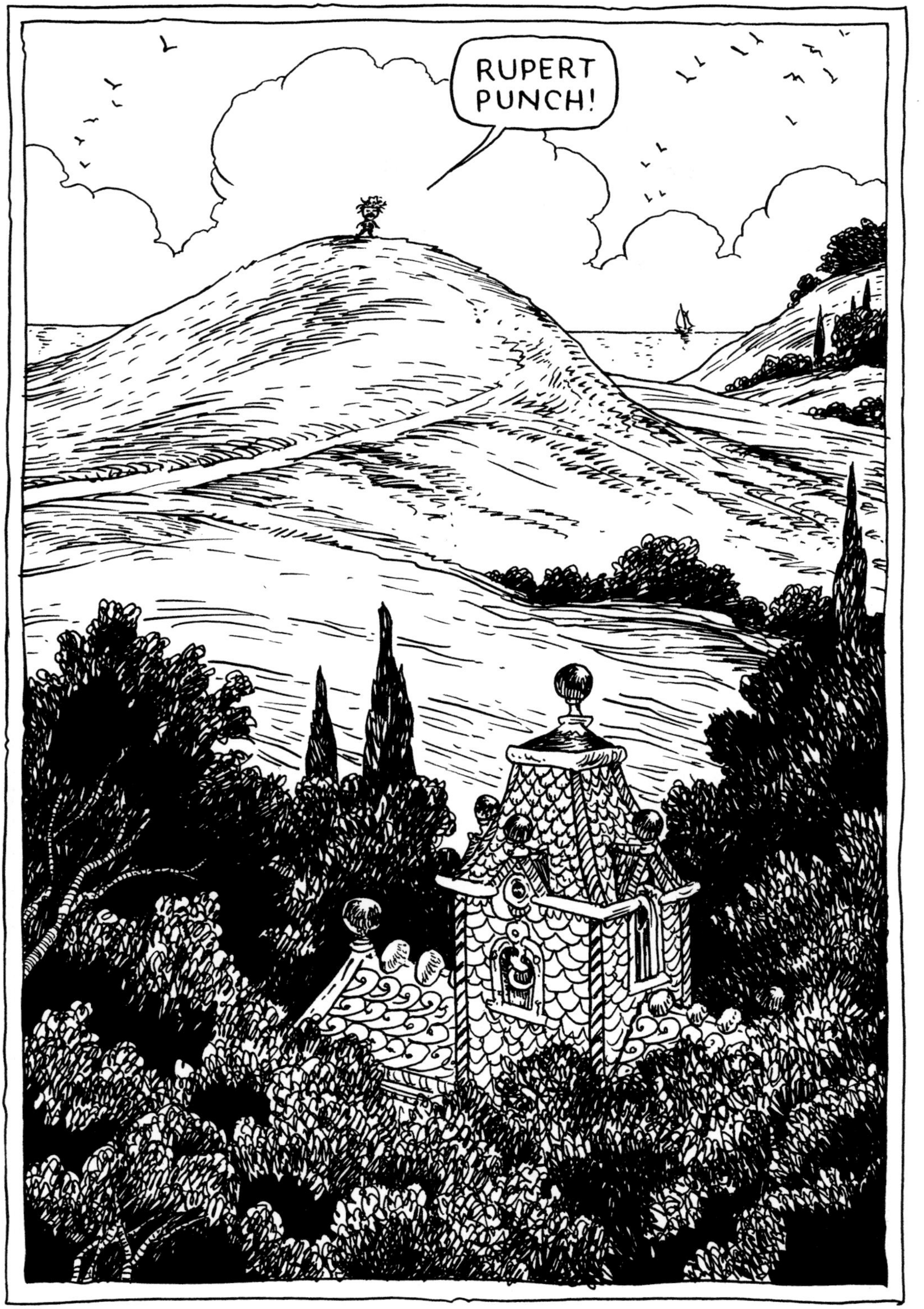
RUPERT PUNCH!

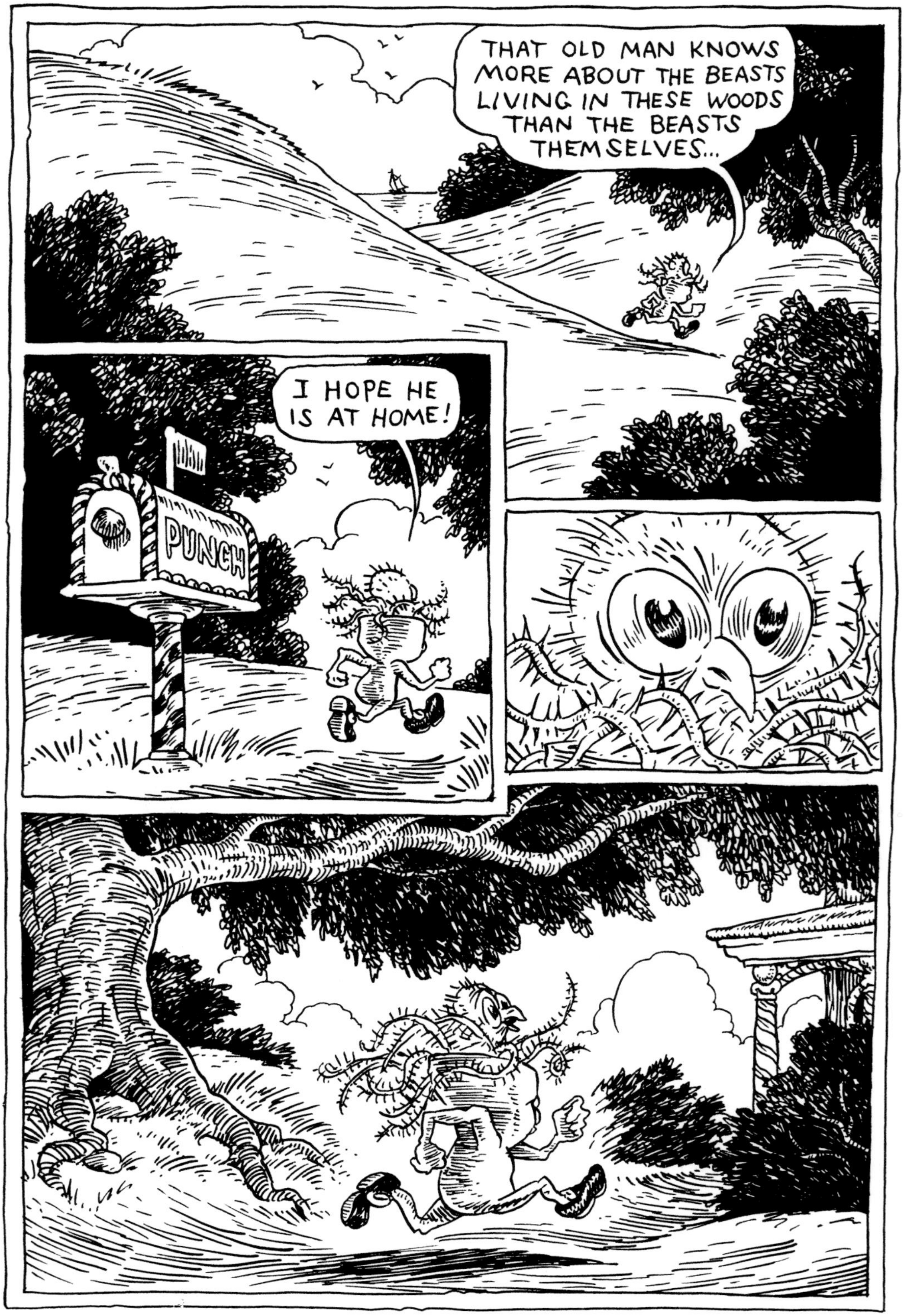
THAT OLD MAN KNOWS MORE ABOUT THE BEASTS LIVING IN THESE WOODS THAN THE BEASTS THEMSELVES...
I HOPE HE IS AT HOME!
PUNCH

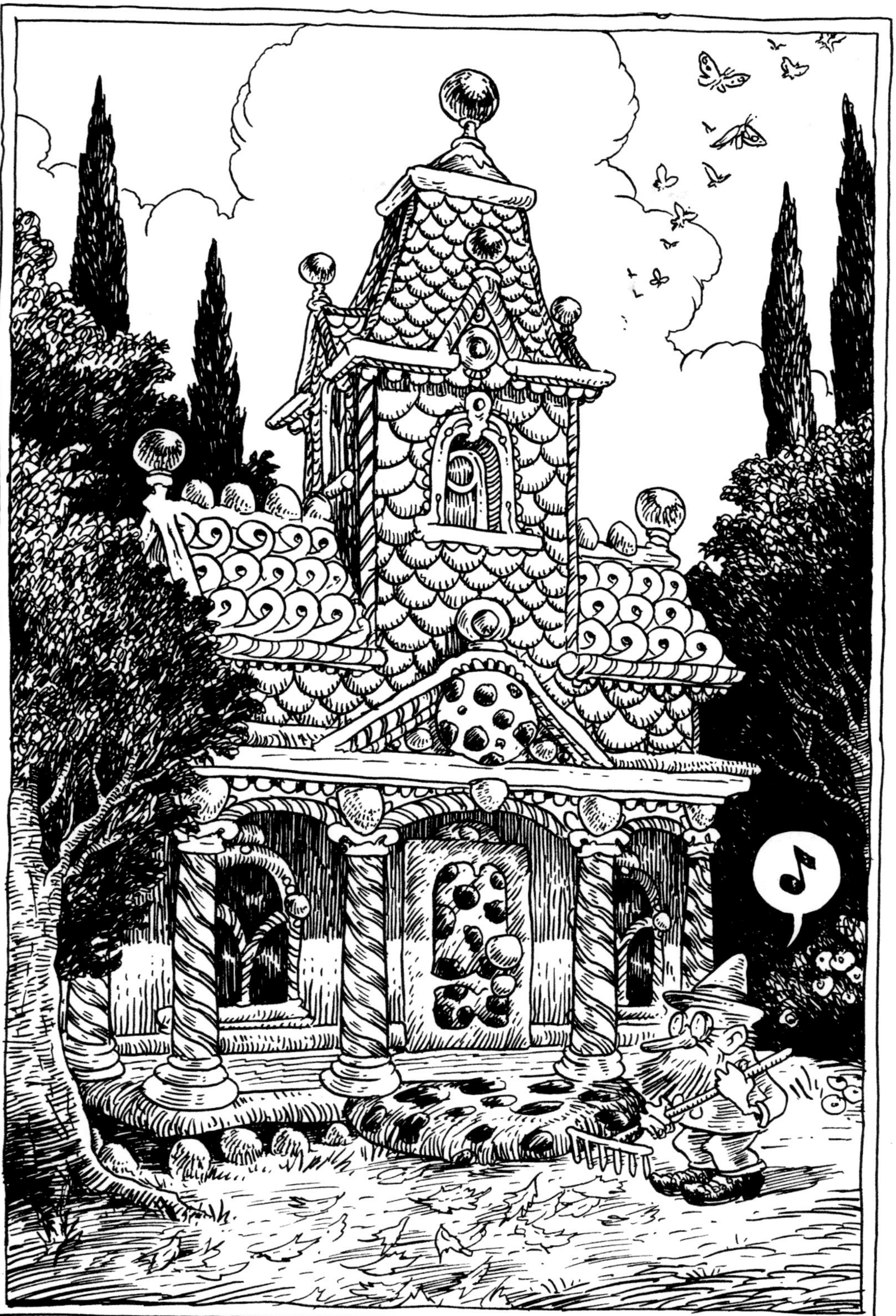

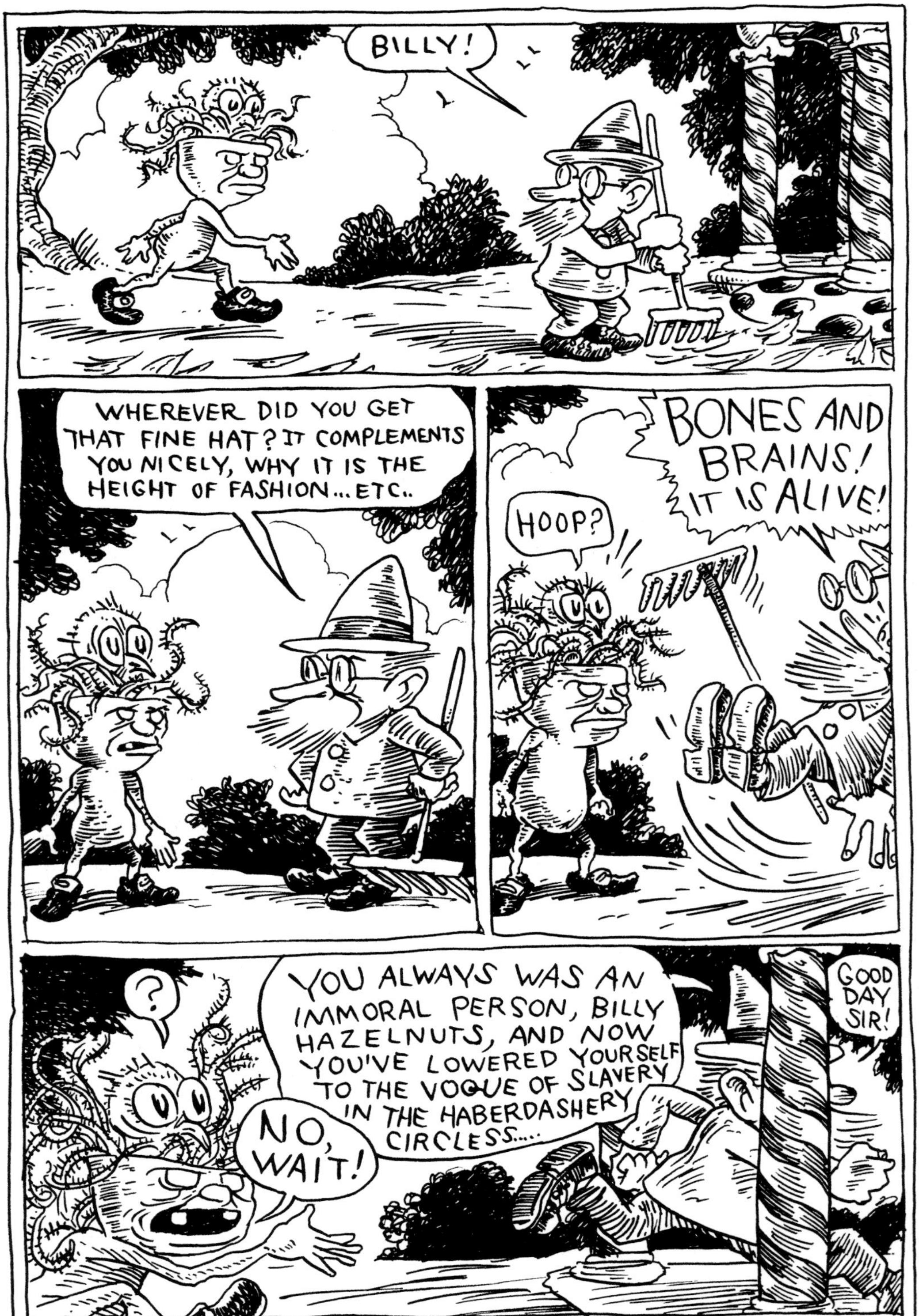
BILLY!
WHEREVER DID YOU GET THAT FINE HAT? IT COMPLEMENTS YOU NICELY, WHY IT IS THE HEIGHT OF FASHION... ETC..
HOOP?
BONES AND BRAINS! IT IS ALIVE!
?
YOU ALWAYS WAS AN IMMORAL PERSON, BILLY HAZELNUTS, AND NOW YOU'VE LOWERED YOURSELF TO THE VOGUE OF SLAVERY IN THE HABERDASHERY CIRCLESS.....
NO, WAIT!
GOOD DAY SIR!

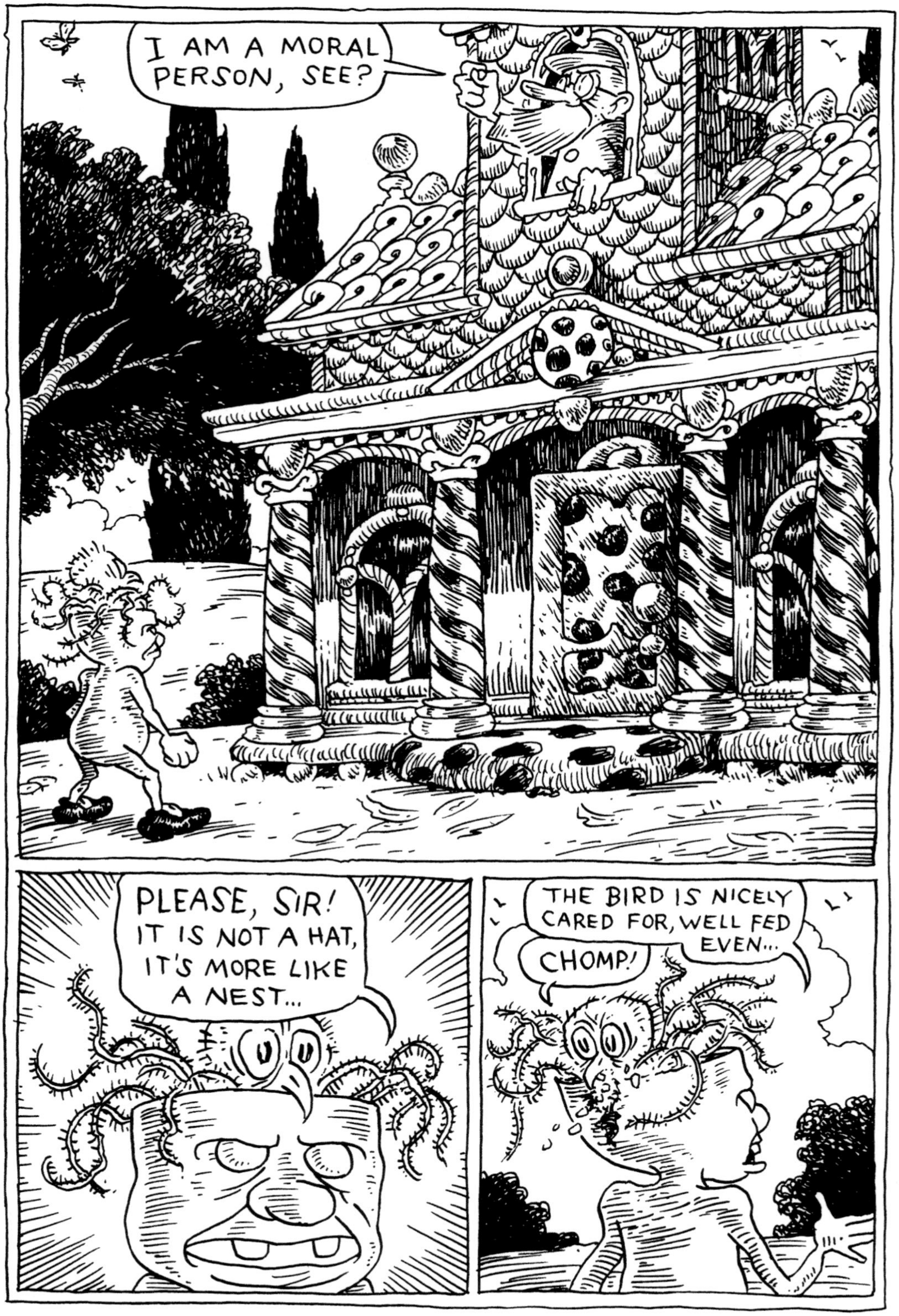
I AM A MORAL PERSON, SEE?
PLEASE, SIR! IT IS NOT A HAT, IT'S MORE LIKE A NEST...
THE BIRD IS NICELY CARED FOR, WELL FED EVEN...
CHOMP!

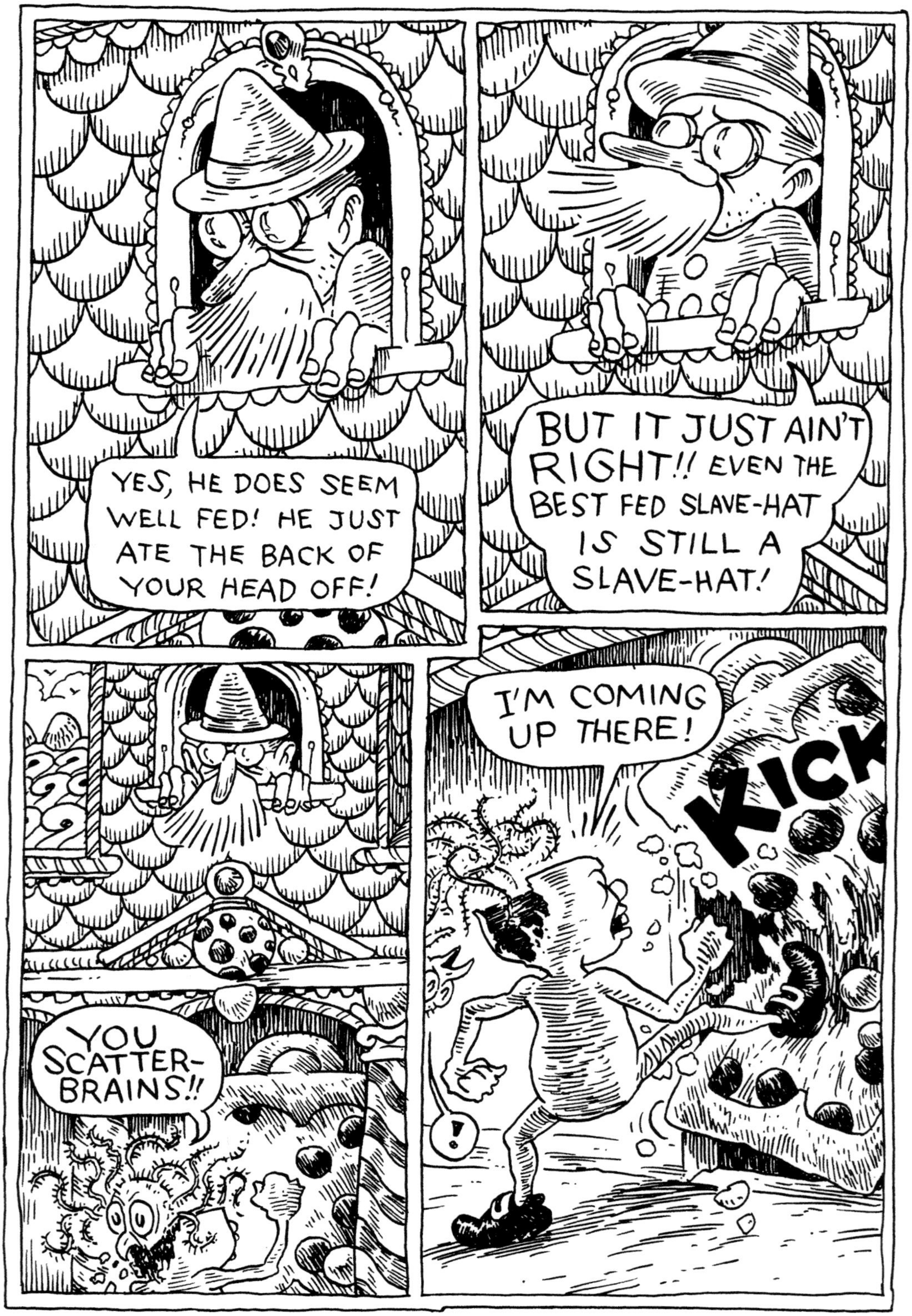
YES, HE DOES SEEM WELL FED! HE JUST ATE THE BACK OF YOUR HEAD OFF!
BUT IT JUST AIN'T RIGHT!! EVEN THE BEST FED SLAVE-HAT IS STILL A SLAVE-HAT!
YOU SCATTER-BRAINS!!
I'M COMING UP THERE!
KICK
!

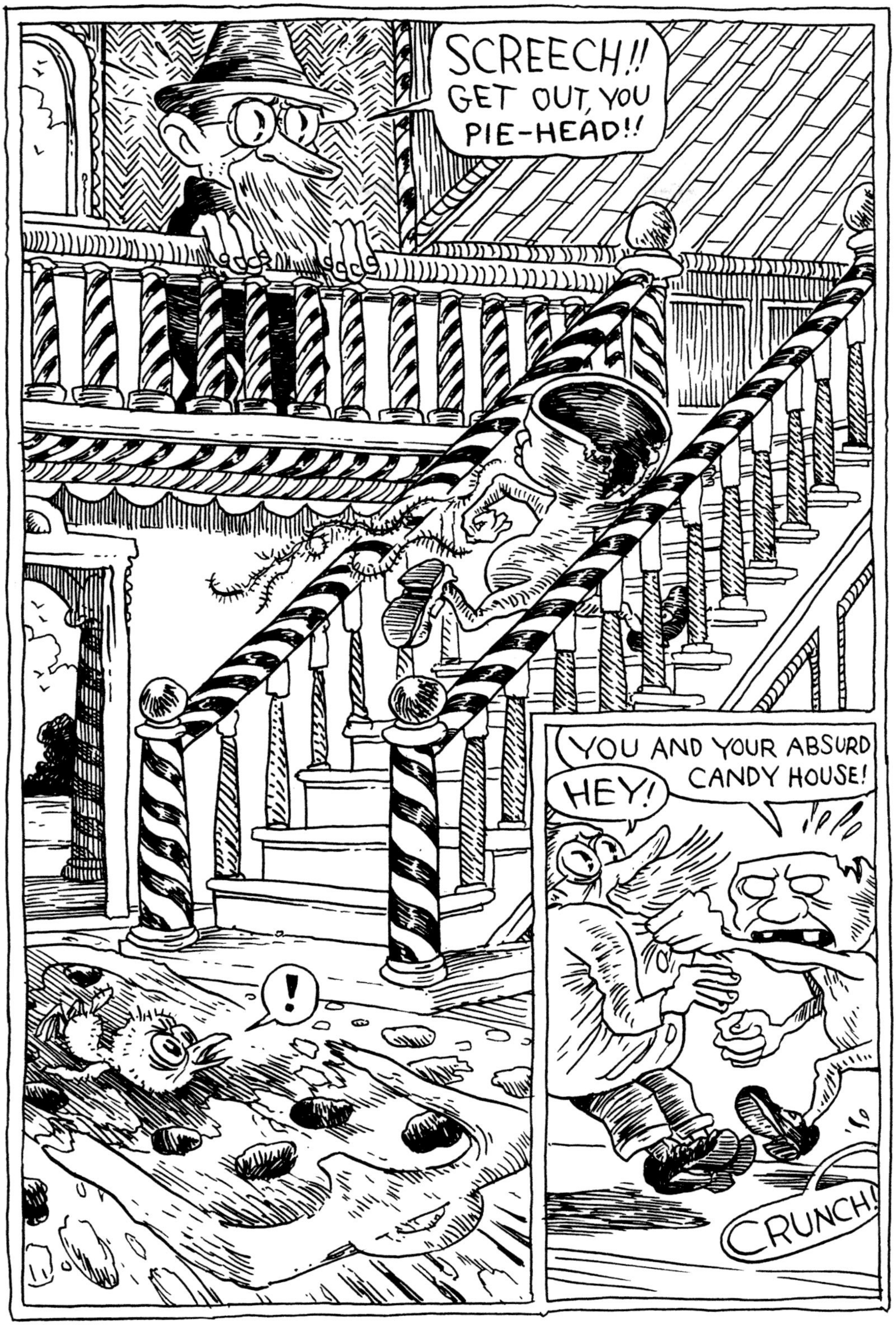
SCREECH!! GET OUT, YOU PIE-HEAD!!
!
YOU AND YOUR ABSURD CANDY HOUSE!
HEY!
CRUNCH!

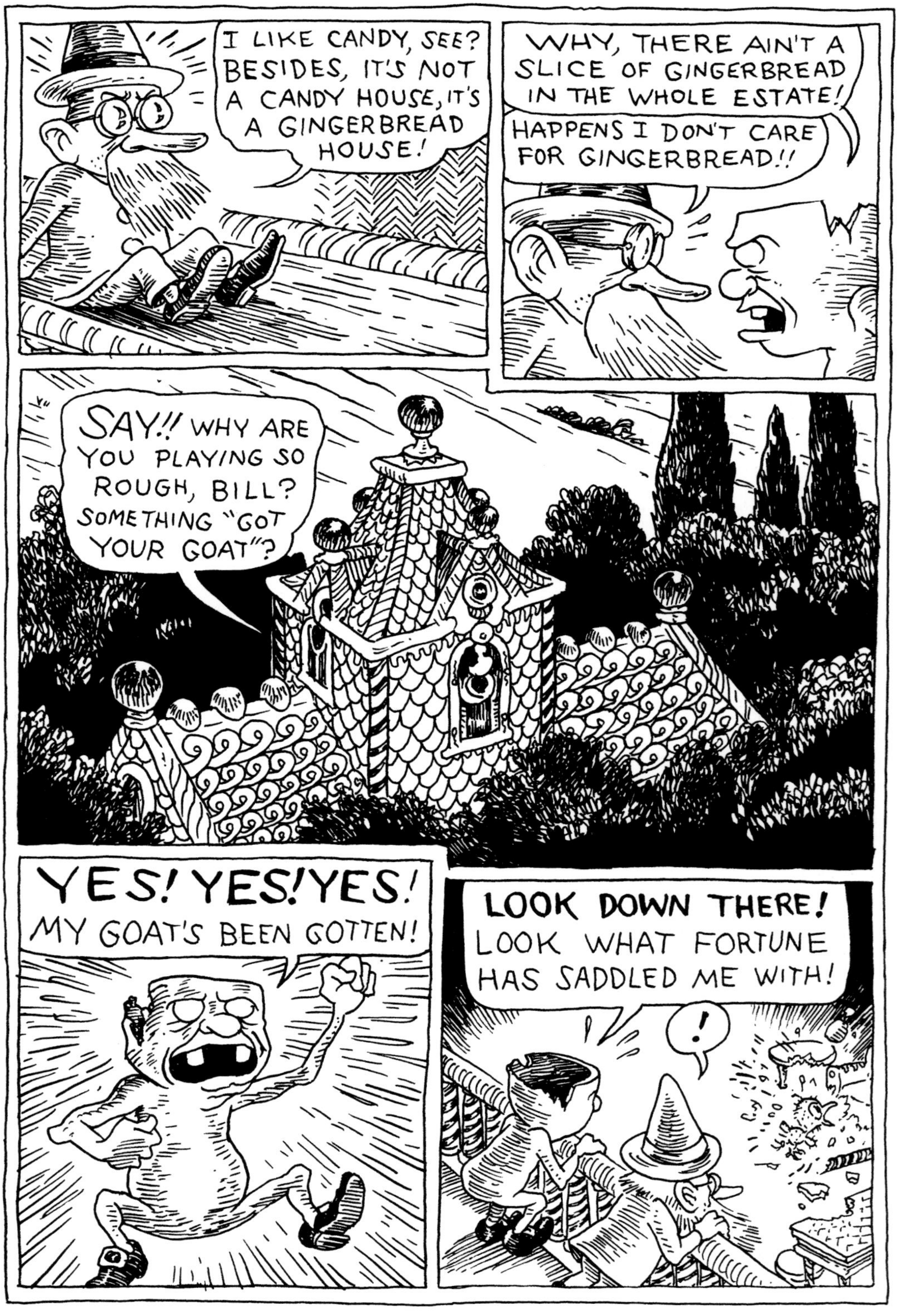
I LIKE CANDY, SEE? BESIDES, IT'S NOT A CANDY HOUSE, IT'S A GINGERBREAD HOUSE!
WHY, THERE AIN'T A SLICE OF GINGERBREAD IN THE WHOLE ESTATE!
HAPPENS I DON'T CARE FOR GINGERBREAD!!
SAY!! WHY ARE YOU PLAYING SO ROUGH, BILL? SOMETHING "GOT YOUR GOAT"?
YES! YES! YES! MY GOAT'S BEEN GOTTEN!
LOOK DOWN THERE! LOOK WHAT FORTUNE HAS SADDLED ME WITH!
!

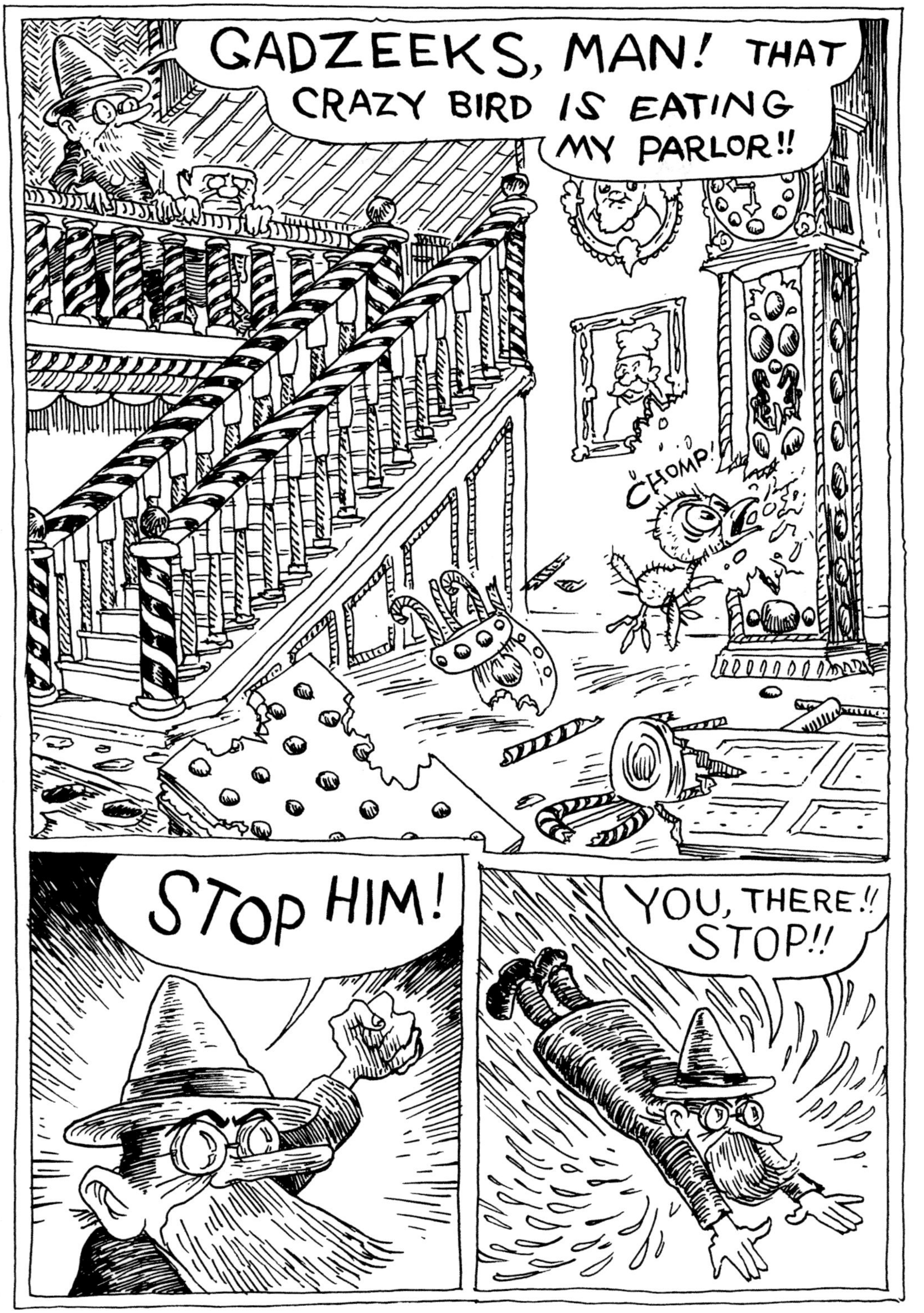
GADZEEKS, MAN! THAT CRAZY BIRD IS EATING MY PARLOR!!
CHOMP!
STOP HIM!
YOU, THERE!! STOP!!

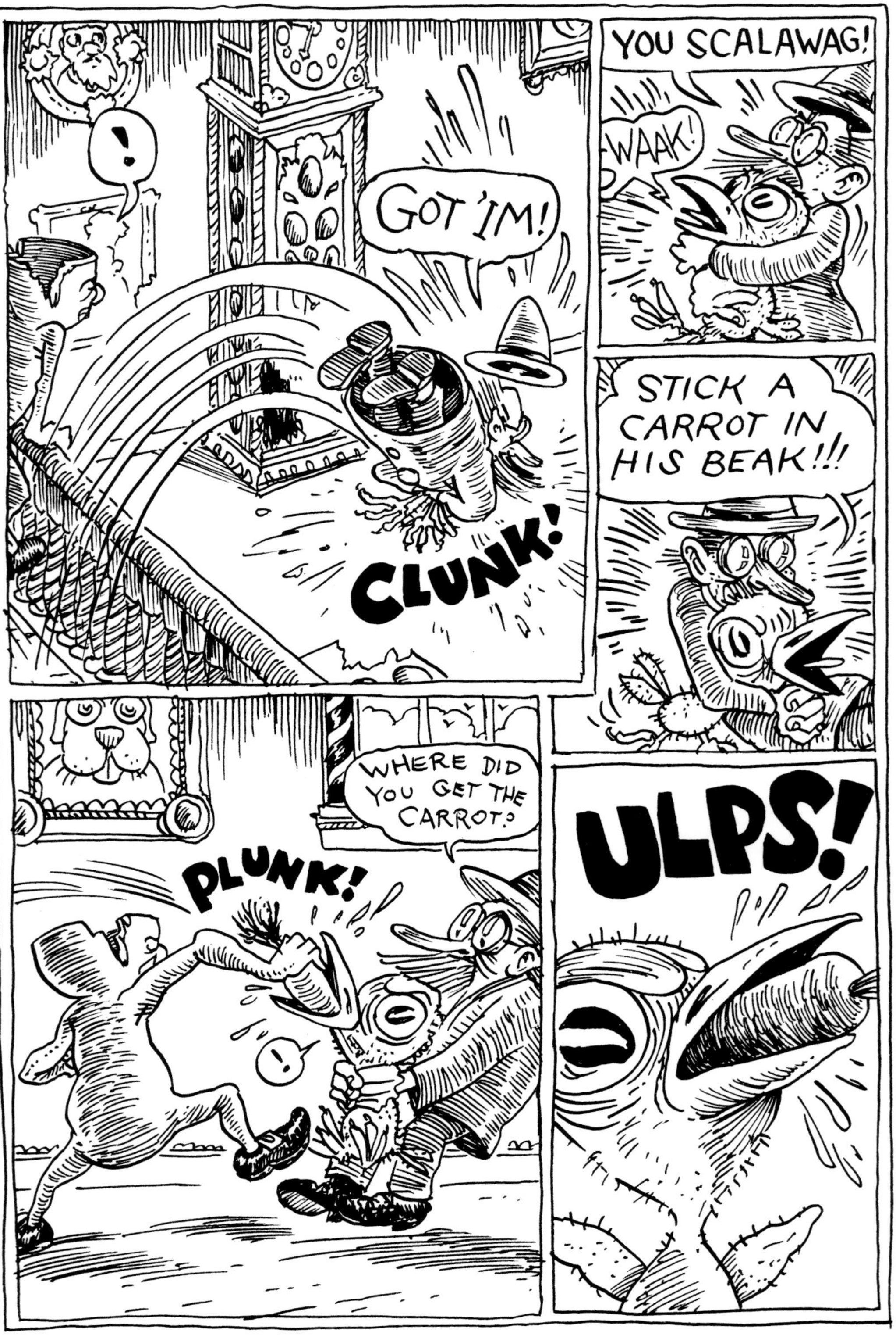
!
GOT 'IM!
CLUNK!
YOU SCALAWAG!
WAAK!
STICK A CARROT IN HIS BEAK!!!
PLUNK!
WHERE DID YOU GET THE CARROT?
!
ULPS!

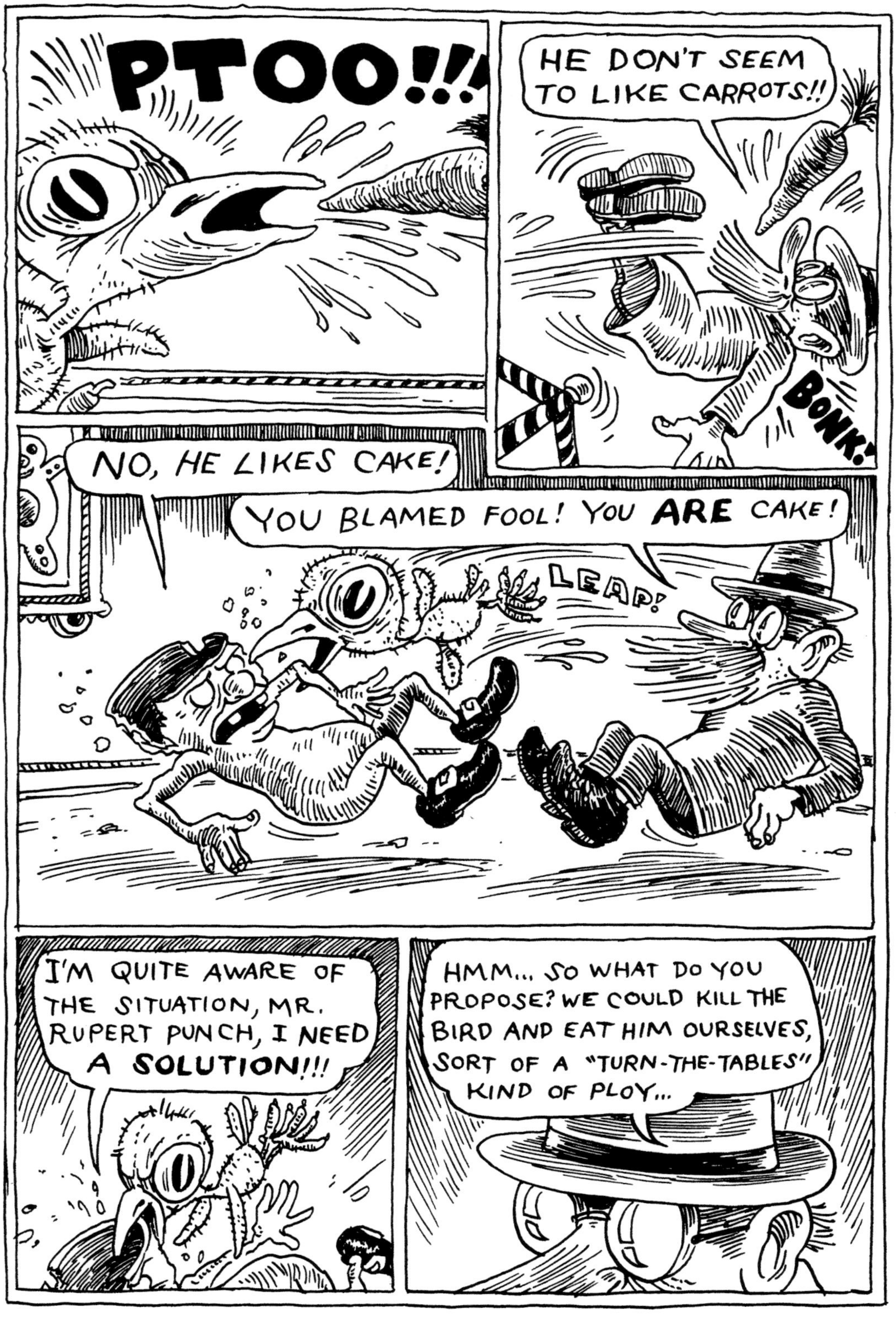
PTOO!!!
HE DON'T SEEM TO LIKE CARROTS!!
BONK!
NO, HE LIKES CAKE!
YOU BLAMED FOOL! YOU **ARE** CAKE!
LEAP!
I'M QUITE AWARE OF THE SITUATION, MR. RUPERT PUNCH, I NEED A **SOLUTION**!!!
HMM... SO WHAT DO YOU PROPOSE? WE COULD KILL THE BIRD AND EAT HIM OURSELVES, SORT OF A "TURN-THE-TABLES" KIND OF PLOY...

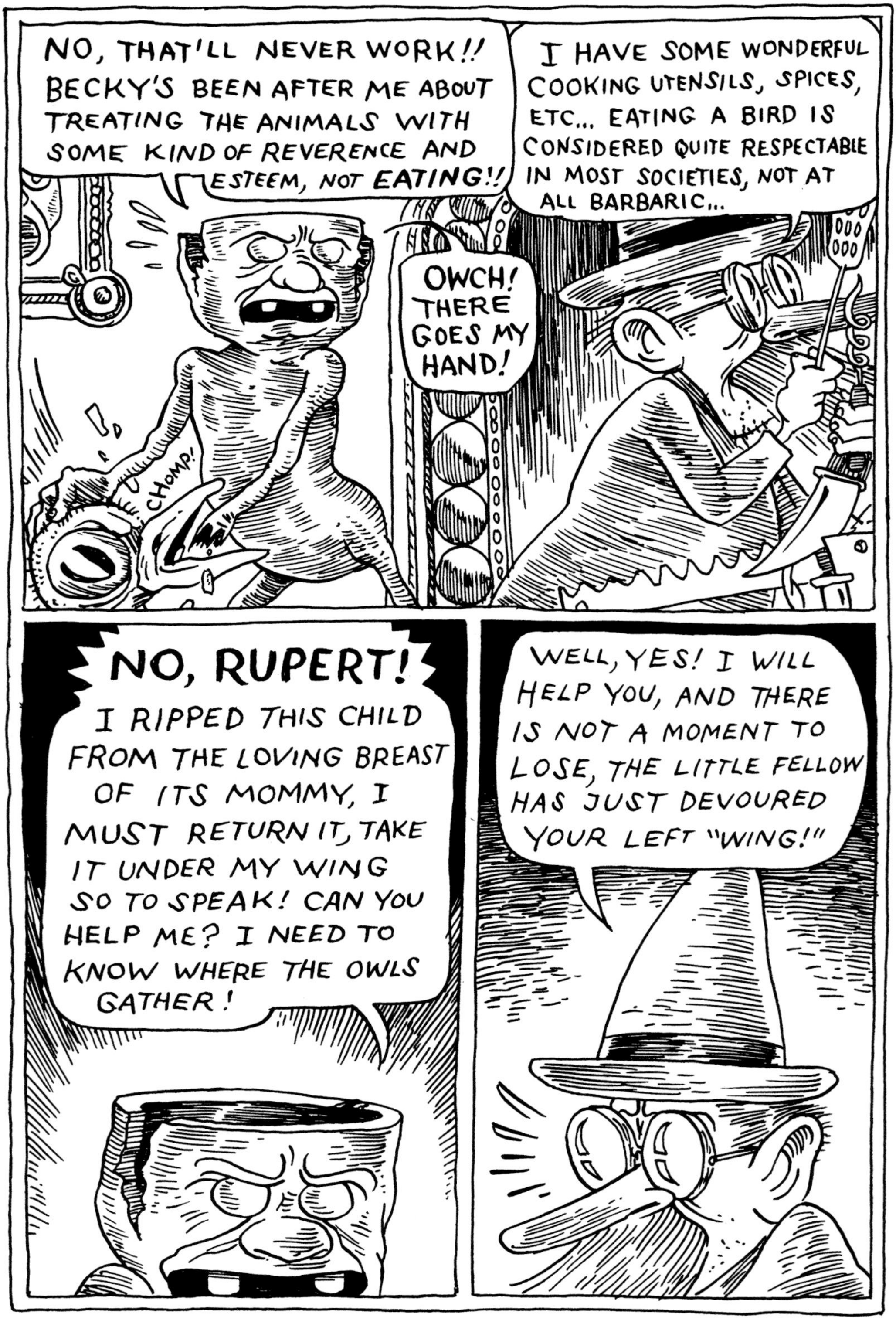
NO, THAT'LL NEVER WORK!! BECKY'S BEEN AFTER ME ABOUT TREATING THE ANIMALS WITH SOME KIND OF REVERENCE AND ESTEEM, NOT EATING!!
I HAVE SOME WONDERFUL COOKING UTENSILS, SPICES, ETC... EATING A BIRD IS CONSIDERED QUITE RESPECTABLE IN MOST SOCIETIES, NOT AT ALL BARBARIC...
OWCH! THERE GOES MY HAND!
CHOMP!
NO, RUPERT!
I RIPPED THIS CHILD FROM THE LOVING BREAST OF ITS MOMMY, I MUST RETURN IT, TAKE IT UNDER MY WING SO TO SPEAK! CAN YOU HELP ME? I NEED TO KNOW WHERE THE OWLS GATHER!
WELL, YES! I WILL HELP YOU, AND THERE IS NOT A MOMENT TO LOSE, THE LITTLE FELLOW HAS JUST DEVOURED YOUR LEFT "WING!"

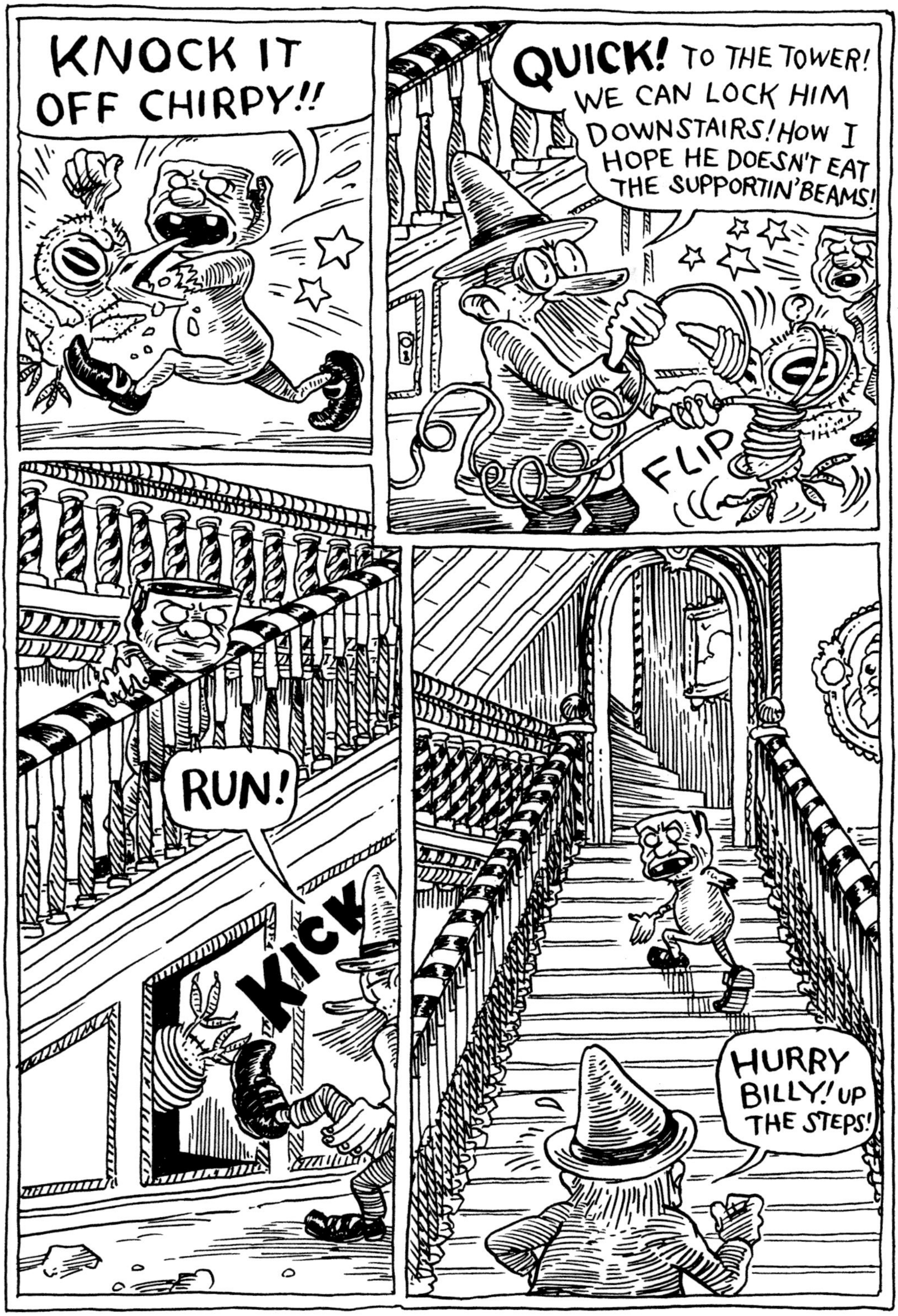
KNOCK IT OFF CHIRPY!!
QUICK! TO THE TOWER! WE CAN LOCK HIM DOWNSTAIRS! HOW I HOPE HE DOESN'T EAT THE SUPPORTIN' BEAMS!
FLIP
RUN!
KICK
HURRY BILLY! UP THE STEPS!

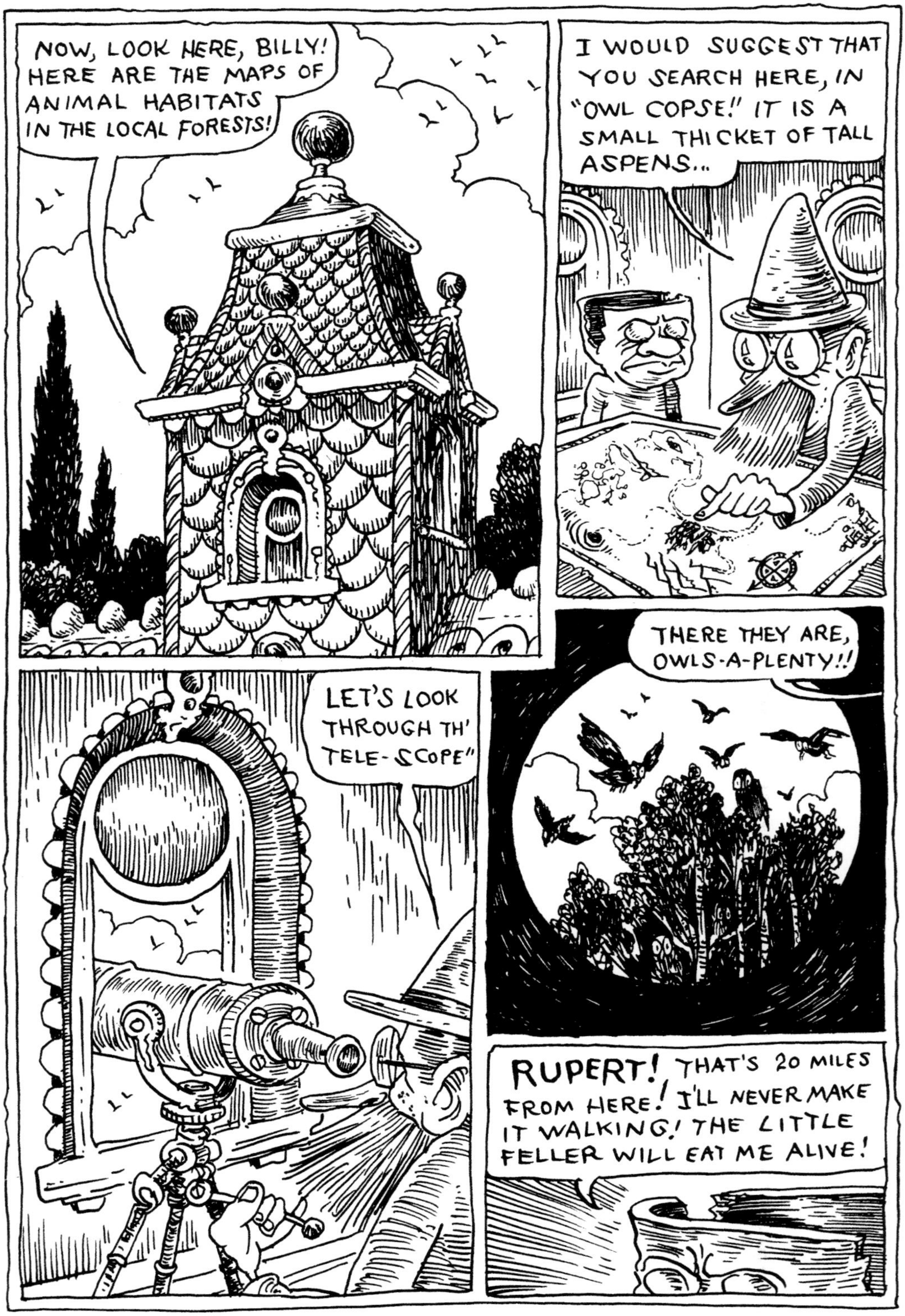
NOW, LOOK HERE, BILLY! HERE ARE THE MAPS OF ANIMAL HABITATS IN THE LOCAL FORESTS!
I WOULD SUGGEST THAT YOU SEARCH HERE, IN "OWL COPSE!" IT IS A SMALL THICKET OF TALL ASPENS...
LET'S LOOK THROUGH TH' TELE-SCOPE"
THERE THEY ARE, OWLS-A-PLENTY!!
RUPERT! THAT'S 20 MILES FROM HERE! I'LL NEVER MAKE IT WALKING! THE LITTLE FELLER WILL EAT ME ALIVE!

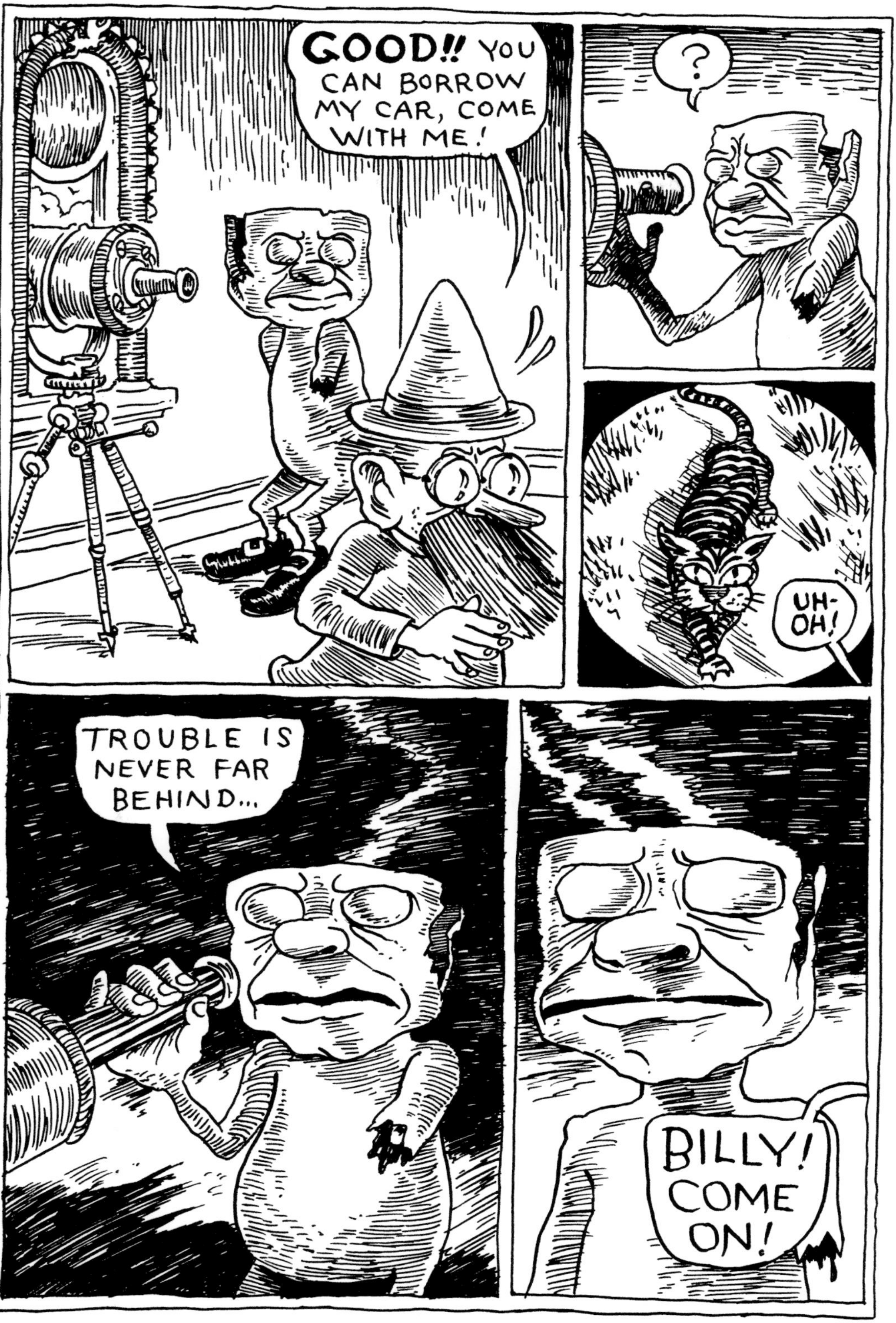
GOOD!! YOU CAN BORROW MY CAR, COME WITH ME!
?
UH-OH!
TROUBLE IS NEVER FAR BEHIND...
BILLY! COME ON!

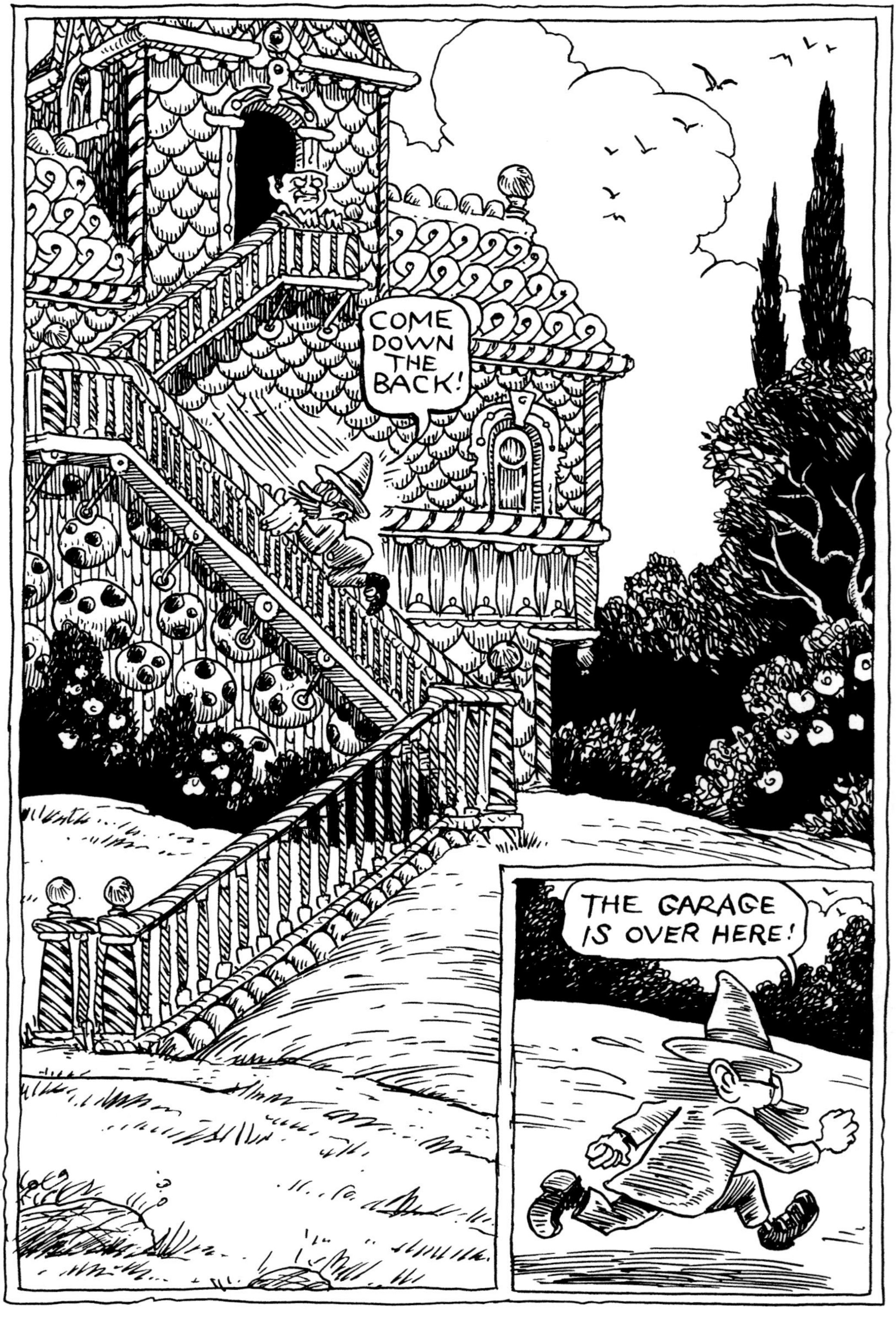
COME DOWN THE BACK!
THE GARAGE IS OVER HERE!

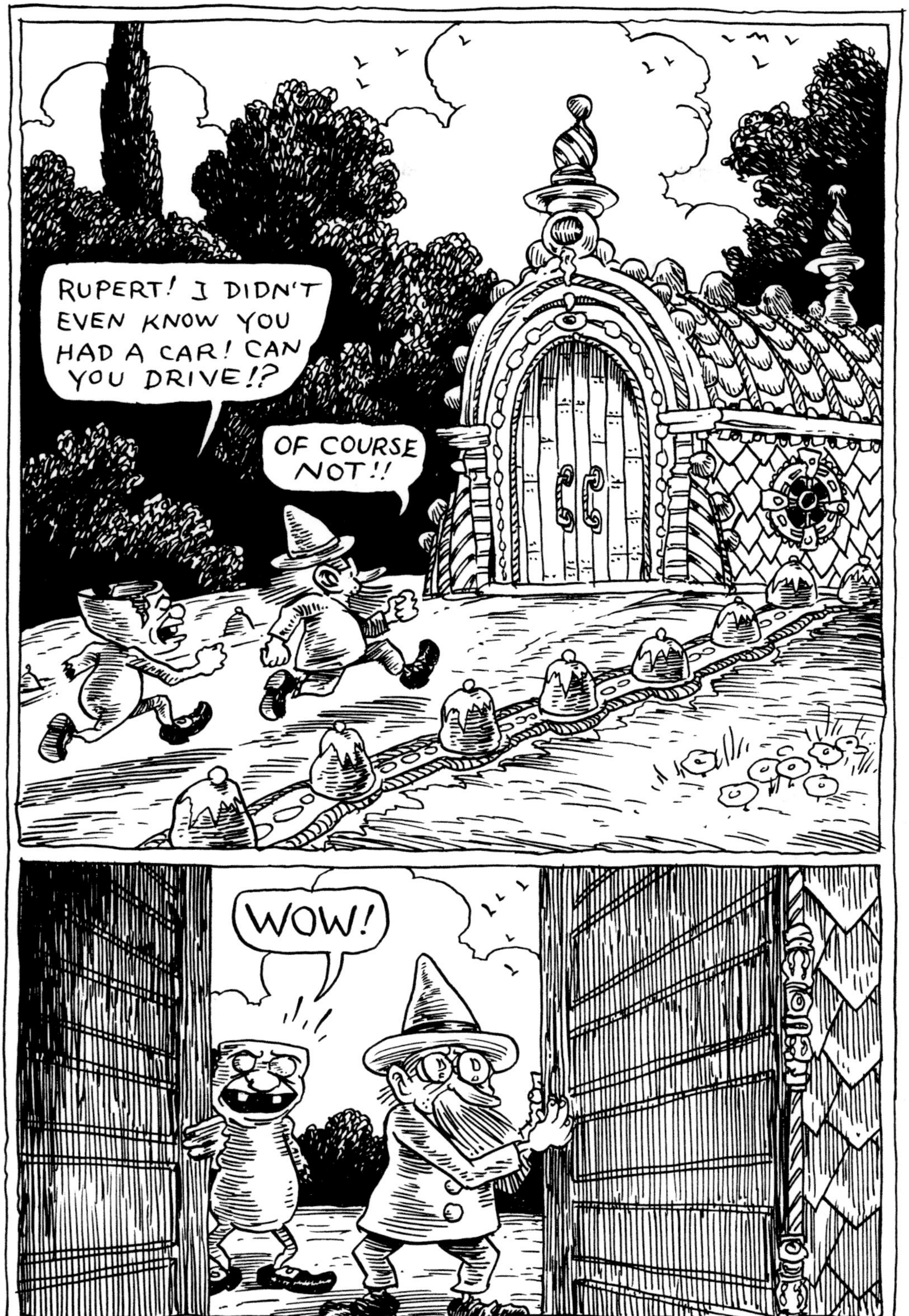
RUPERT! I DIDN'T EVEN KNOW YOU HAD A CAR! CAN YOU DRIVE!?
OF COURSE NOT!!
WOW!

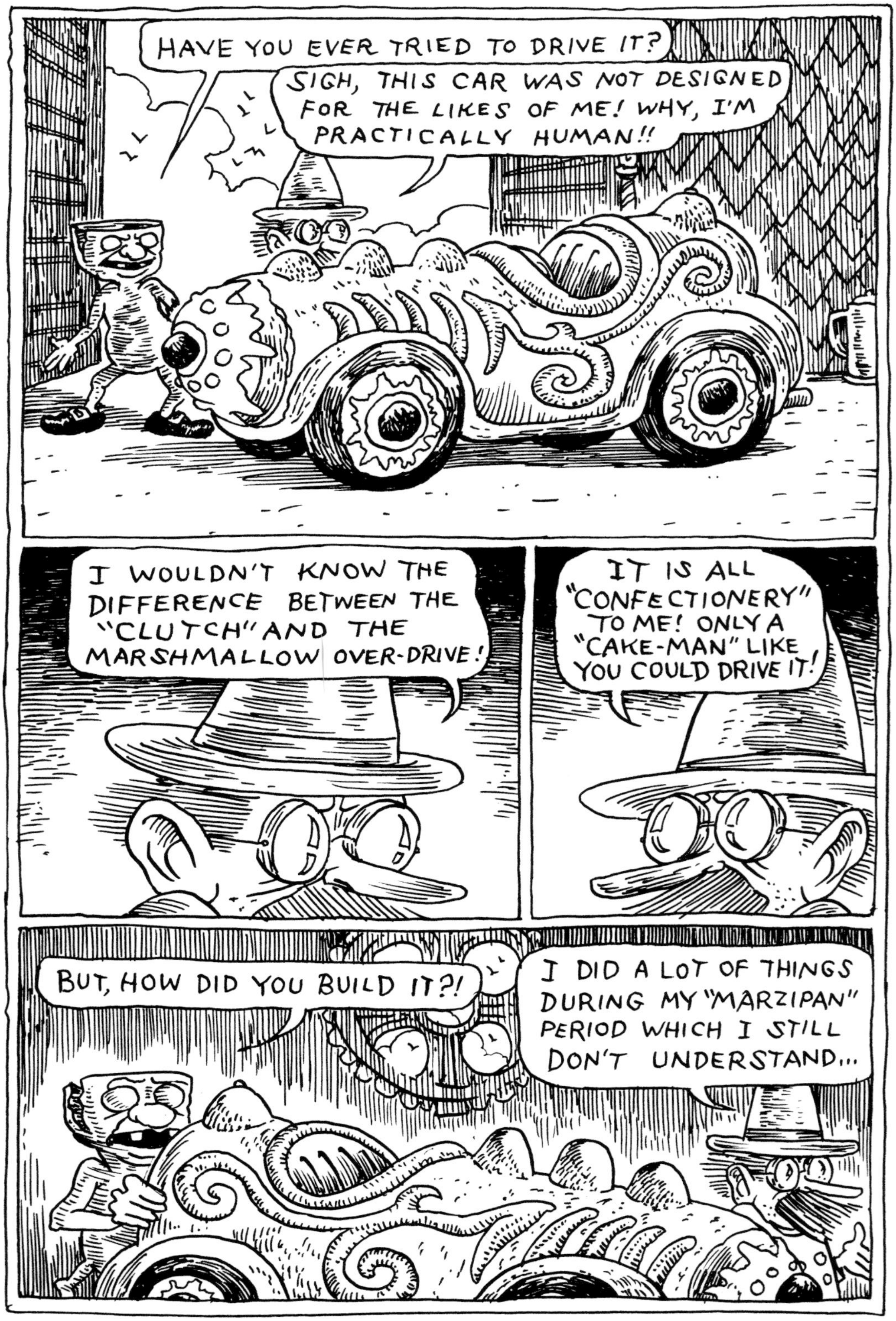
HAVE YOU EVER TRIED TO DRIVE IT?
SIGH, THIS CAR WAS NOT DESIGNED FOR THE LIKES OF ME! WHY, I'M PRACTICALLY HUMAN!!
I WOULDN'T KNOW THE DIFFERENCE BETWEEN THE "CLUTCH" AND THE MARSHMALLOW OVER-DRIVE!
IT IS ALL "CONFECTIONERY" TO ME! ONLY A "CAKE-MAN" LIKE YOU COULD DRIVE IT!
BUT, HOW DID YOU BUILD IT?!
I DID A LOT OF THINGS DURING MY "MARZIPAN" PERIOD WHICH I STILL DON'T UNDERSTAND...

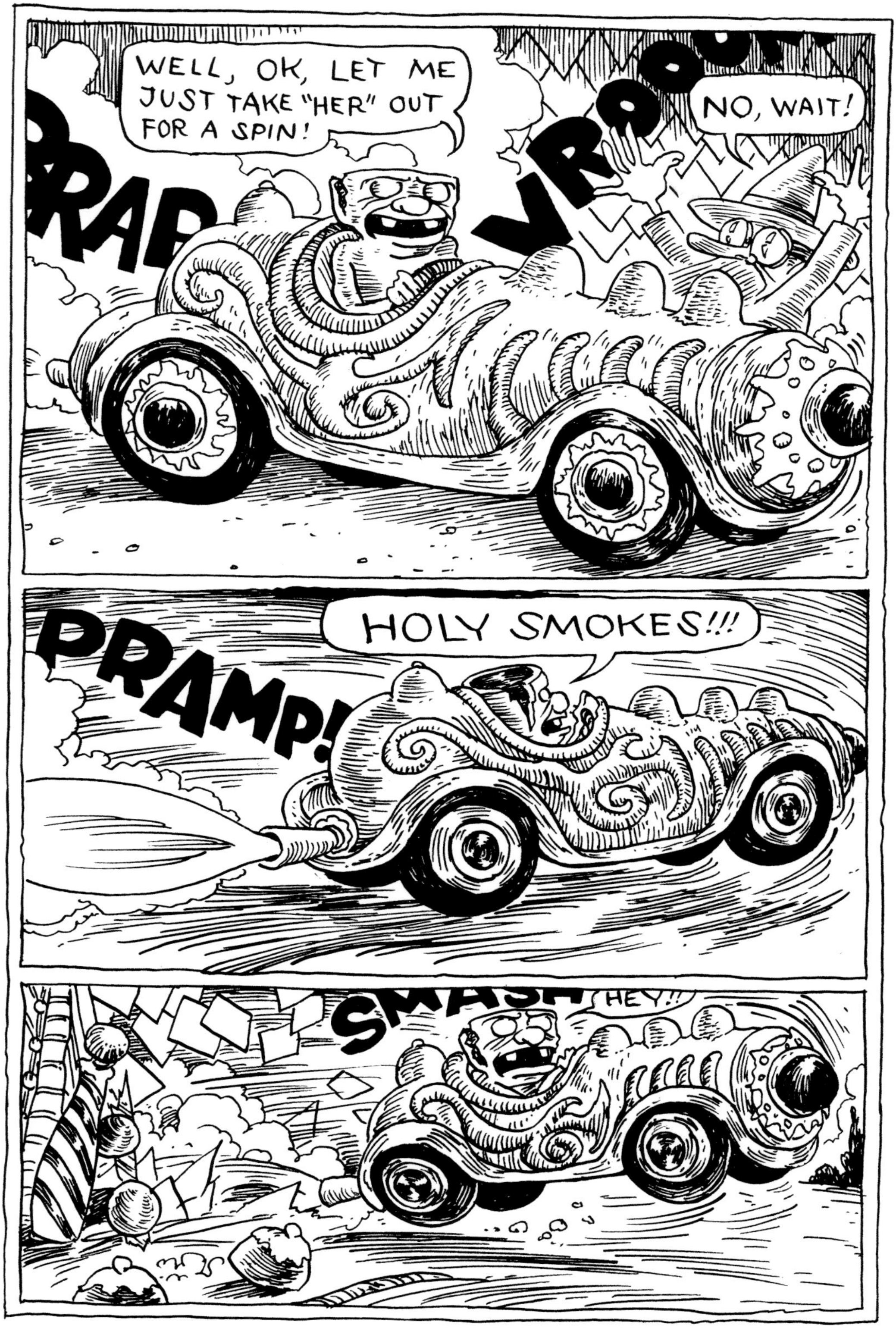
WELL, OK, LET ME JUST TAKE "HER" OUT FOR A SPIN!
RAP
VROO
NO, WAIT!
PRAMP!
HOLY SMOKES!!!
SMASH
HEY!!

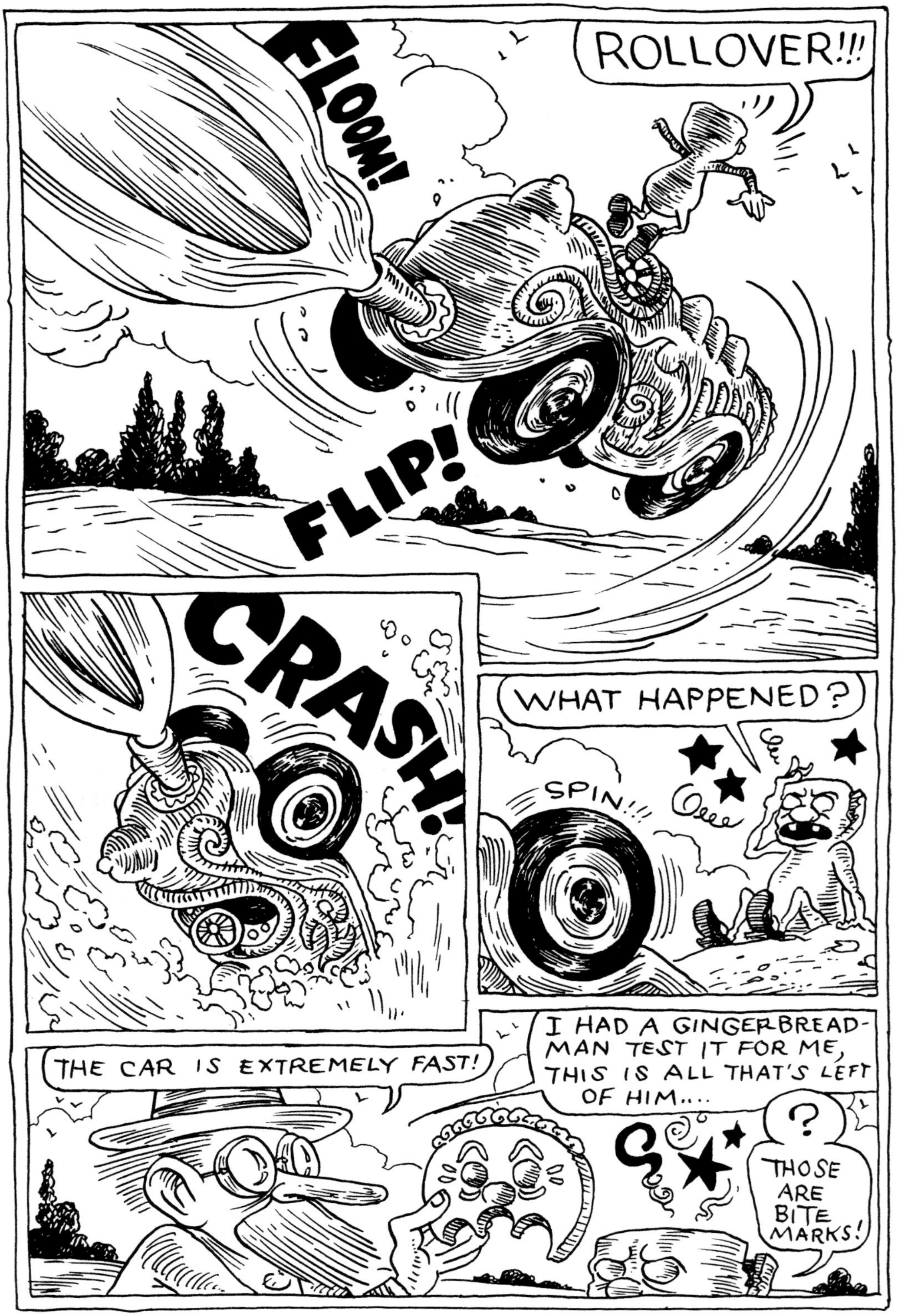

FLOOM!
ROLLOVER!!!
FLIP!
CRASH!
WHAT HAPPENED?
SPIN!!!
THE CAR IS EXTREMELY FAST!
I HAD A GINGERBREAD-MAN TEST IT FOR ME, THIS IS ALL THAT'S LEFT OF HIM....
?
THOSE ARE BITE MARKS!

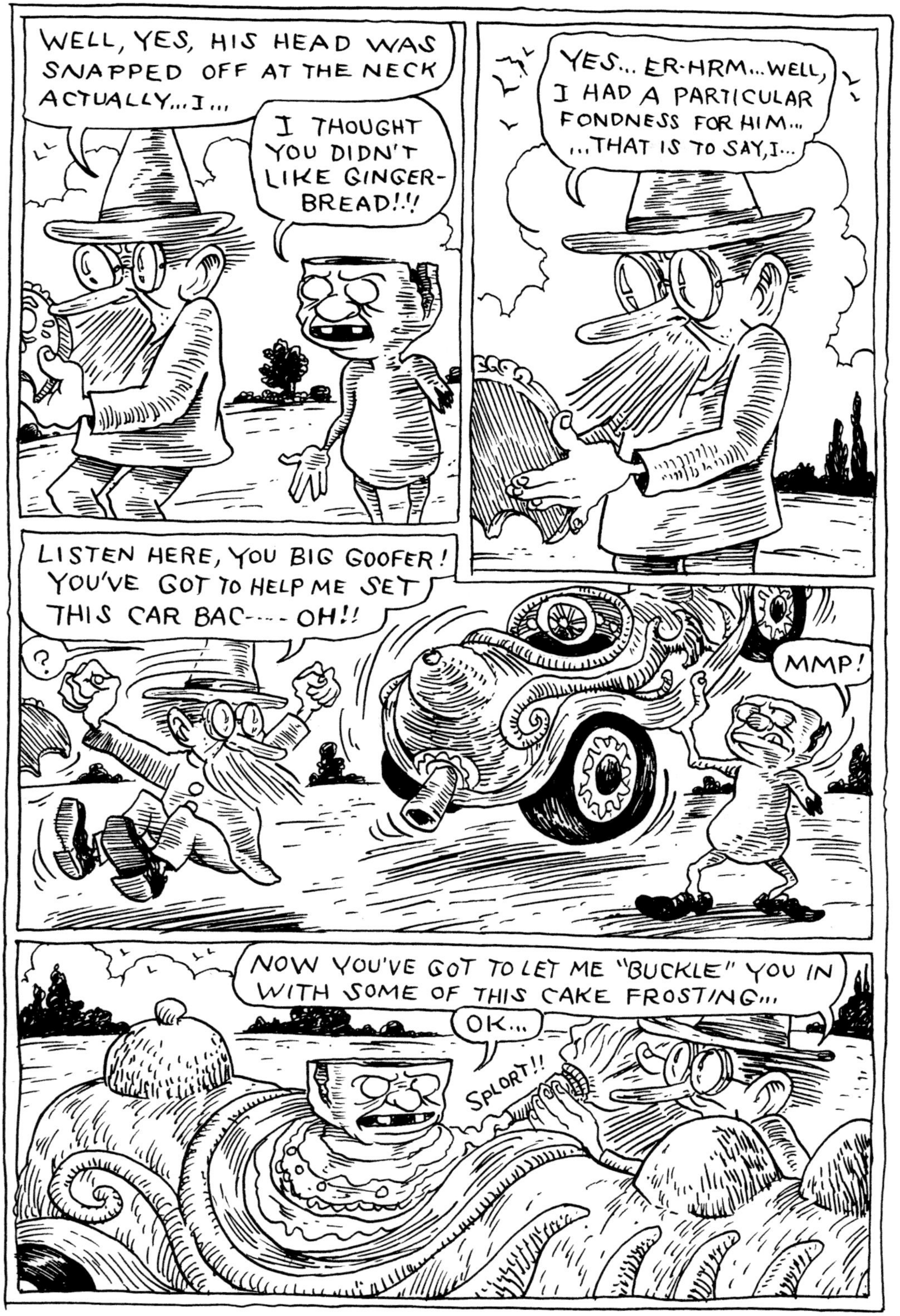
WELL, YES, HIS HEAD WAS SNAPPED OFF AT THE NECK ACTUALLY...I...
I THOUGHT YOU DIDN'T LIKE GINGER-BREAD!!!
YES... ER-HRM...WELL, I HAD A PARTICULAR FONDNESS FOR HIM... ...THAT IS TO SAY, I...
LISTEN HERE, YOU BIG GOOFER! YOU'VE GOT TO HELP ME SET THIS CAR BAC----OH!!
?
MMP!
NOW YOU'VE GOT TO LET ME "BUCKLE" YOU IN WITH SOME OF THIS CAKE FROSTING...
OK...
SPLORT!!

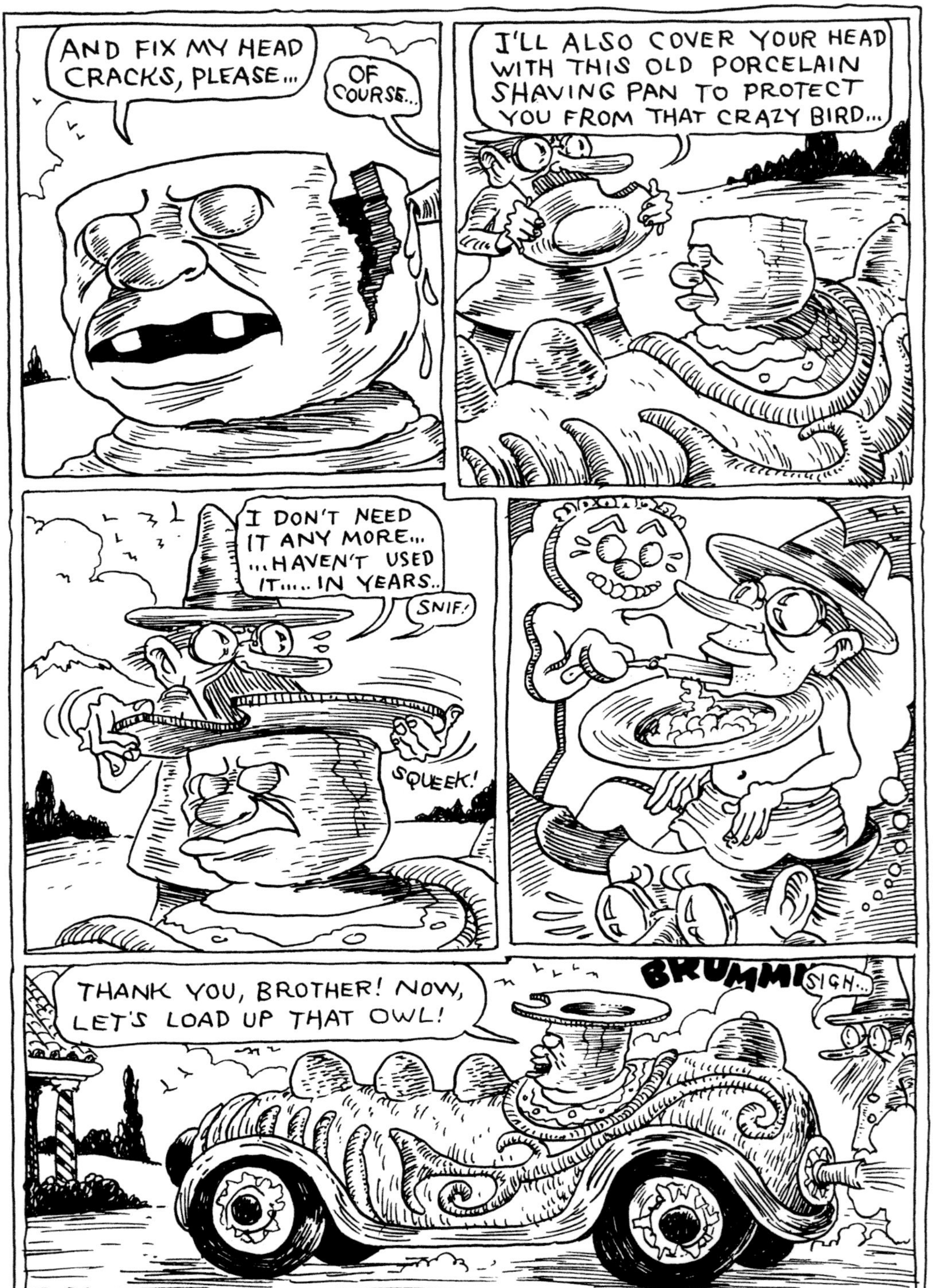
AND FIX MY HEAD CRACKS, PLEASE...
OF COURSE...
I'LL ALSO COVER YOUR HEAD WITH THIS OLD PORCELAIN SHAVING PAN TO PROTECT YOU FROM THAT CRAZY BIRD...
I DON'T NEED IT ANY MORE... ...HAVEN'T USED IT..... IN YEARS..
SNIF!
SQUEEK!
THANK YOU, BROTHER! NOW, LET'S LOAD UP THAT OWL!
BRUMM
SIGH...

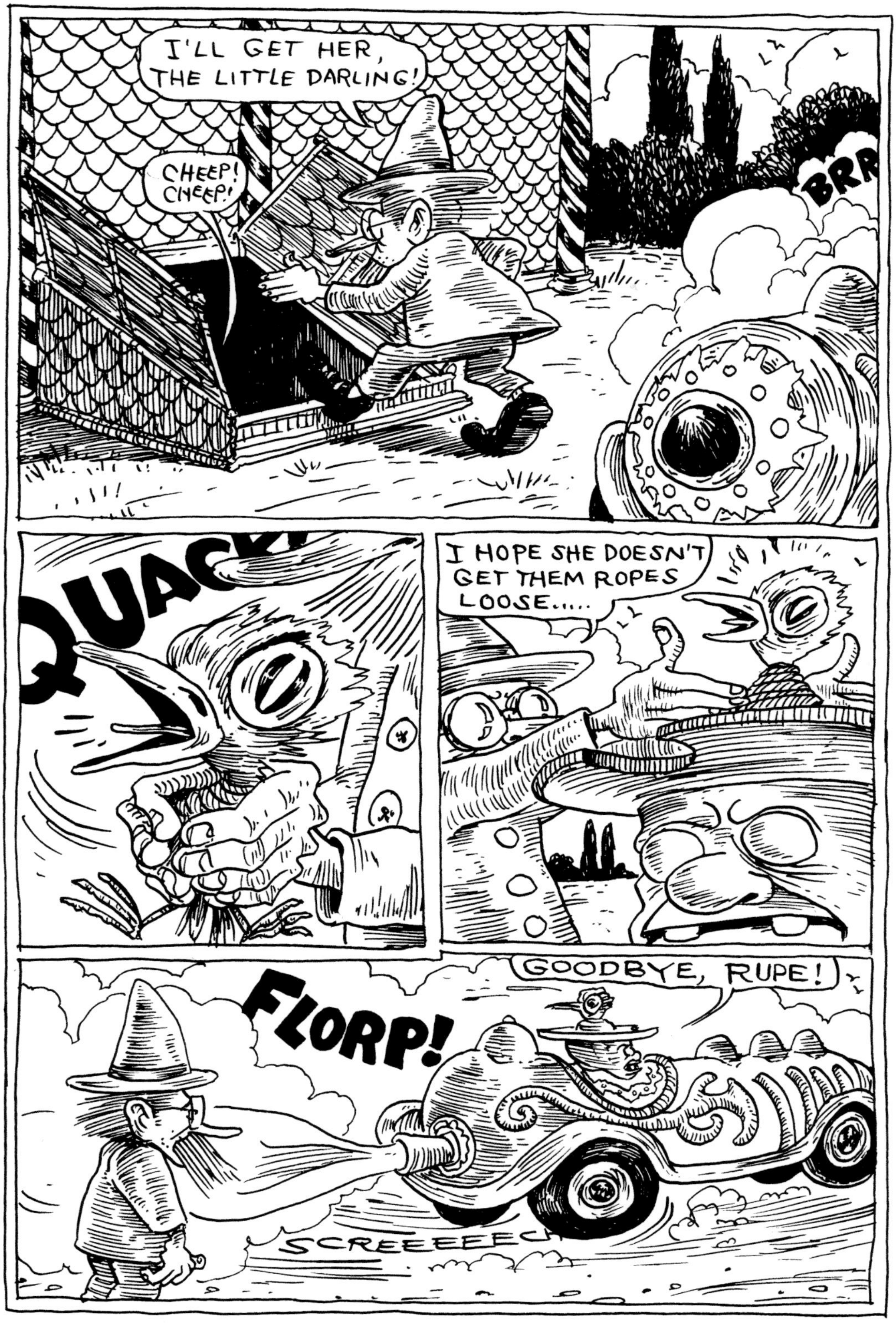

I'LL GET HER, THE LITTLE DARLING!
CHEEP! CHEEP!
BRR
I HOPE SHE DOESN'T GET THEM ROPES LOOSE.....
GOODBYE, RUPE!
FLORP!
SCREEEEEECH

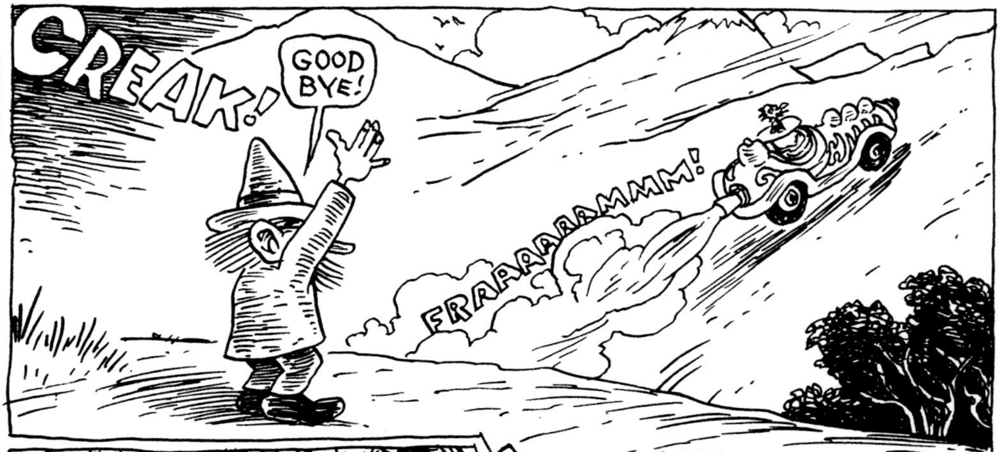
CREAK!
GOOD BYE!
FRRAAAARAAMMMM!

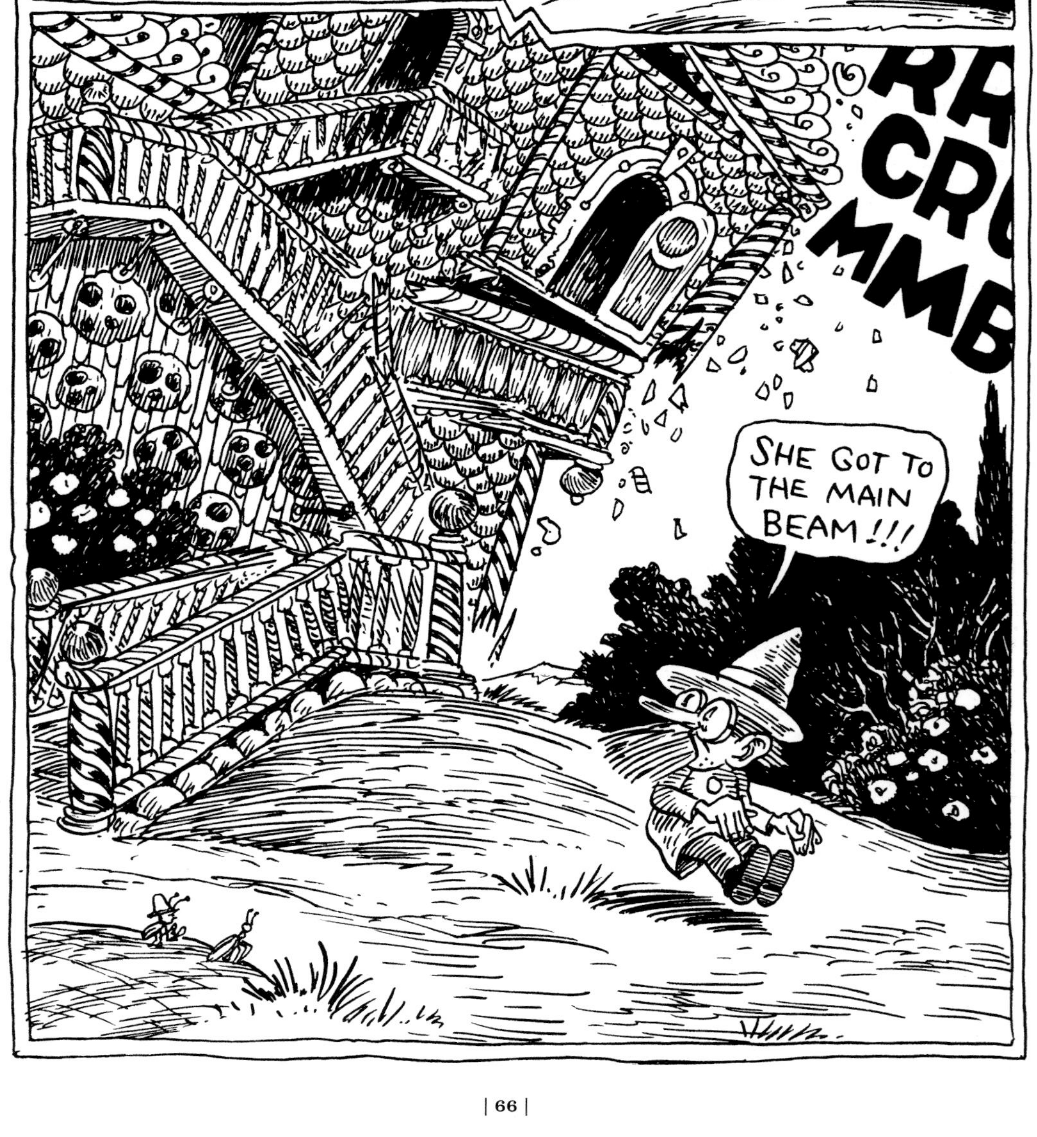
RA CRU MMB
SHE GOT TO THE MAIN BEAM!!!

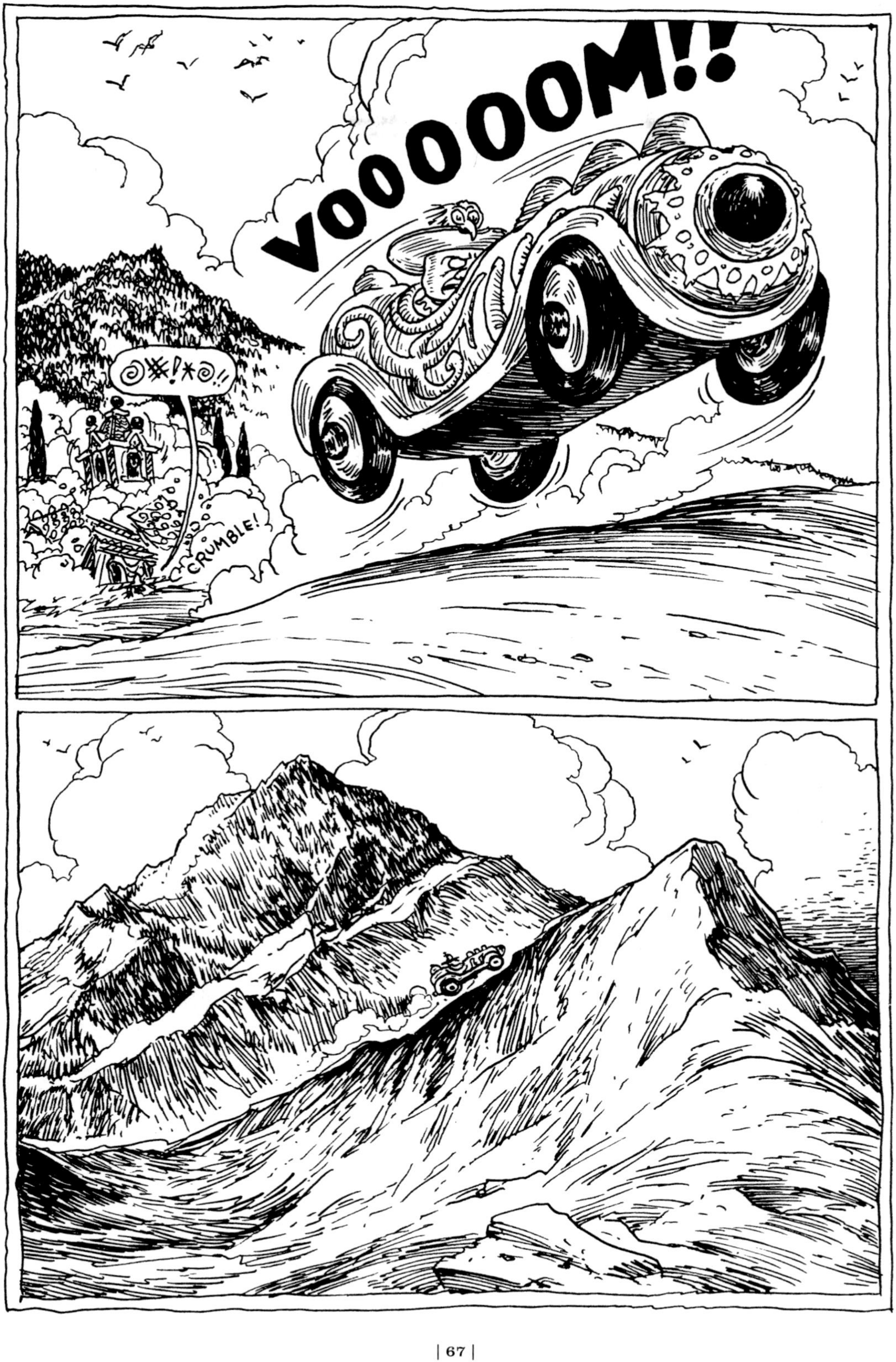
VOOOOOM!!
CRUMBLE!

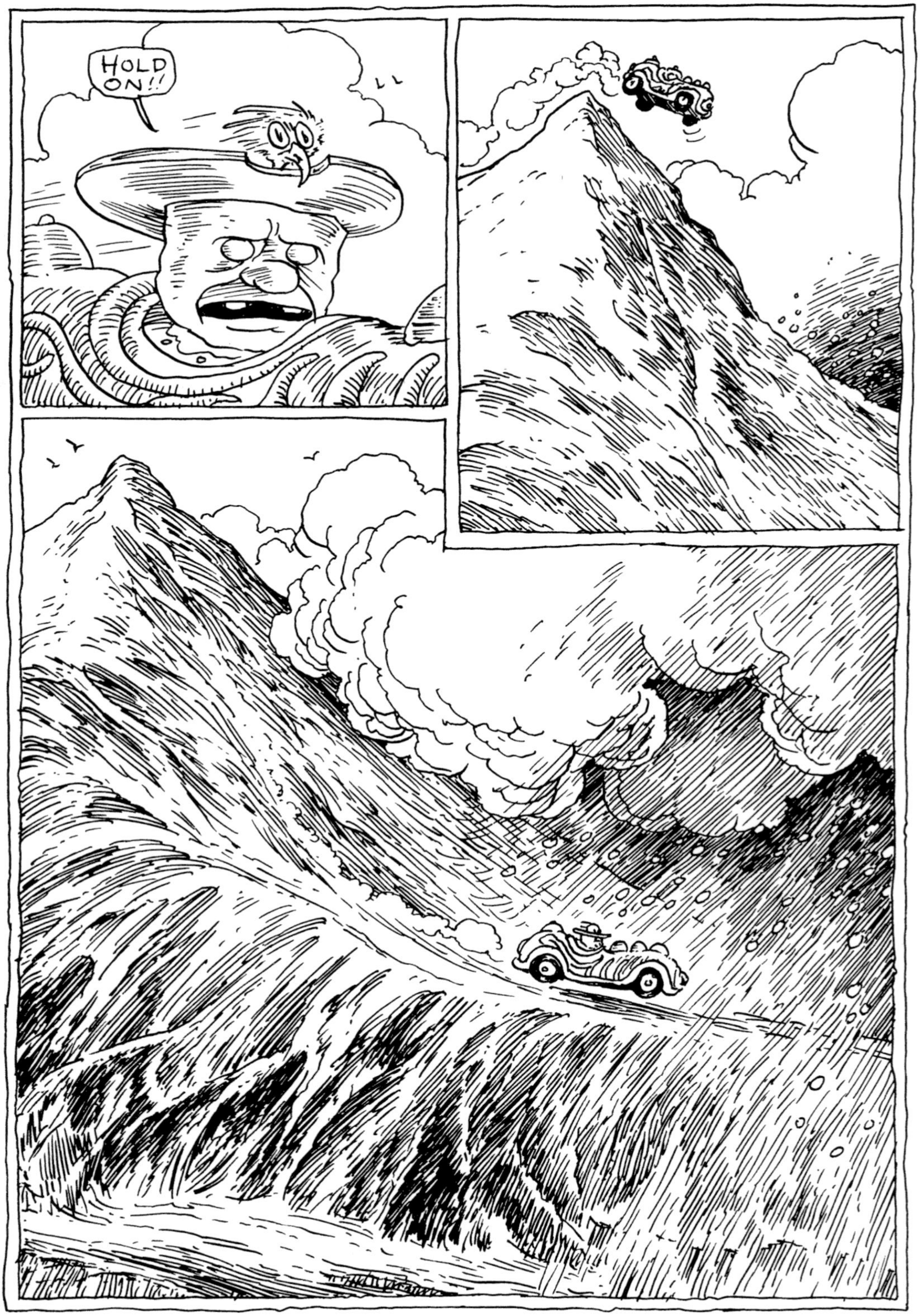
HOLD ON!!

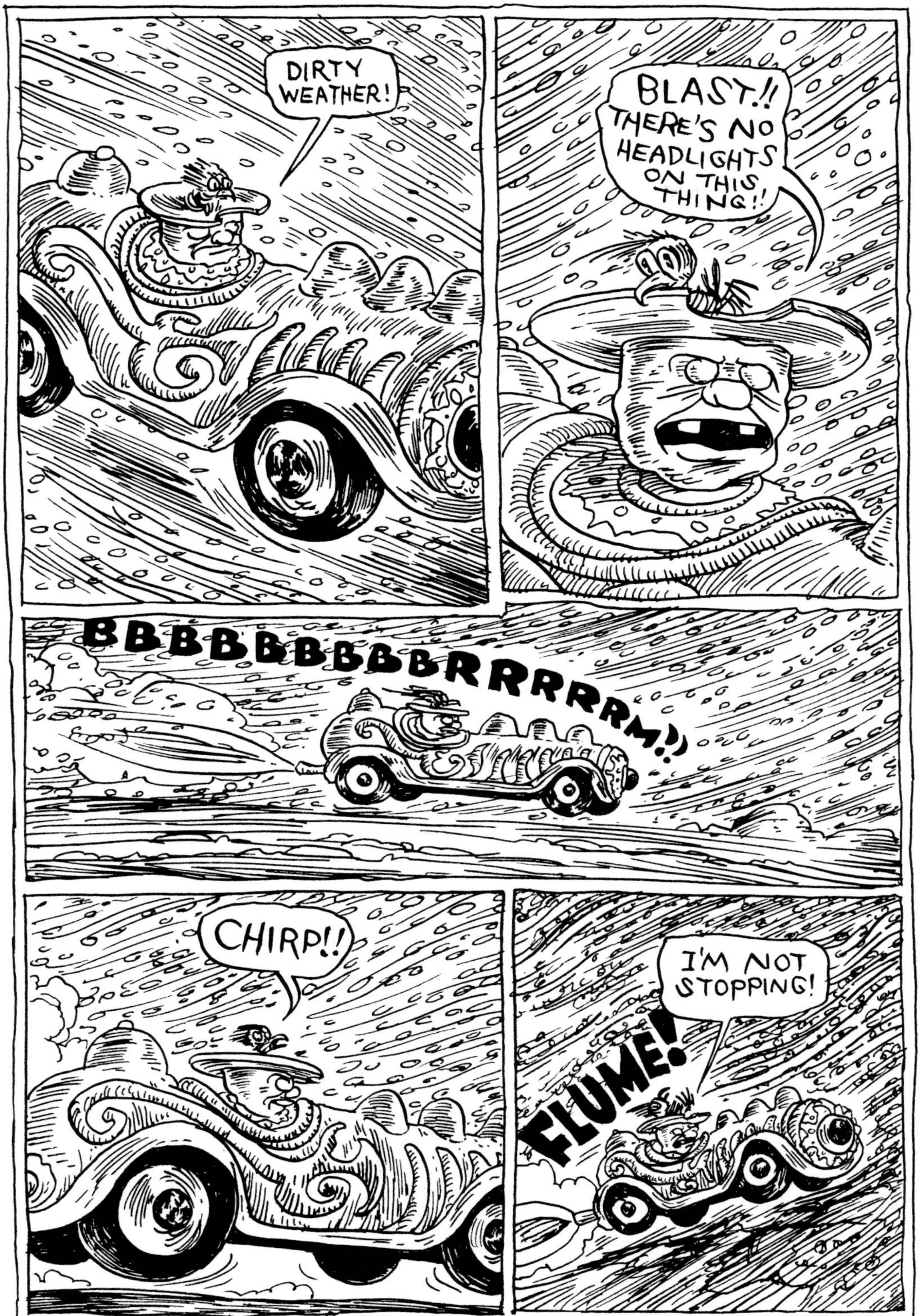
DIRTY WEATHER!
BLAST!! THERE'S NO HEADLIGHTS ON THIS THING!!
BBBBBBBBBRRRRRRRM!!
CHIRP!!
I'M NOT STOPPING!
FLUME!

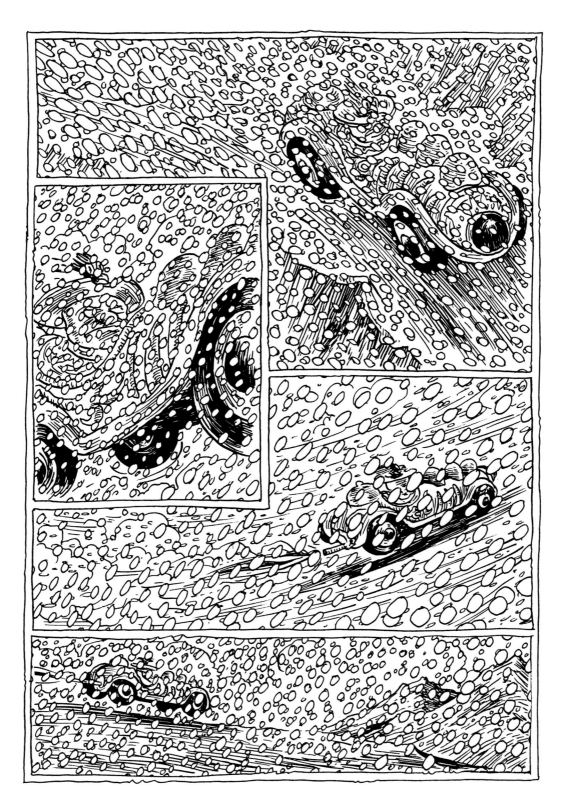

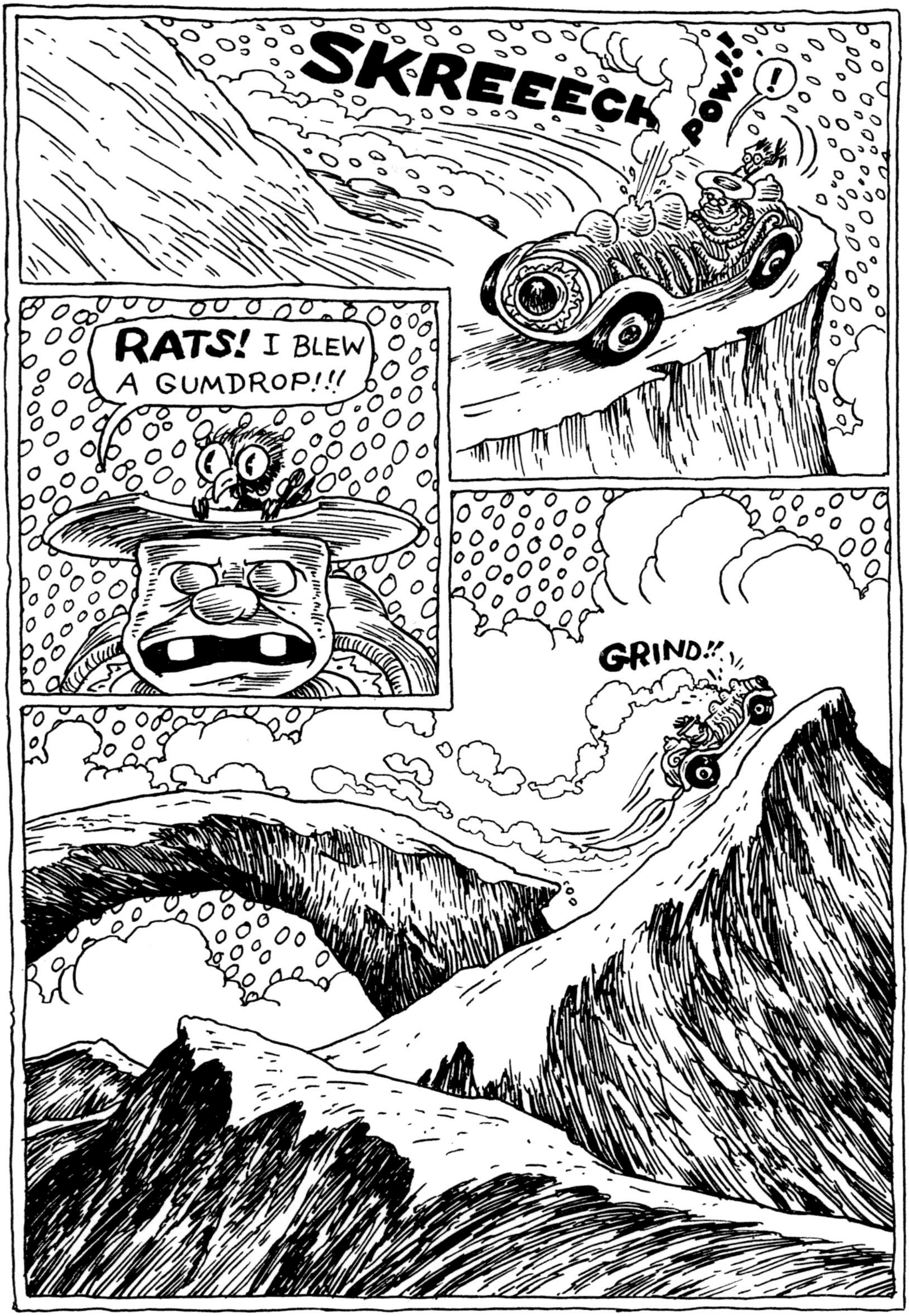
SKREEECH
POW!!
!
RATS! I BLEW A GUMDROP!!!
GRIND!!
!

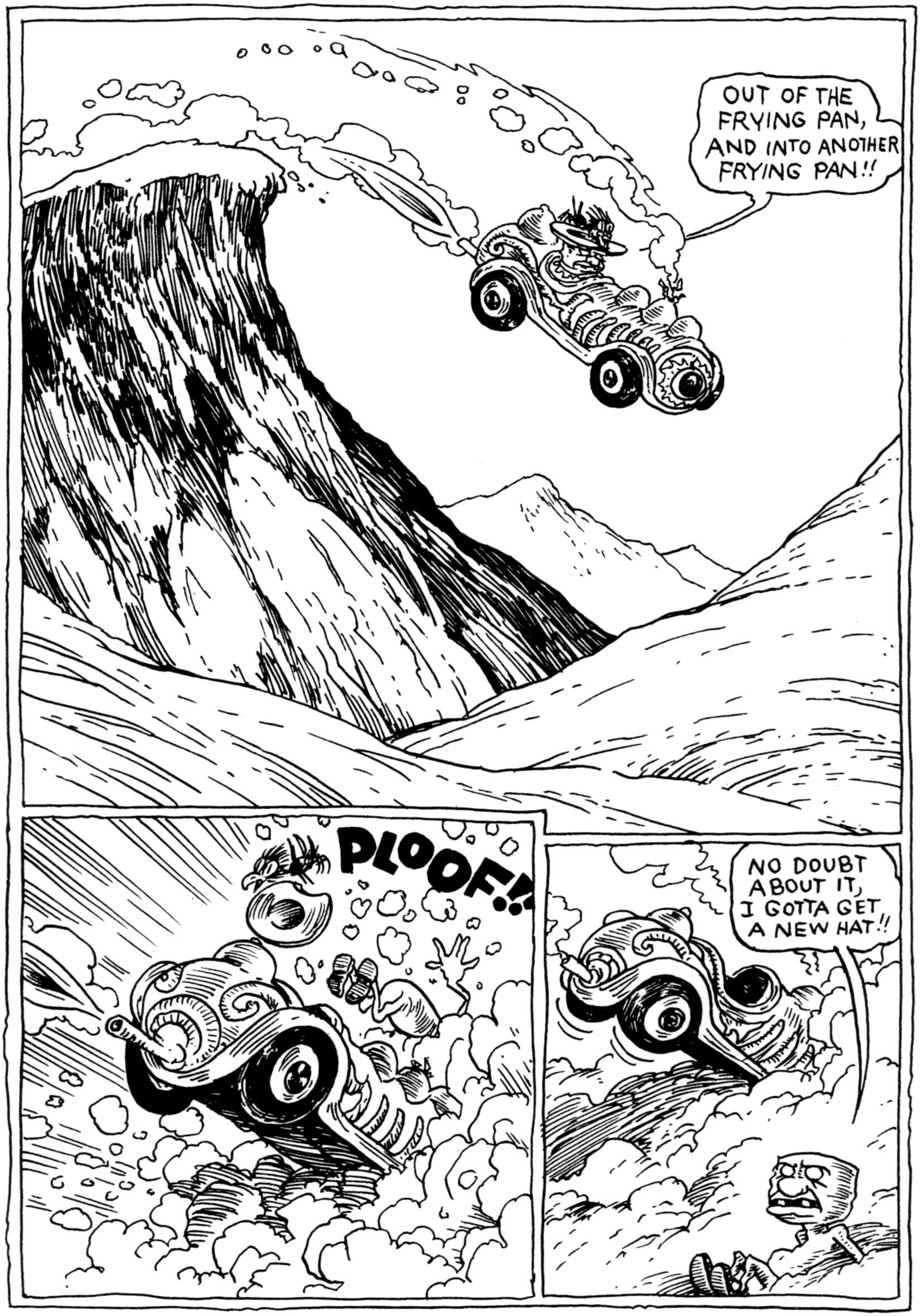
OUT OF THE FRYING PAN, AND INTO ANOTHER FRYING PAN!!
PLOOF!!
NO DOUBT ABOUT IT, I GOTTA GET A NEW HAT!!

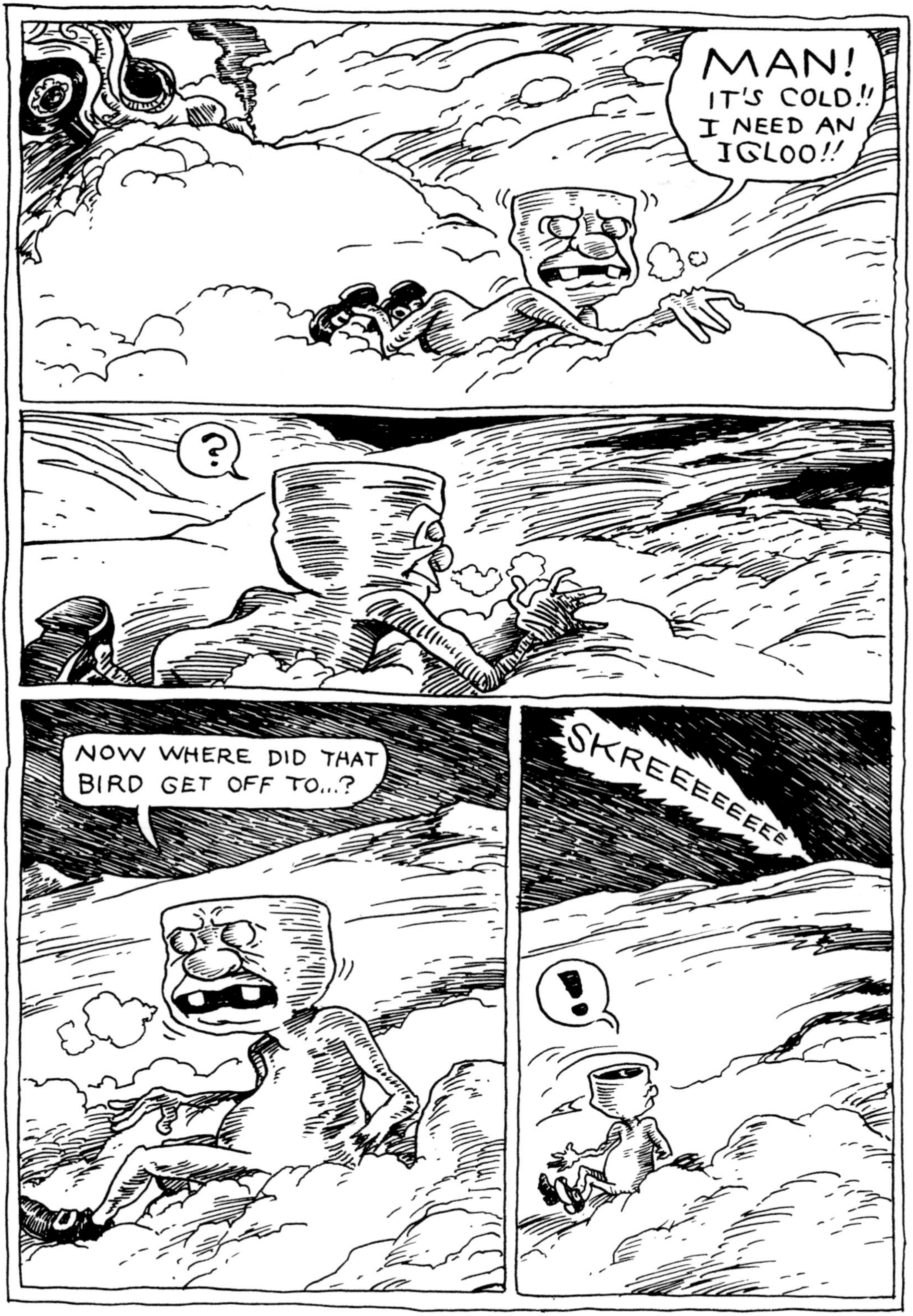
MAN! IT'S COLD!! I NEED AN IGLOO!!
?
NOW WHERE DID THAT BIRD GET OFF TO...?
SKREEEEEEEEE
!

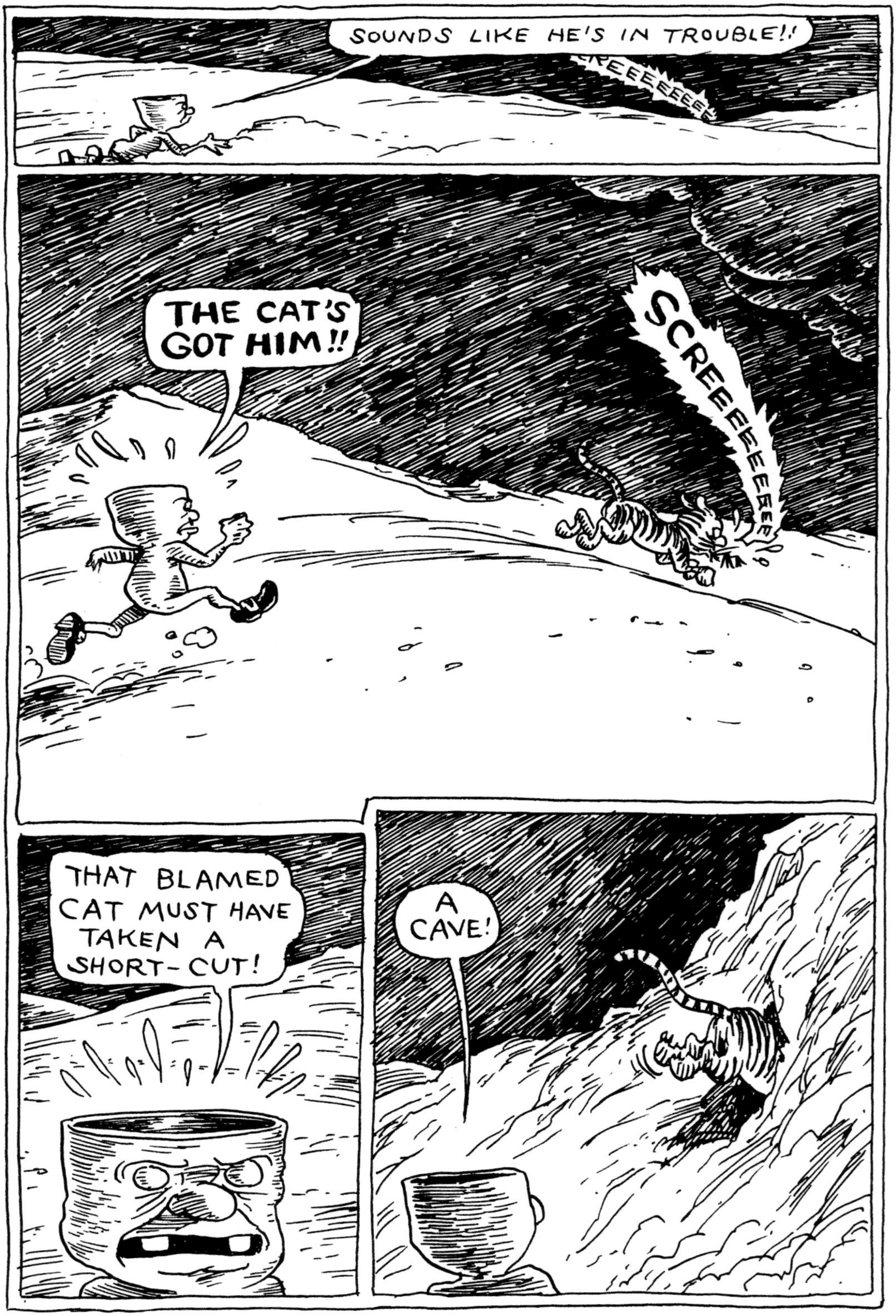
SOUNDS LIKE HE'S IN TROUBLE!!
THE CAT'S GOT HIM!!
SCREEEEEEEEEEE
THAT BLAMED CAT MUST HAVE TAKEN A SHORT-CUT!
A CAVE!

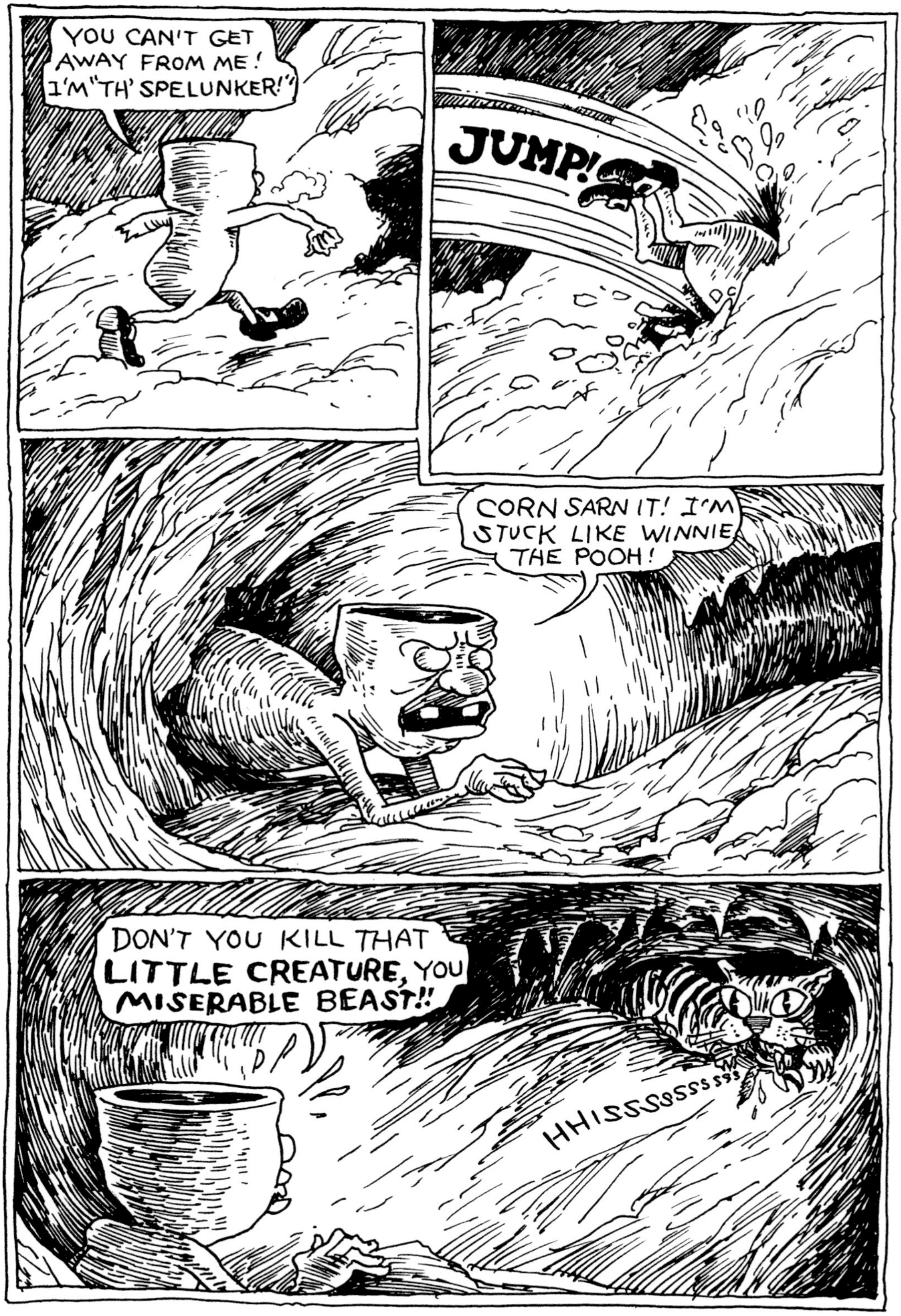
YOU CAN'T GET AWAY FROM ME! I'M "TH' SPELUNKER!"
JUMP!
CORN SARN IT! I'M STUCK LIKE WINNIE THE POOH!
DON'T YOU KILL THAT LITTLE CREATURE, YOU MISERABLE BEAST!!
HHISSSSSSSSSSS

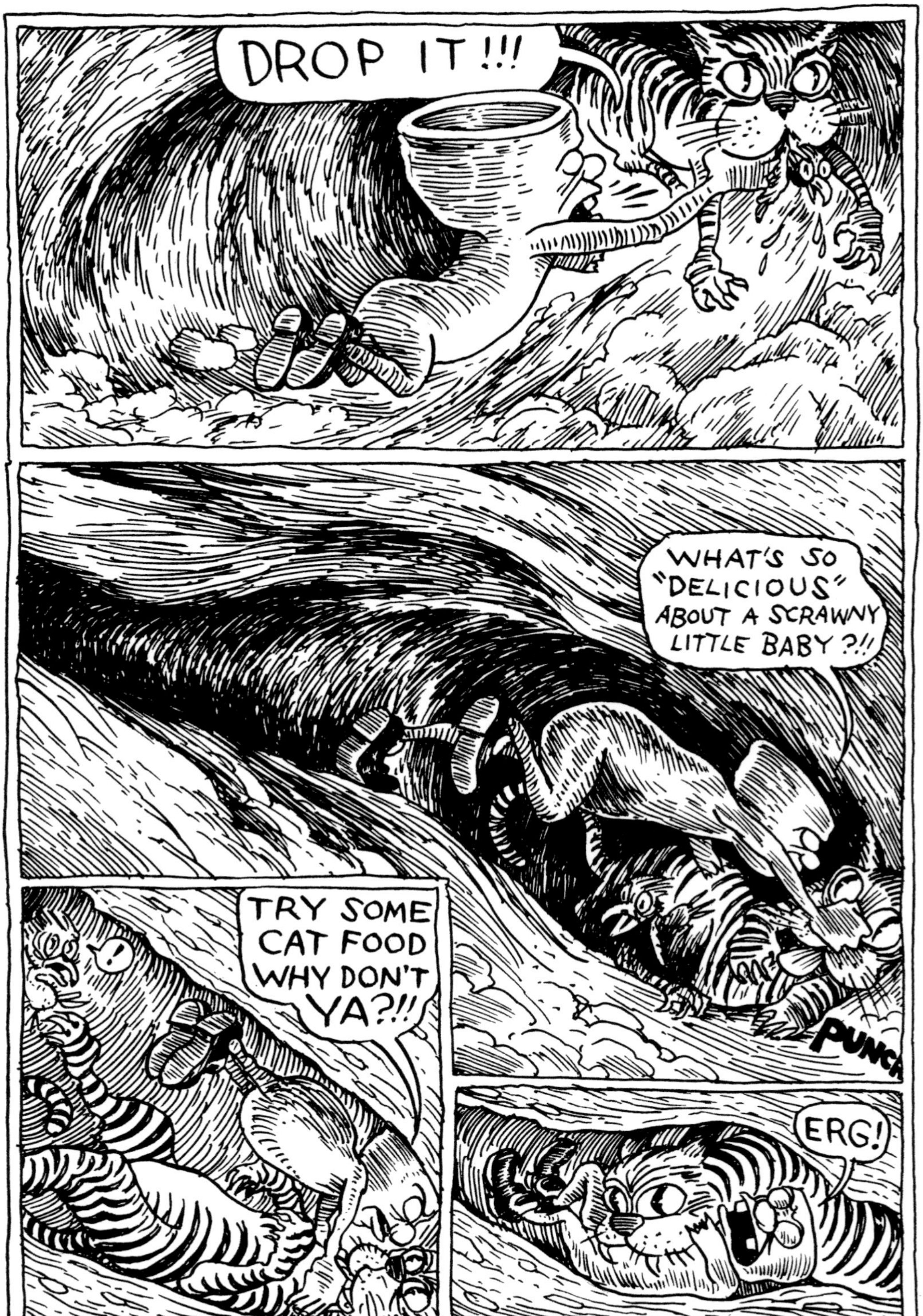
DROP IT!!!
WHAT'S SO "DELICIOUS" ABOUT A SCRAWNY LITTLE BABY?!!
TRY SOME CAT FOOD WHY DON'T YA?!!
PUNCH
ERG!

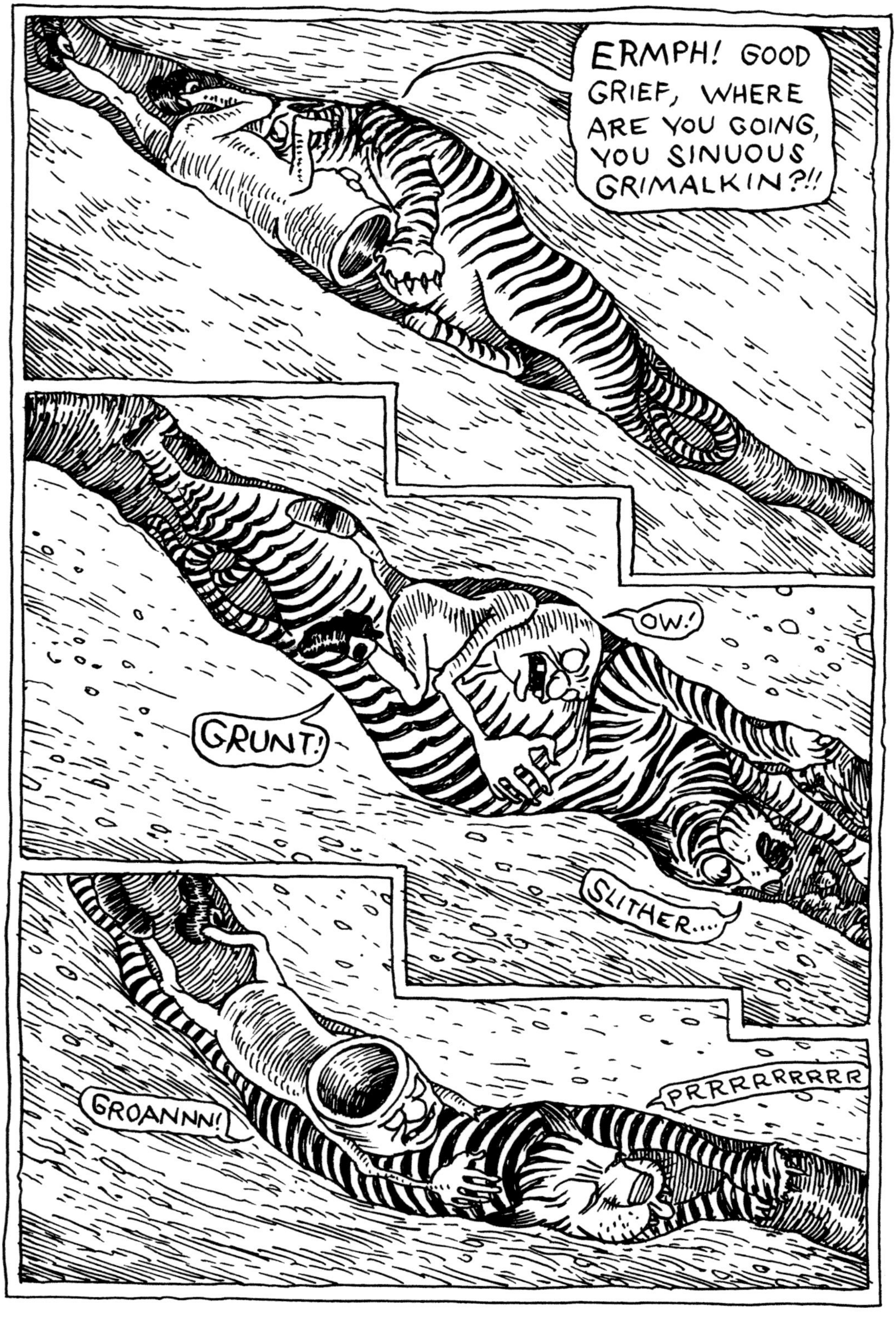

ERMPH! GOOD GRIEF, WHERE ARE YOU GOING, YOU SINUOUS GRIMALKIN?!!
OW!
GRUNT!
SLITHER....
GROANNN!
PRRRRRRRRRR

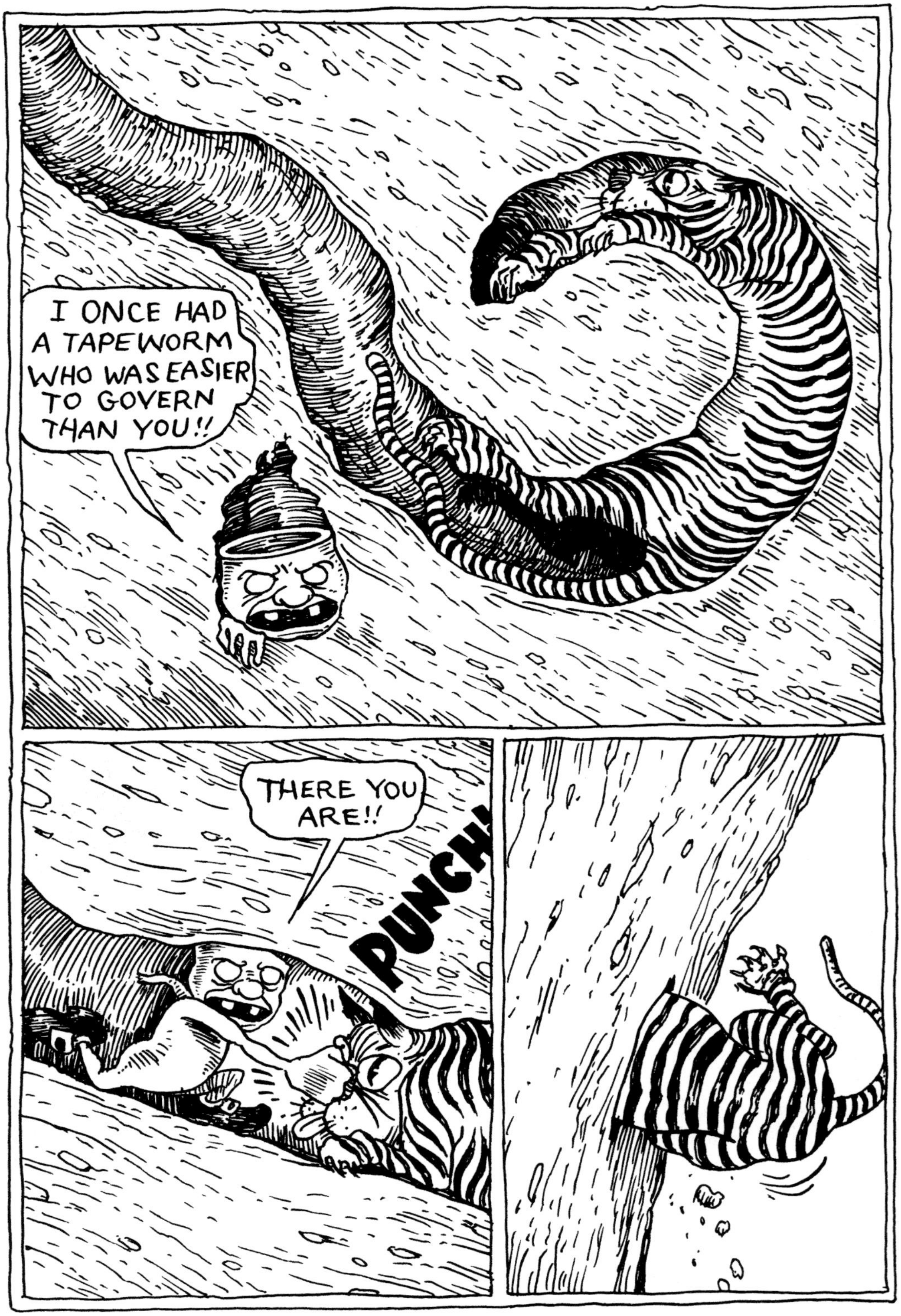
I ONCE HAD A TAPEWORM WHO WAS EASIER TO GOVERN THAN YOU!!
THERE YOU ARE!!
PUNCH!

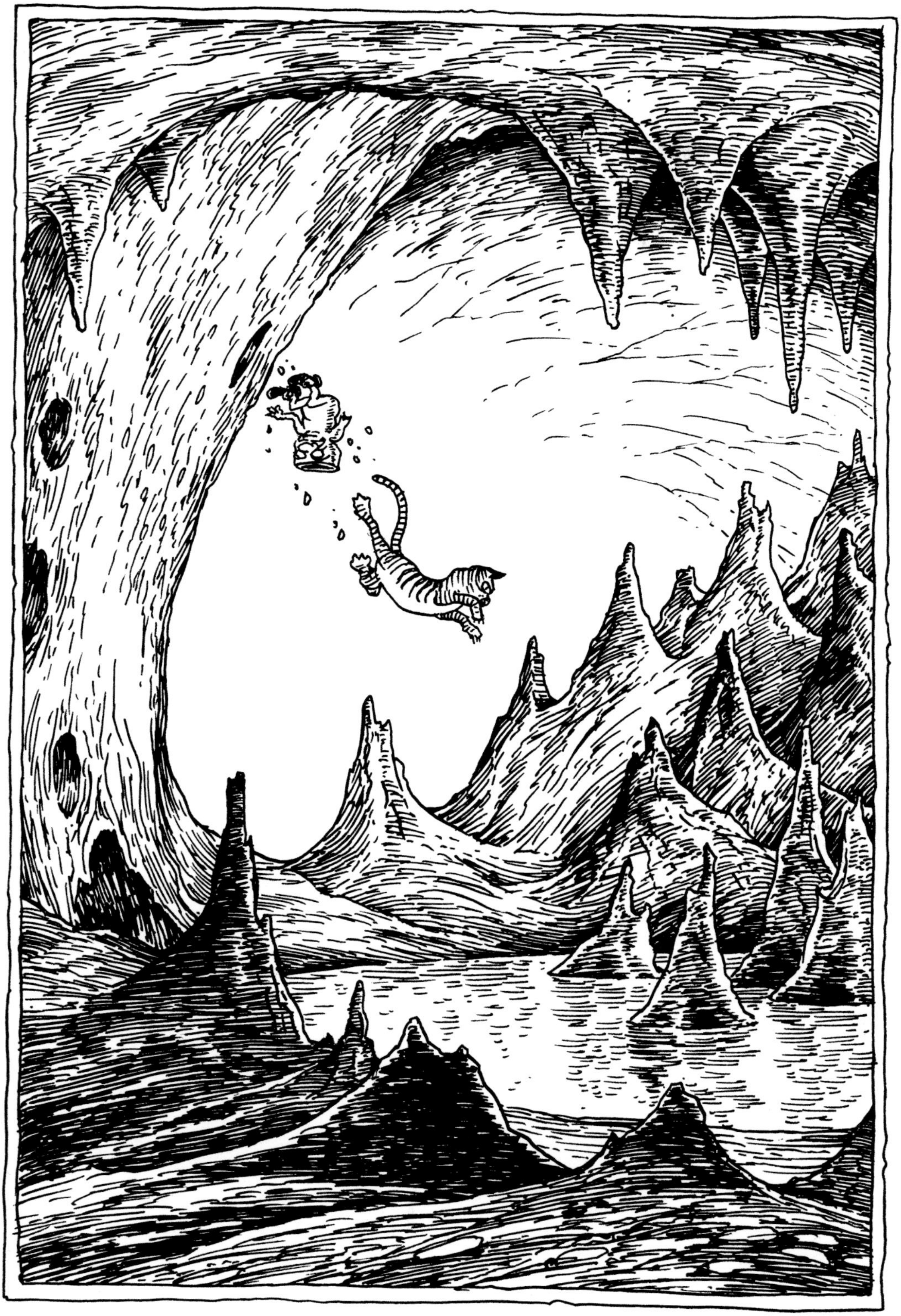

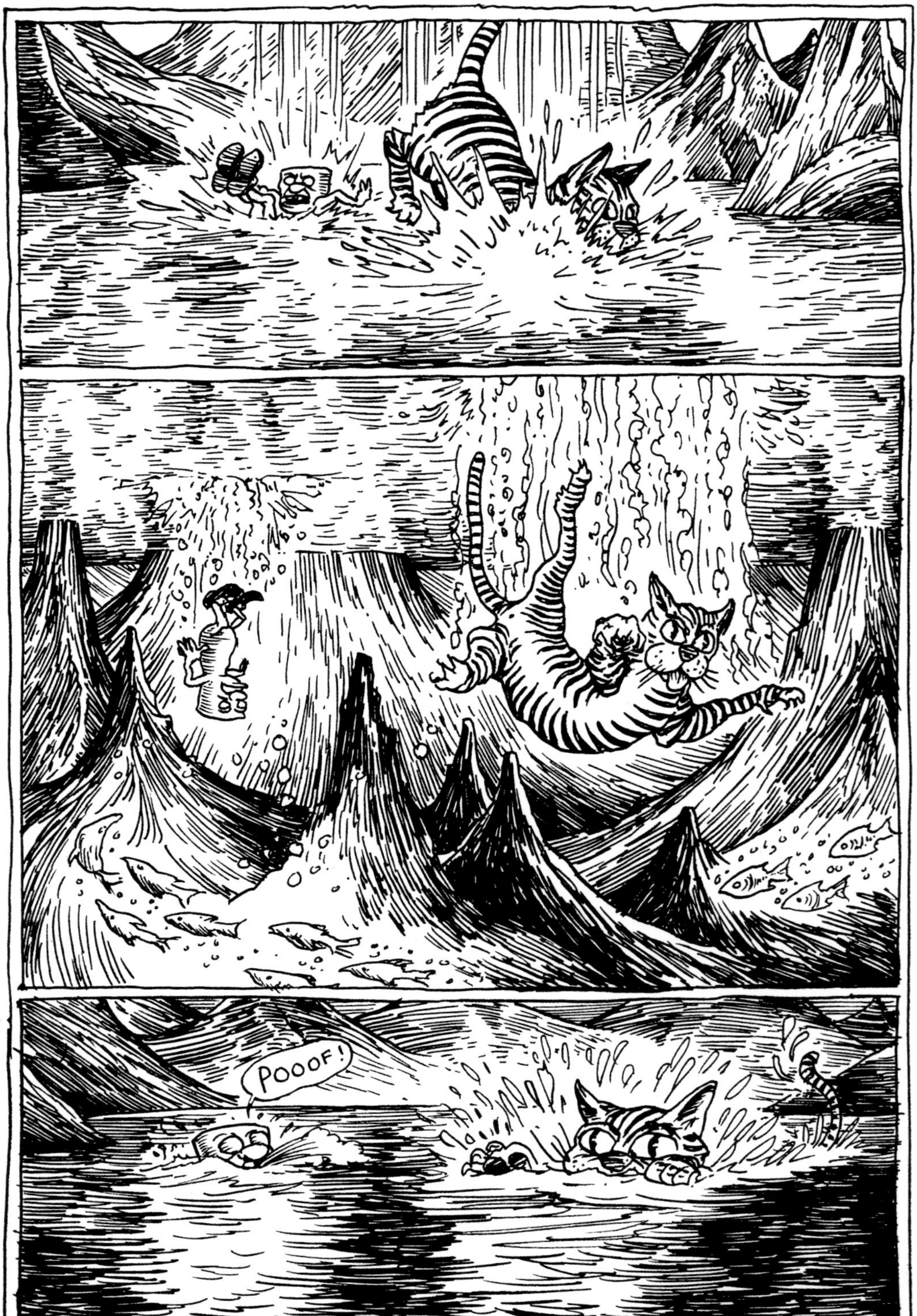
POOOF!

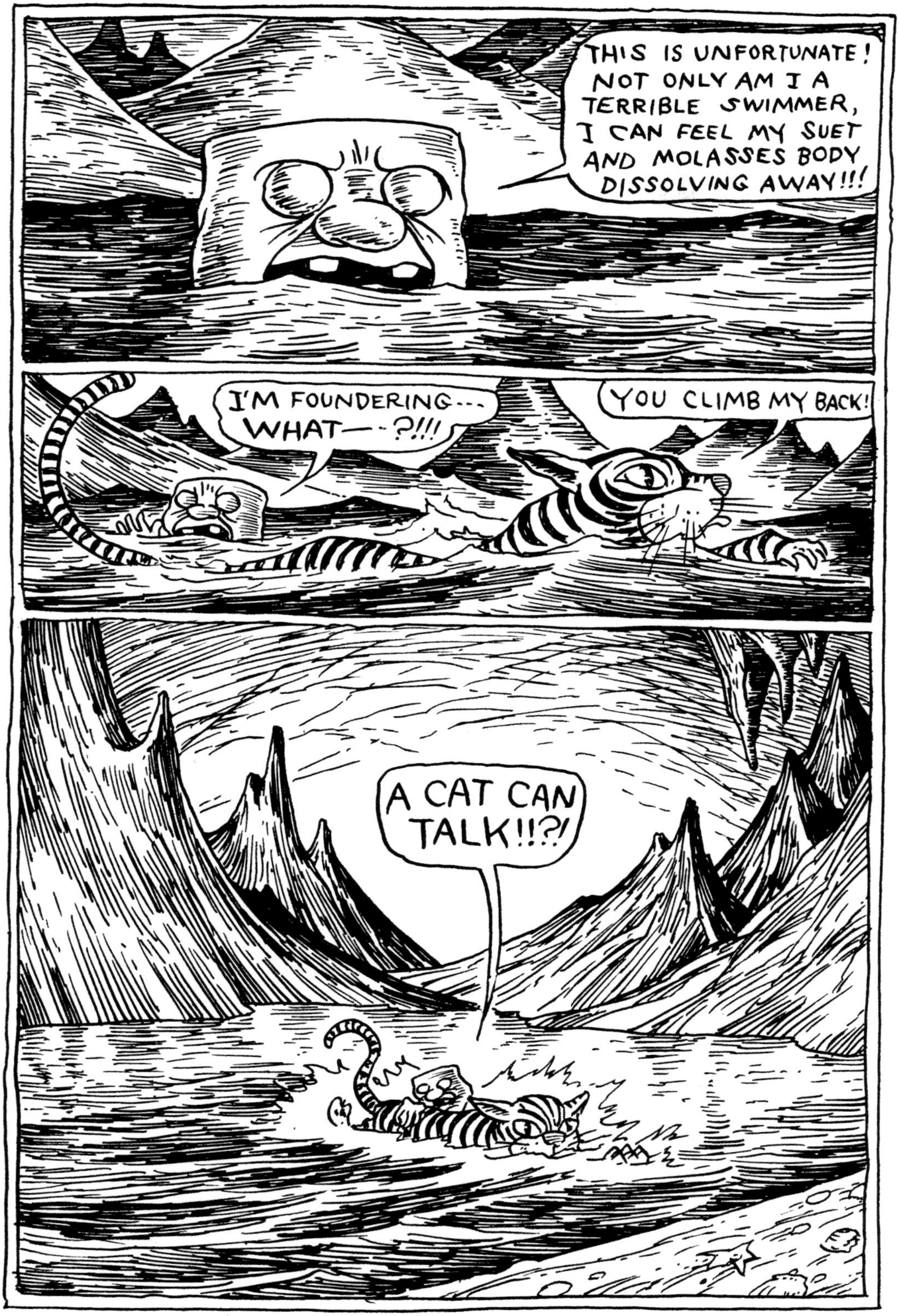
THIS IS UNFORTUNATE! NOT ONLY AM I A TERRIBLE SWIMMER, I CAN FEEL MY SUET AND MOLASSES BODY DISSOLVING AWAY!!!
I'M FOUNDERING... WHAT—?!!!
YOU CLIMB MY BACK!
A CAT CAN TALK!!?!

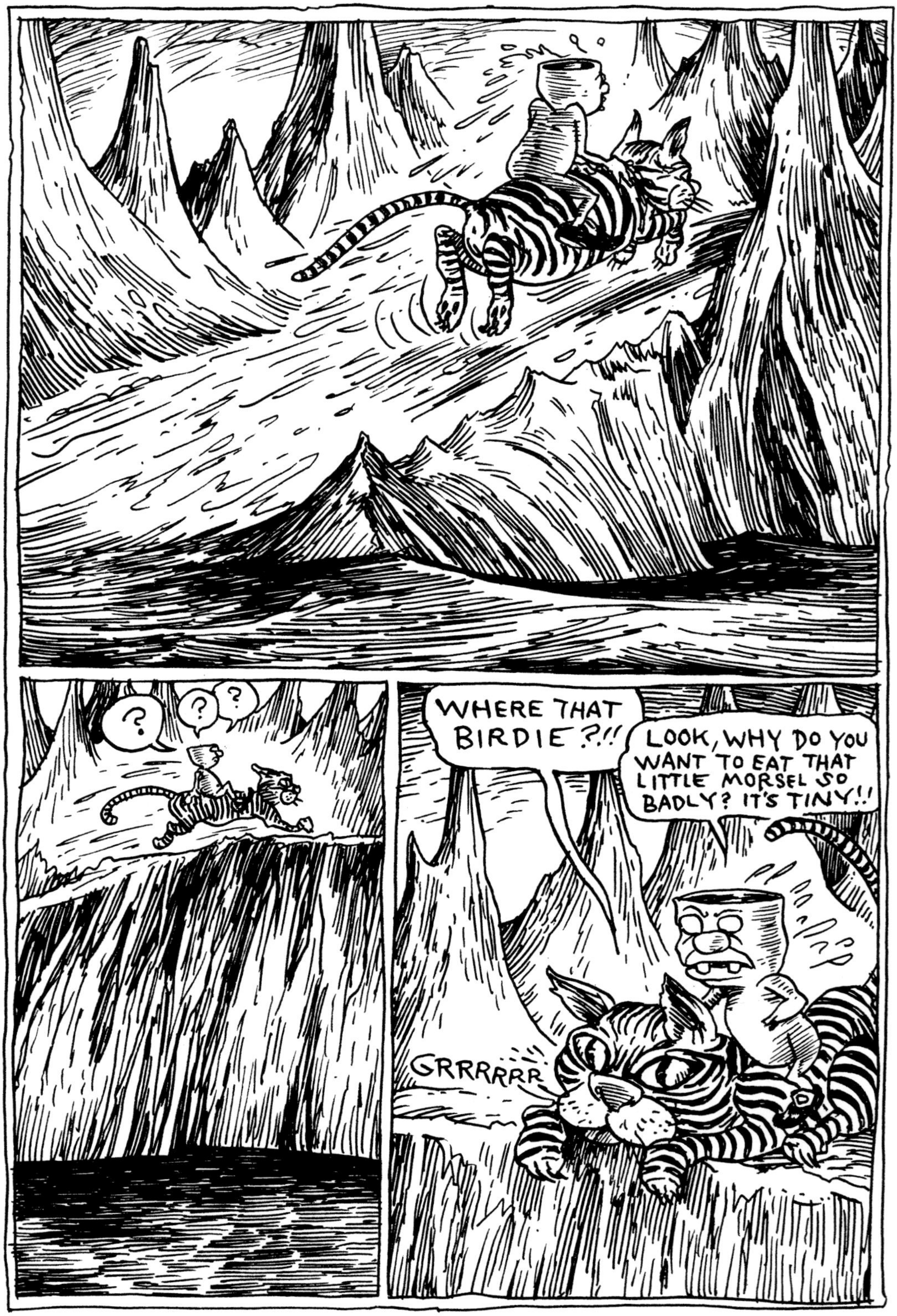
?
?
?
WHERE THAT BIRDIE ?!!
LOOK, WHY DO YOU WANT TO EAT THAT LITTLE MORSEL SO BADLY? IT'S TINY!!
GRRRRRR

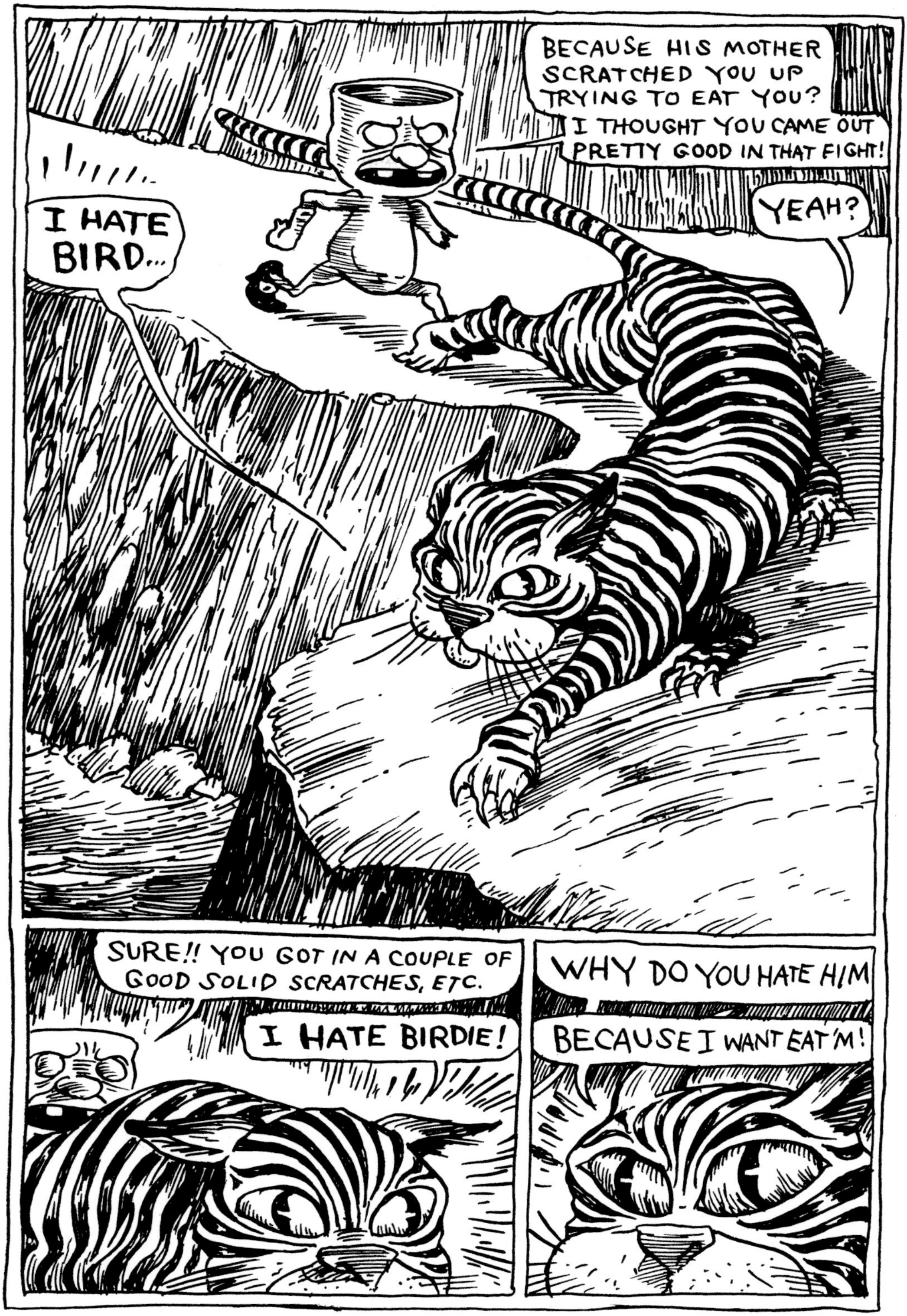

BECAUSE HIS MOTHER SCRATCHED YOU UP TRYING TO EAT YOU?
I THOUGHT YOU CAME OUT PRETTY GOOD IN THAT FIGHT!
I HATE BIRD...
YEAH?
SURE!! YOU GOT IN A COUPLE OF GOOD SOLID SCRATCHES, ETC.
I HATE BIRDIE!
WHY DO YOU HATE HIM
BECAUSE I WANT EAT 'M!

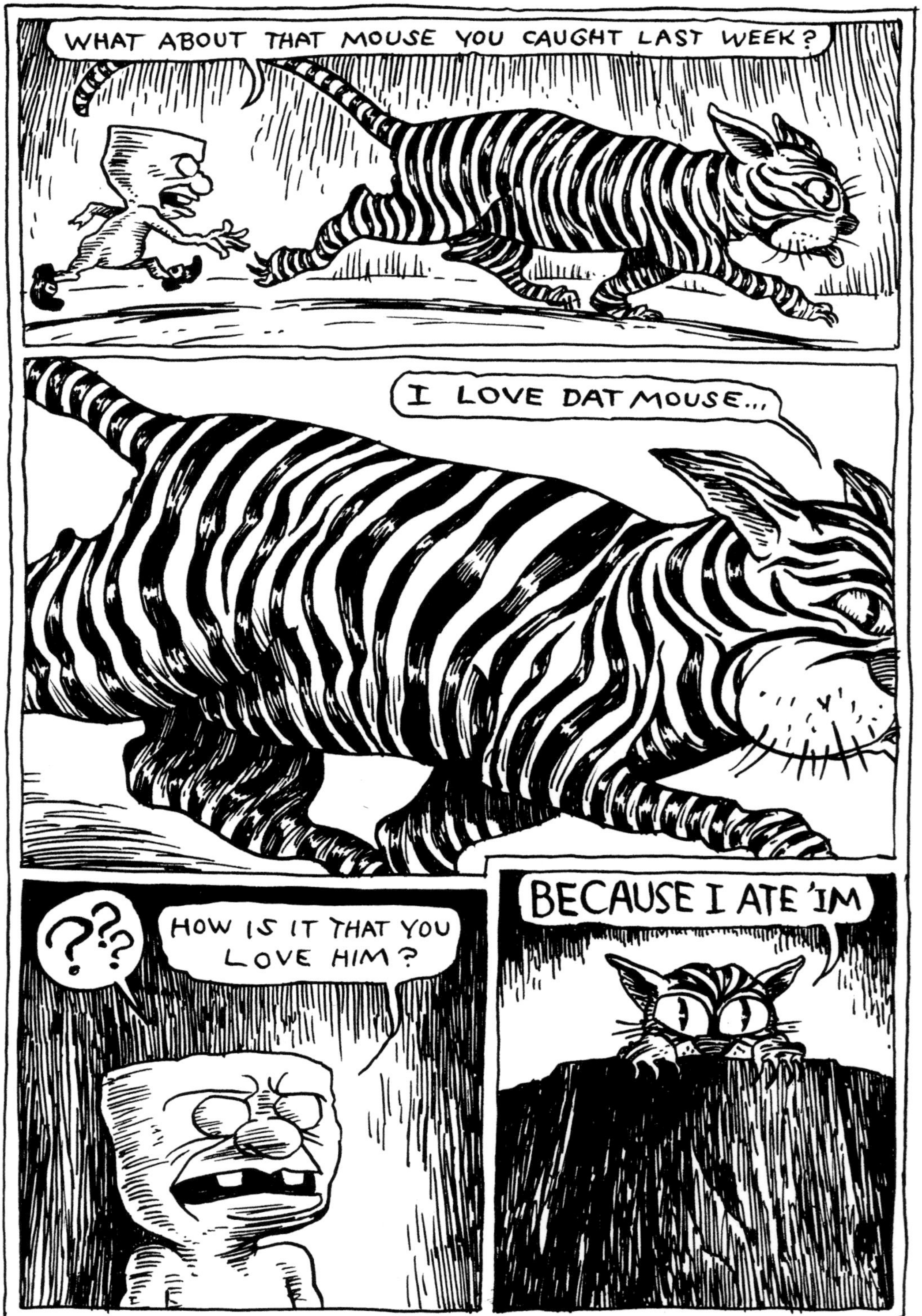
WHAT ABOUT THAT MOUSE YOU CAUGHT LAST WEEK?
I LOVE DAT MOUSE...
??
HOW IS IT THAT YOU LOVE HIM?
BECAUSE I ATE 'IM

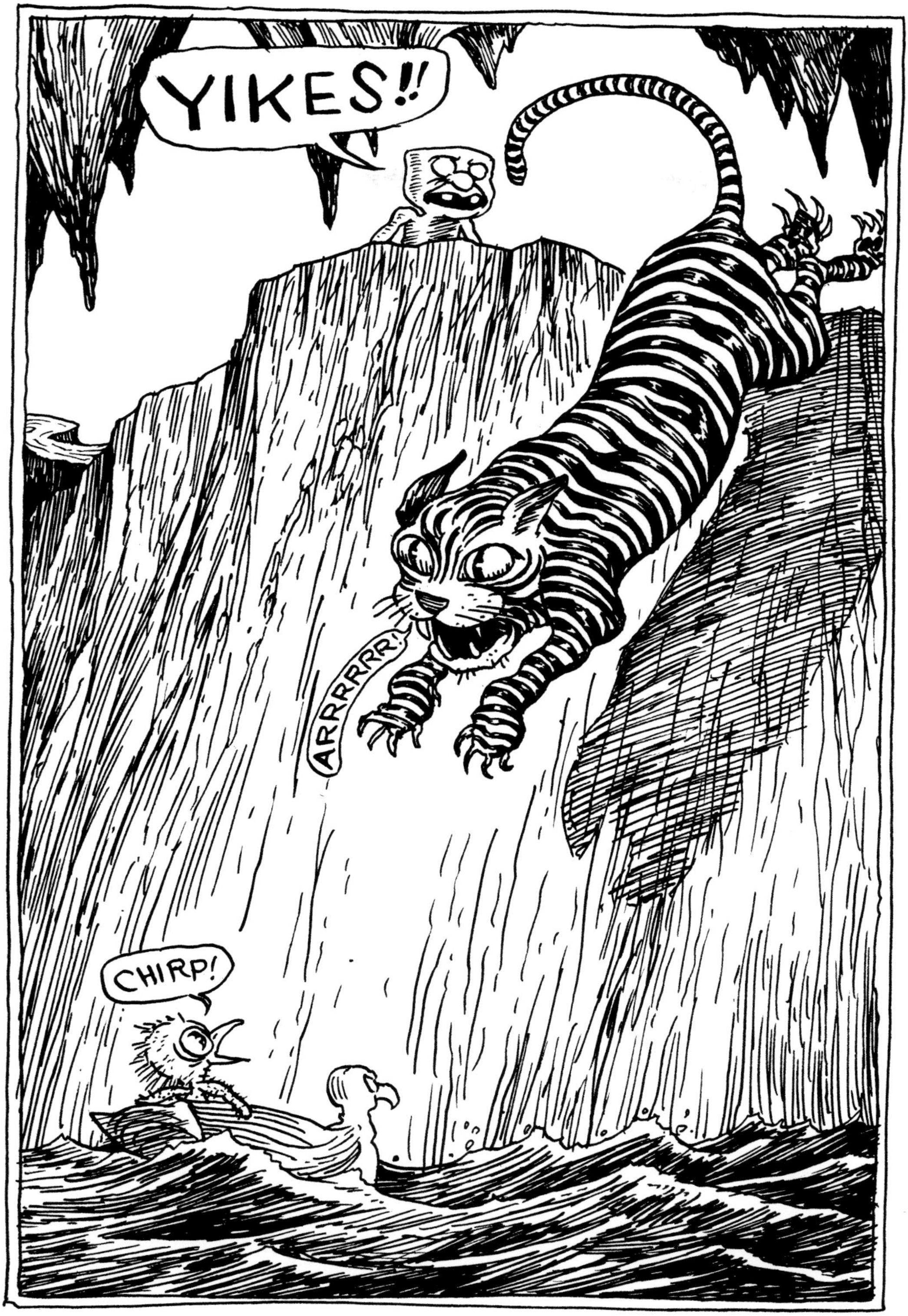
YIKES!!
ARRRRRRR!
CHIRP!

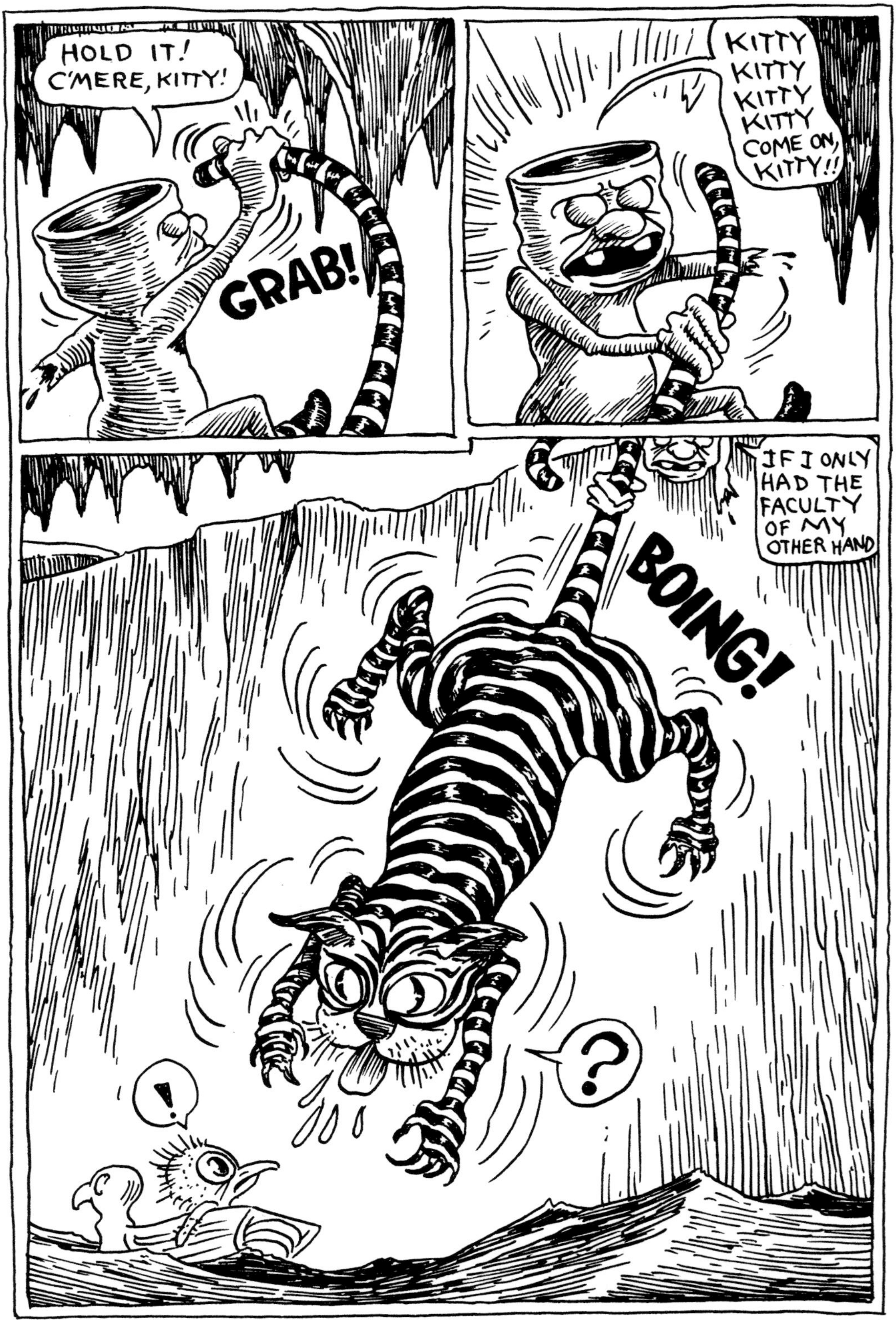
HOLD IT! C'MERE, KITTY!
GRAB!
KITTY KITTY KITTY KITTY COME ON, KITTY!!
IF I ONLY HAD THE FACULTY OF MY OTHER HAND
BOING!
?
!

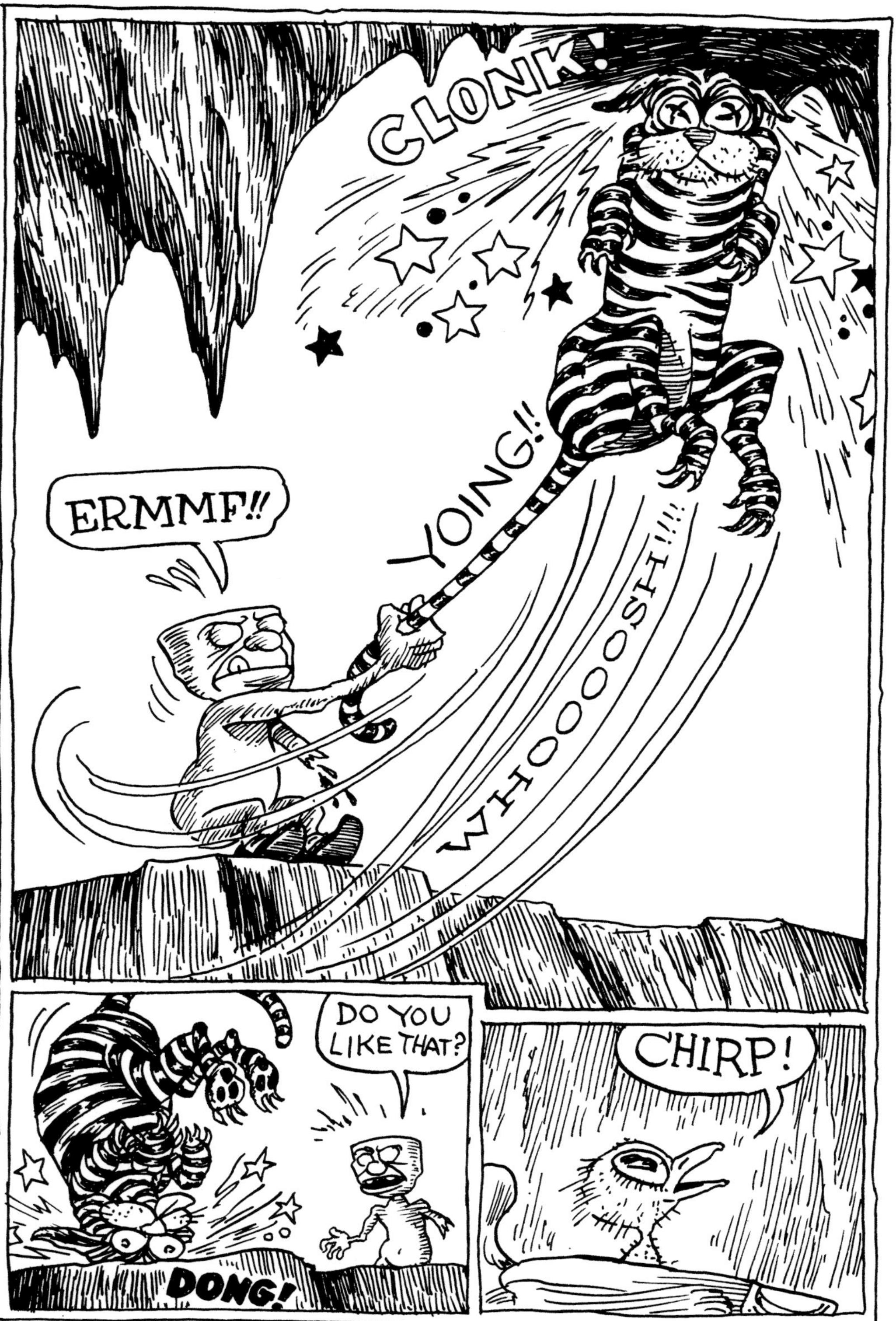
CLONK!
YOING!!
ERMMF!!
WHOOOOOSH!!!
DO YOU LIKE THAT?
DONG!
CHIRP!

WHAT'S GOT YOU TALKING ALL OF A SUDDEN, ANYWAY? I AIN'T NEVER HEARD A CAT TALK!!!

OH, YEAH, I SEE IT! IT'S BECAUSE YOUR'E SO FULL OF **WRATH** THAT YOU'RE SPITTIN' OUT WORDS!

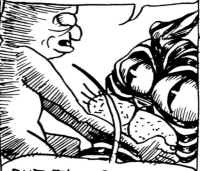

BUT I'VE SEEN YOU MAD BEFORE, YOU WEREN'T LIKE THIS! WHAT IS IT?

IT'S FOOD!!! HOW DO YOU EXPECT A PERSON TO KILL AND EAT A CUTE LITTLE BUNNY OR BIRD IF HE DON'T GET A BURNING RAGE GOING!!! AND I CAN TELL YOU, THAT BIRD'S MOTHER WAS EXTREMELY HELPFUL!

IF I DON'T HATE IT, HOW CAN I EAT IT!!?

NOW, I GET YOU!! HERE, TRY OUT YOUR **INSTINKS** ON THIS TURNIP!

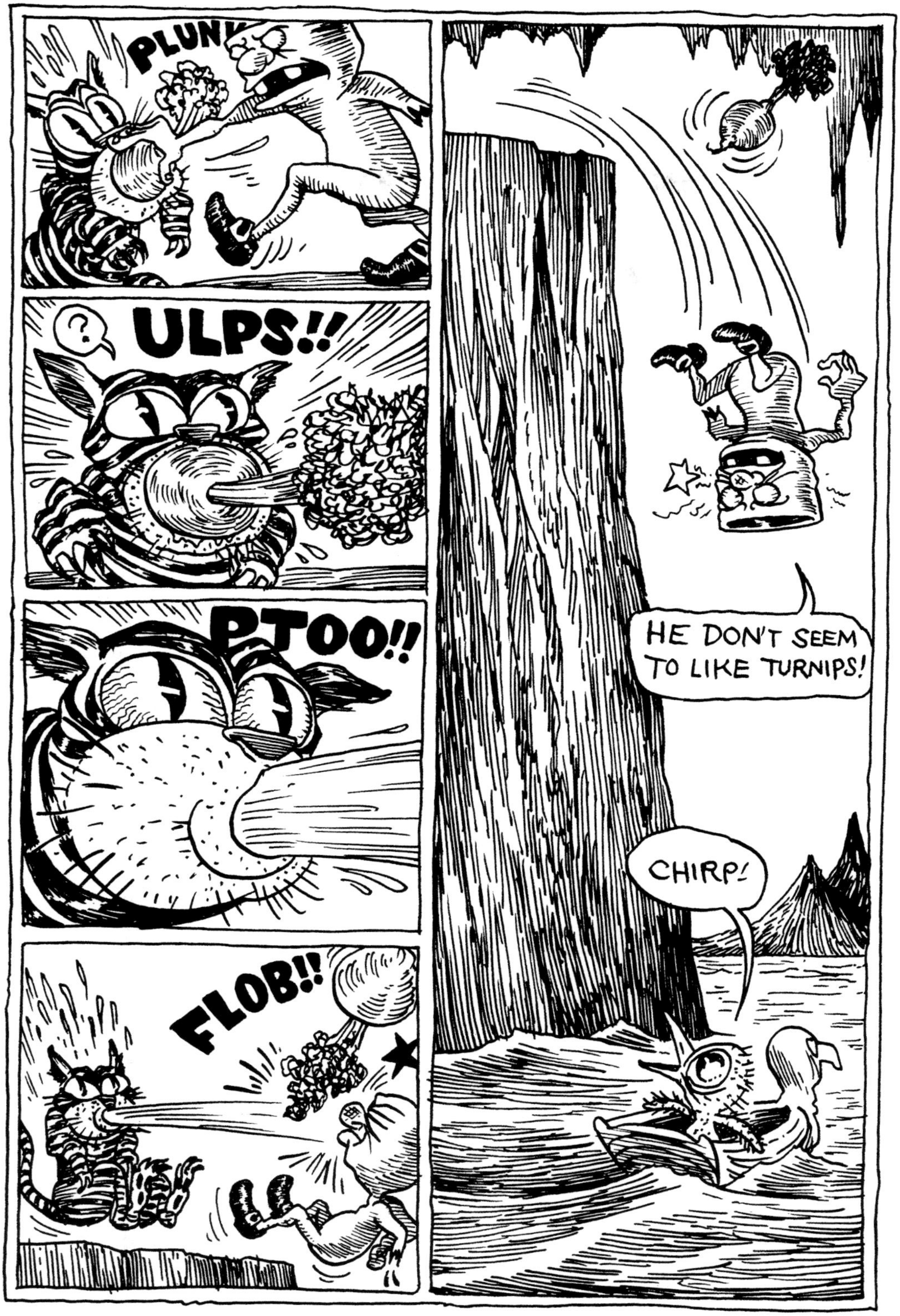

PLUNK
?
ULPS!!
PTOO!!
FLOB!!
HE DON'T SEEM TO LIKE TURNIPS!
CHIRP!

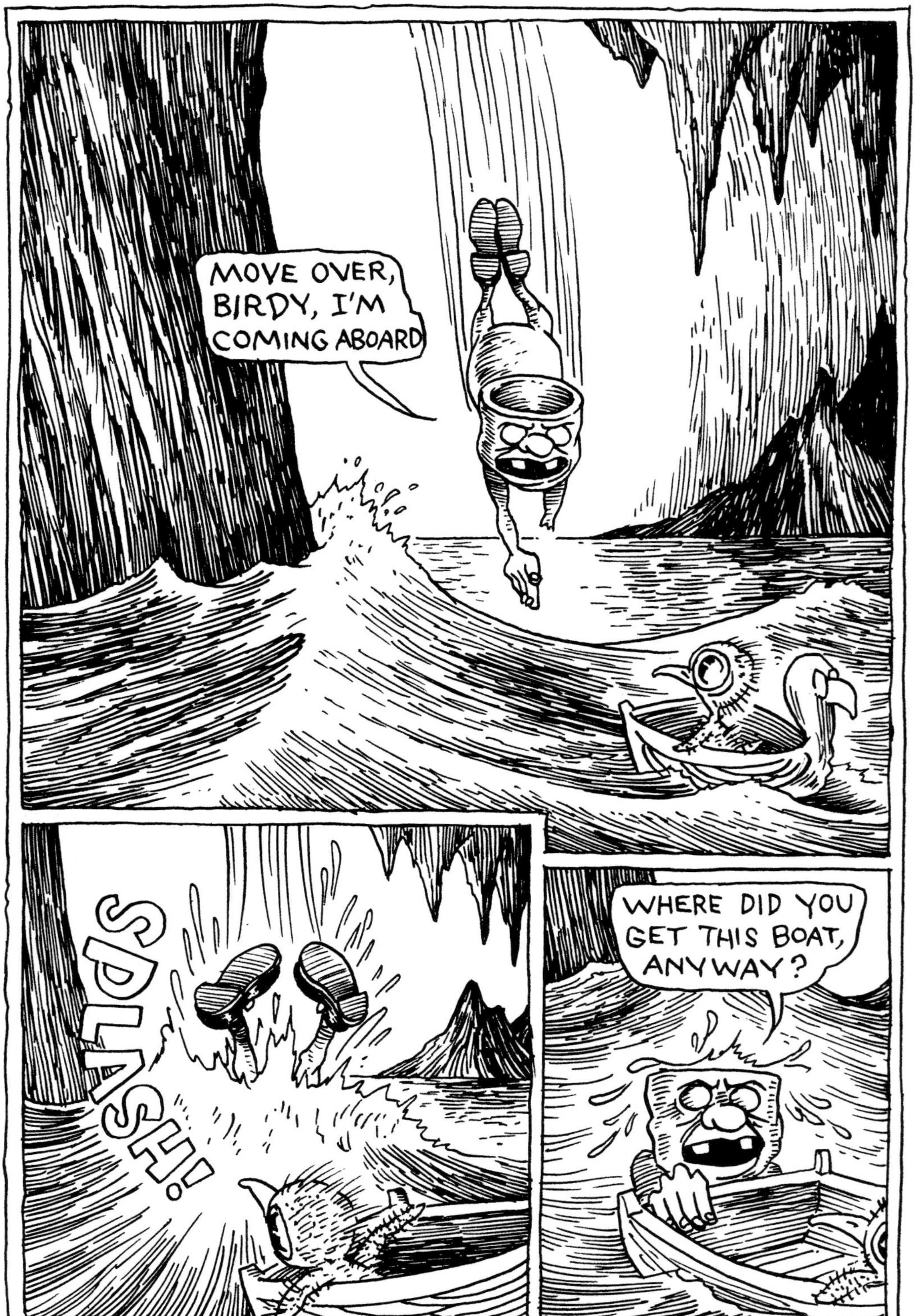
MOVE OVER, BIRDY, I'M COMING ABOARD
SPLASH!
WHERE DID YOU GET THIS BOAT, ANYWAY?

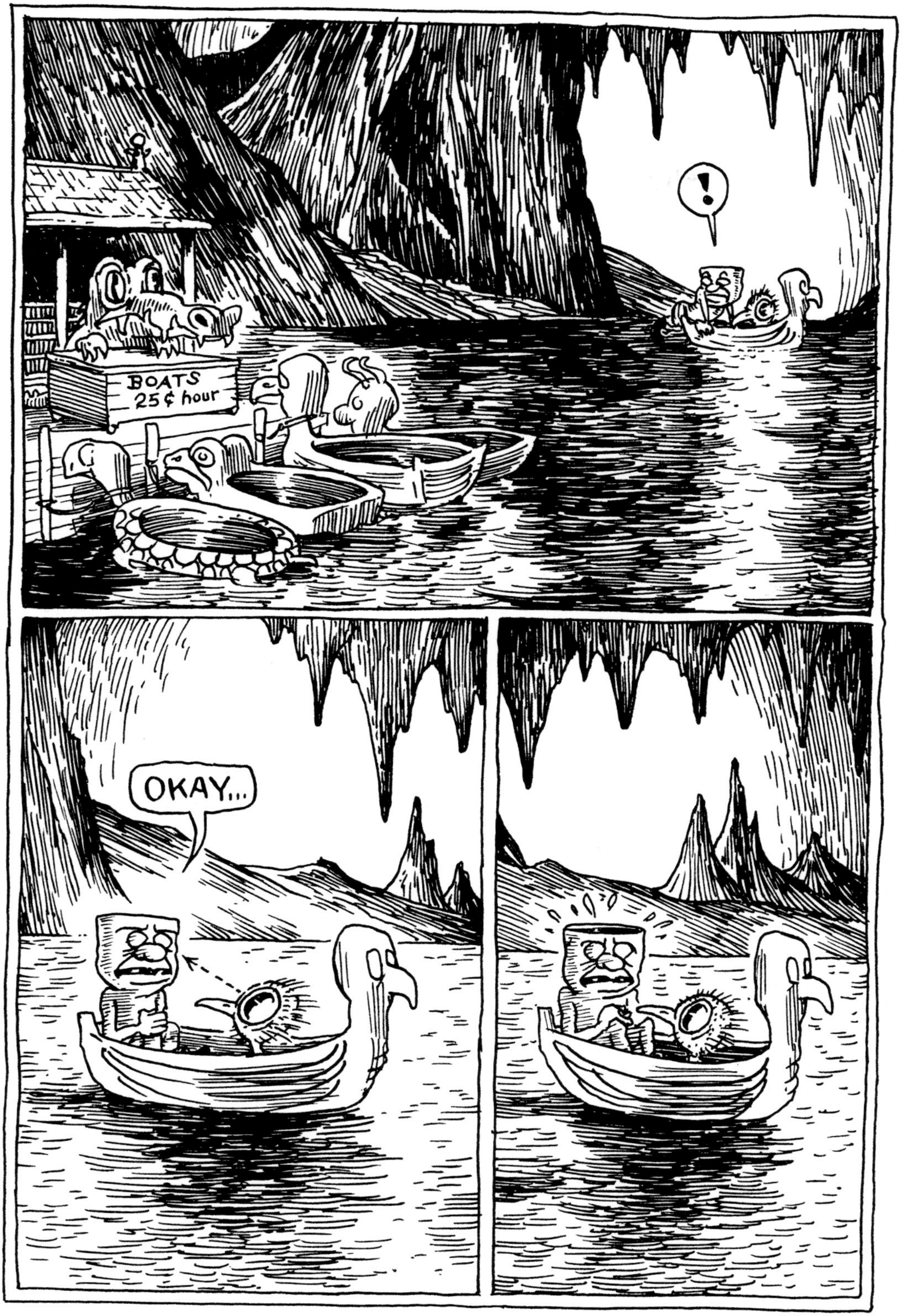
BOATS
25¢ hour
!
OKAY...

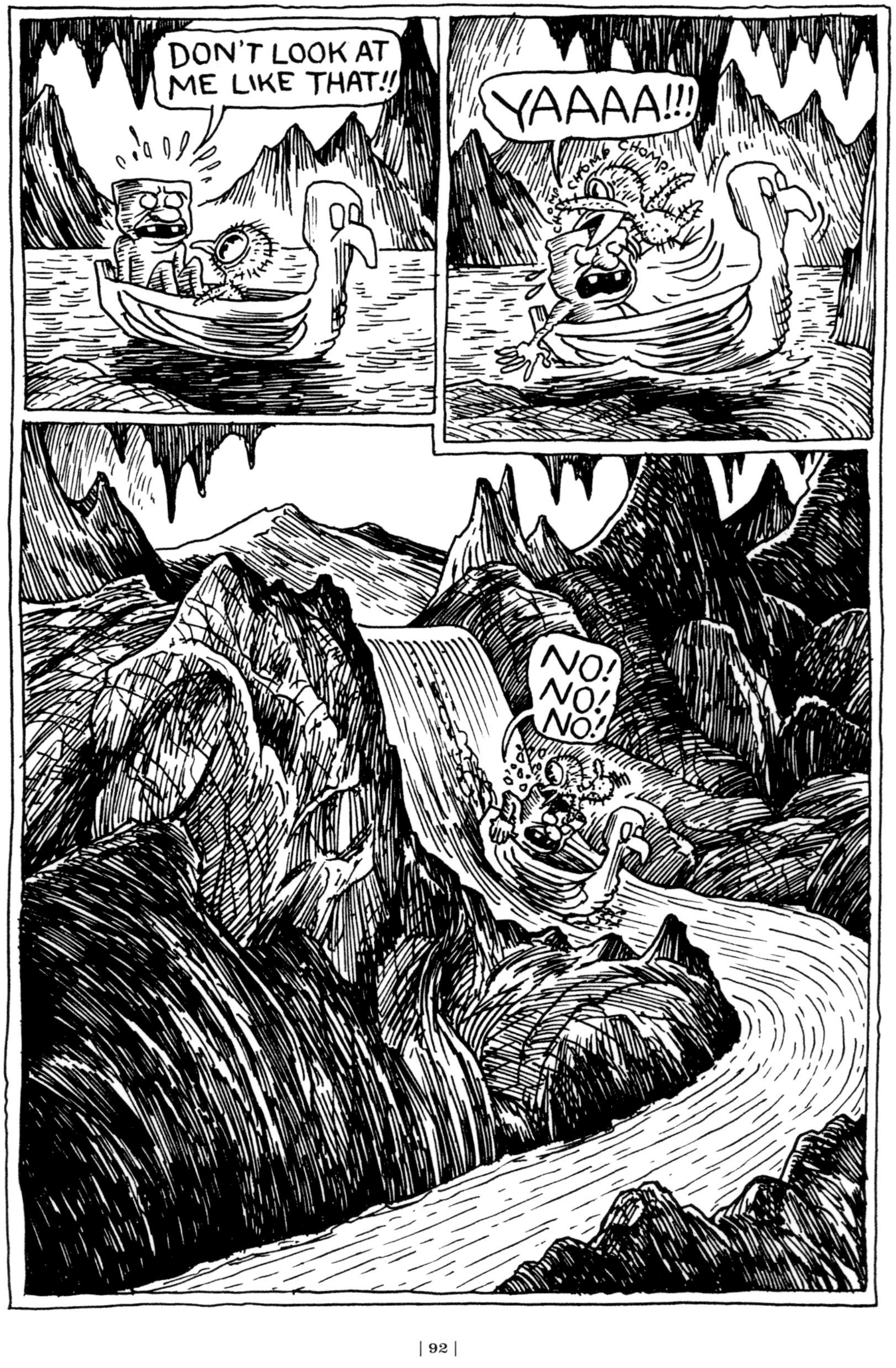
DON'T LOOK AT ME LIKE THAT!!
YAAAA!!!
CHOMP CHOMP CHOMP!
NO! NO! NO!

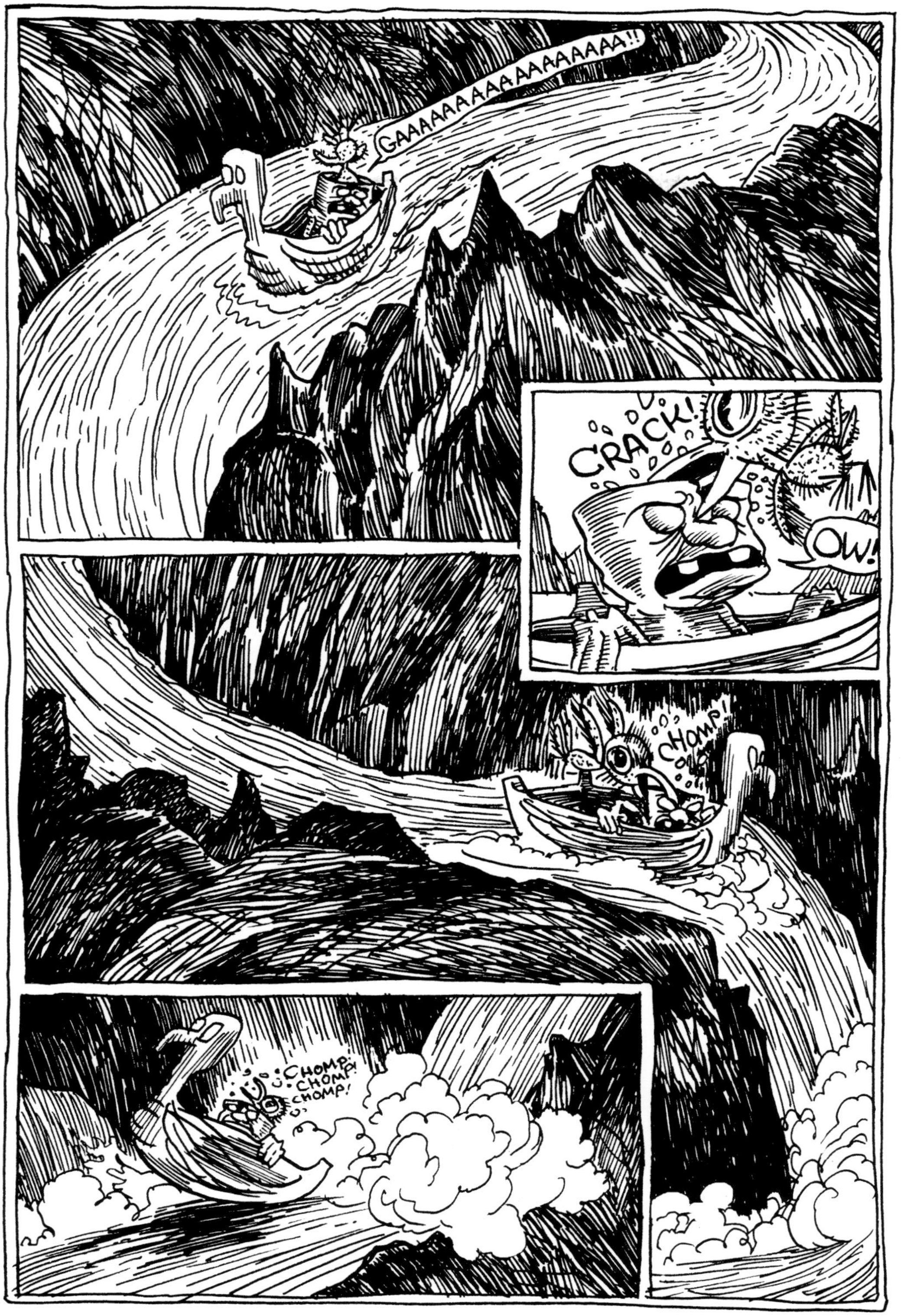
GAAAAAAAAAAAAAAAAAAA!!
CRACK!
OW!
CHOMP!
CHOMP!
CHOMP!
CHOMP!

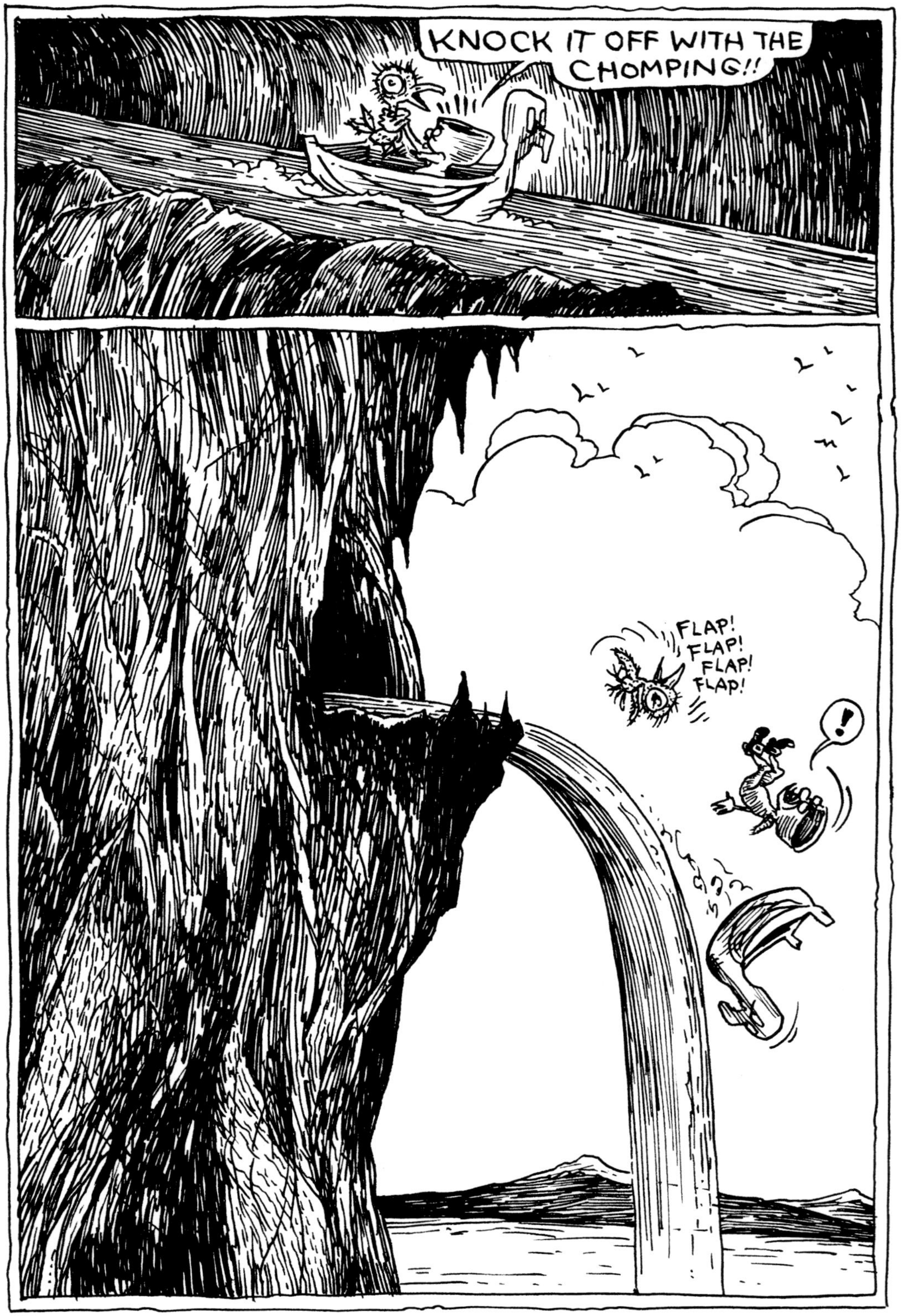
KNOCK IT OFF WITH THE CHOMPING!!
FLAP! FLAP! FLAP! FLAP!
!

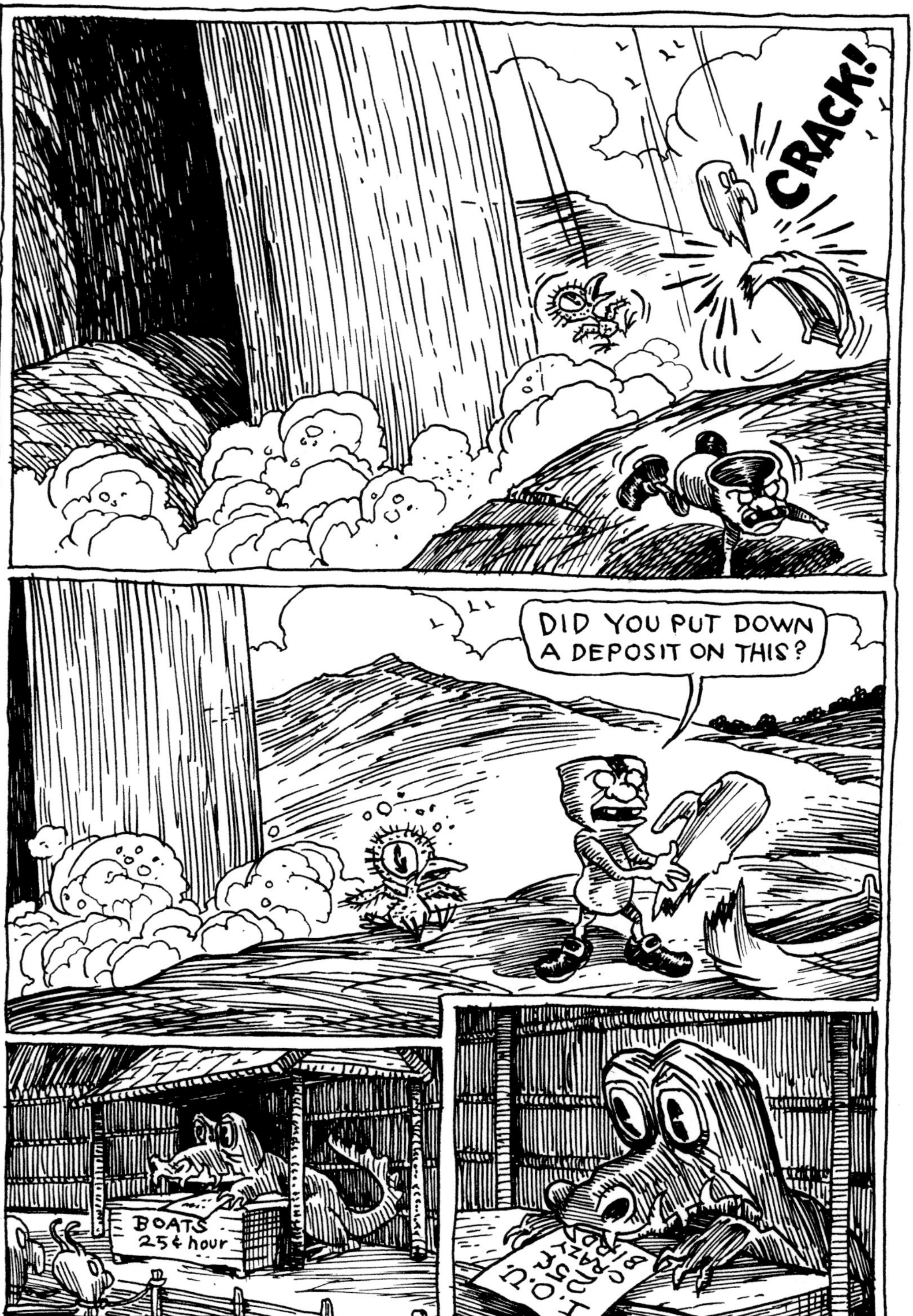
CRACK!
DID YOU PUT DOWN A DEPOSIT ON THIS?
BOATS 25¢ hour
I.O.U. 25¢
CRAZY BIRD

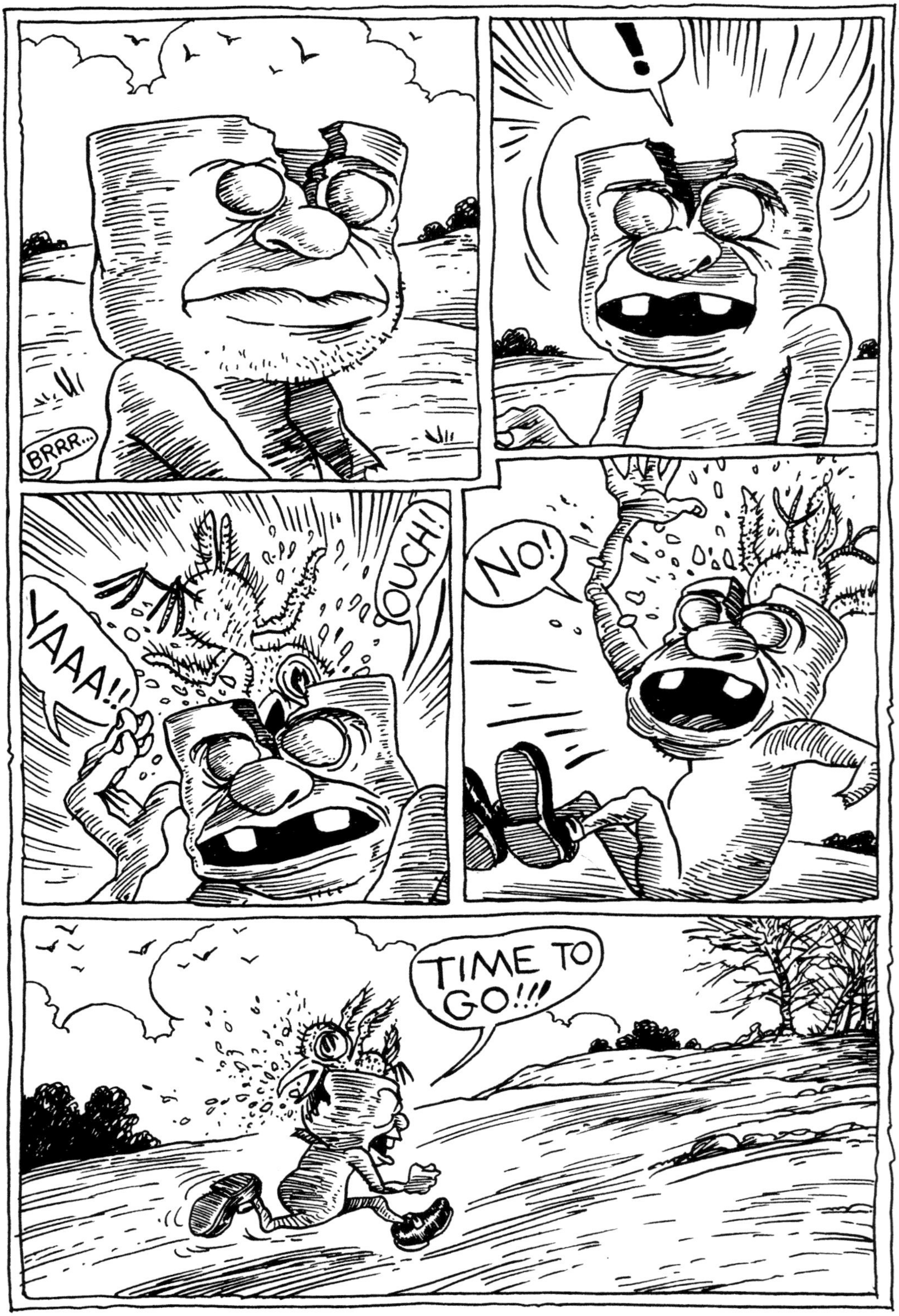
BRRR...
!
YAAAA!!!
OUCH!
NO!
TIME TO GO!!!

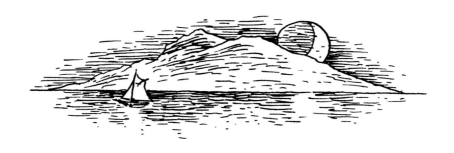

❅ Chapter Three ❆

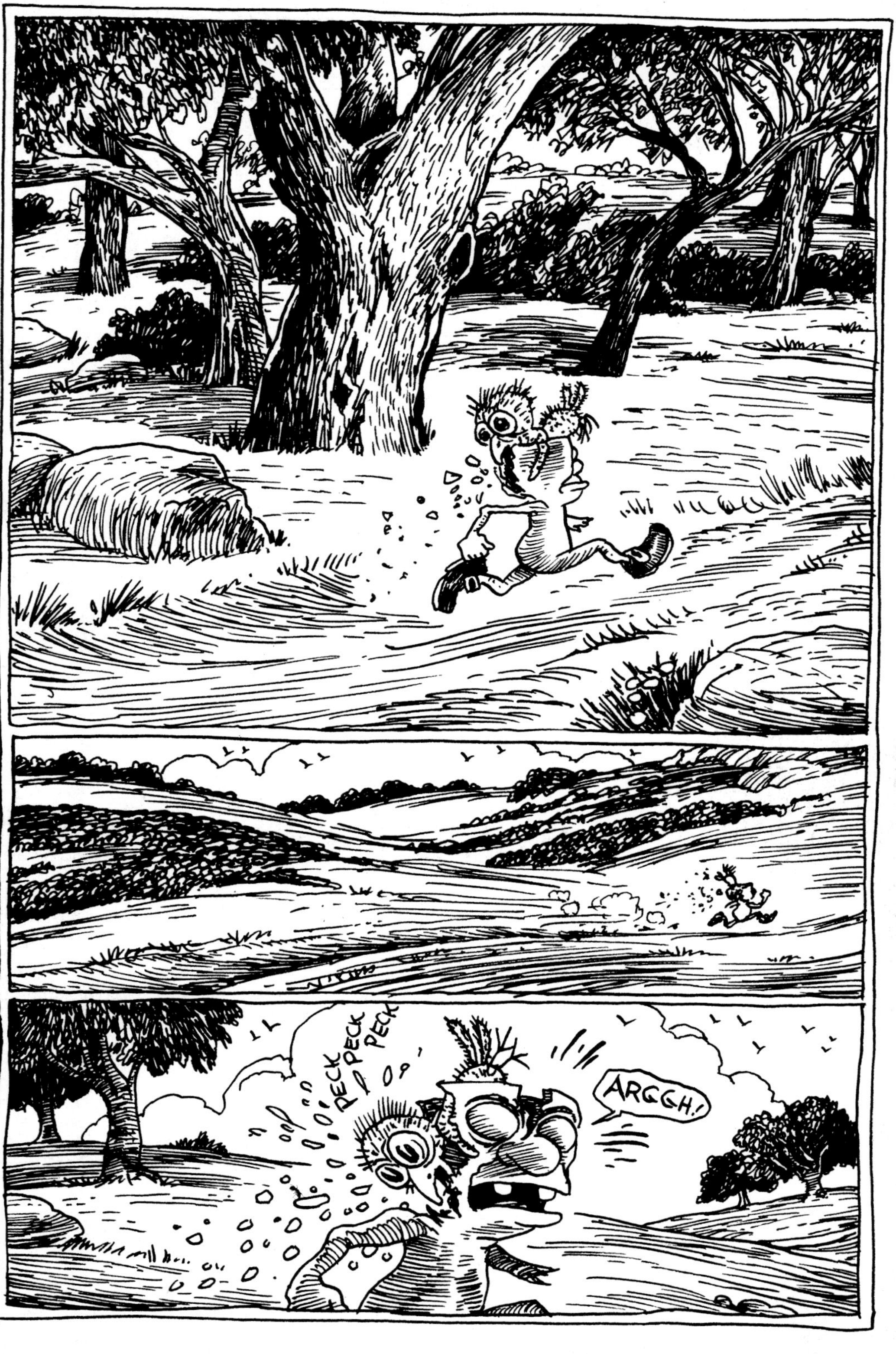
PECK PECK PECK
ARGGH!

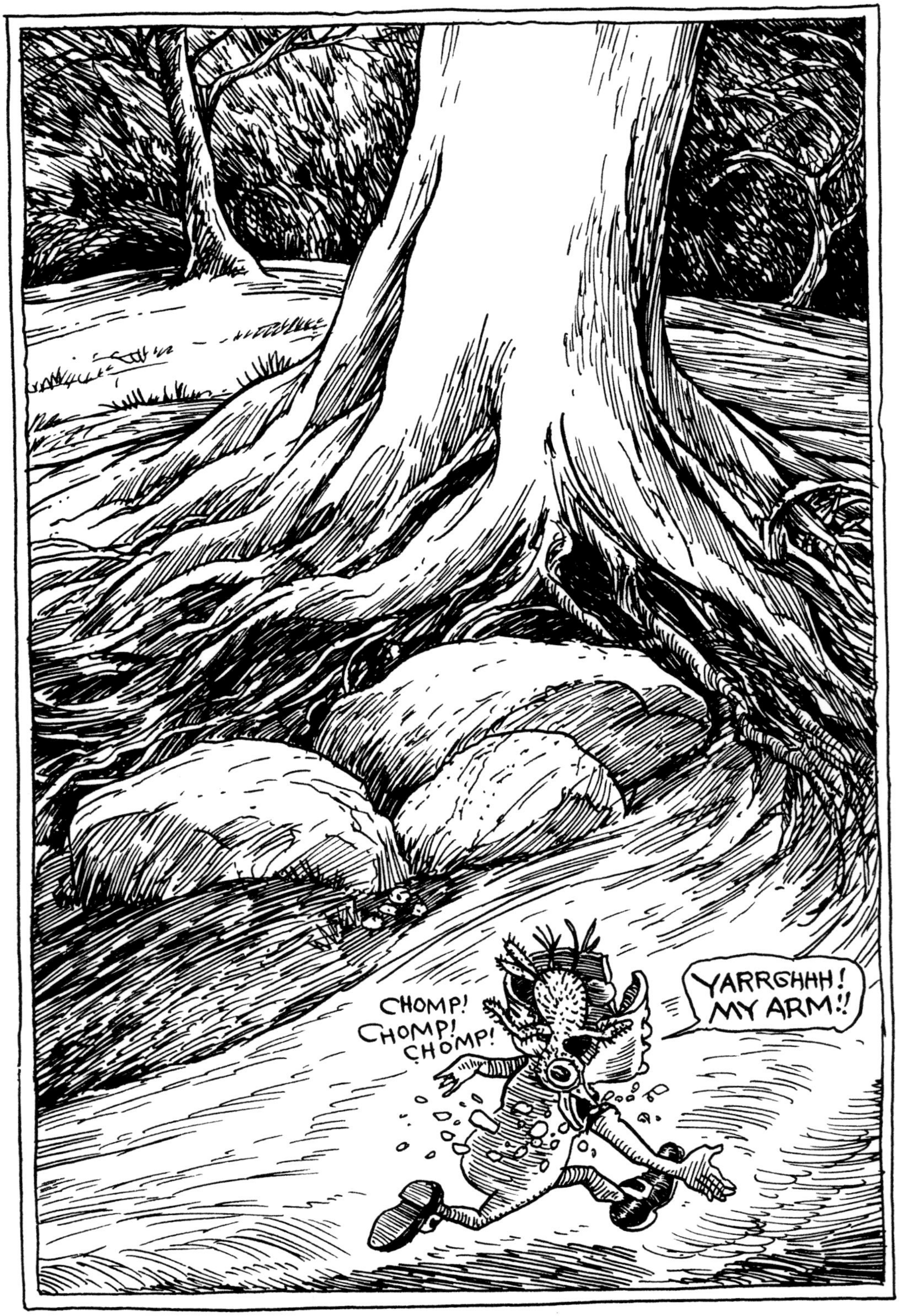
CHOMP! CHOMP! CHOMP!
YARRGHHH! MY ARM!!

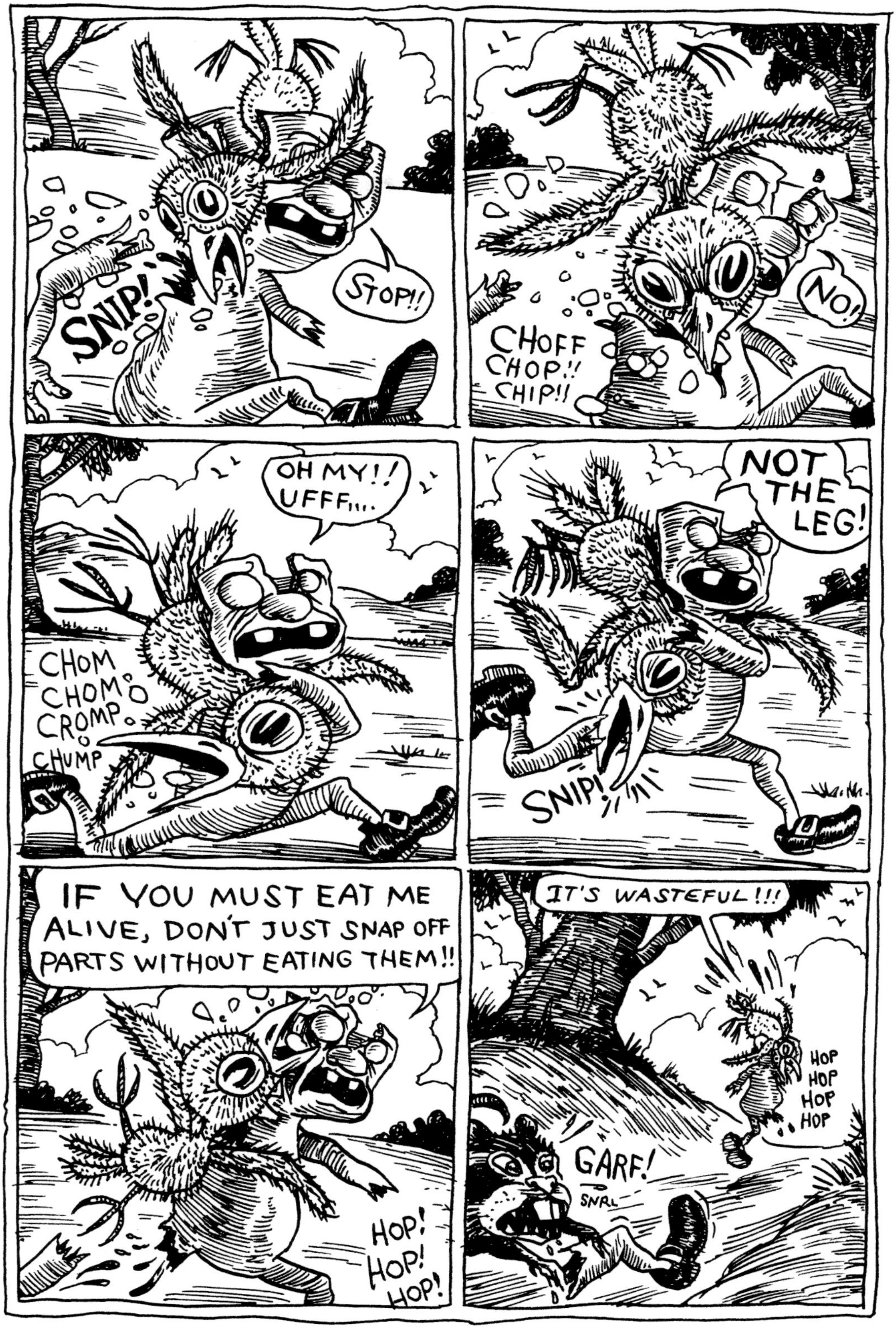
SNIP!
STOP!!
CHOFF
CHOP!!
CHIP!!
NO!
OH MY!! UFFF....
CHOM
CHOM
CROMP
CHUMP
NOT THE LEG!
SNIP!
IF YOU MUST EAT ME ALIVE, DON'T JUST SNAP OFF PARTS WITHOUT EATING THEM!!
HOP!
HOP!
HOP!
IT'S WASTEFUL!!!
HOP
HOP
HOP
HOP
GARF!
SNRL

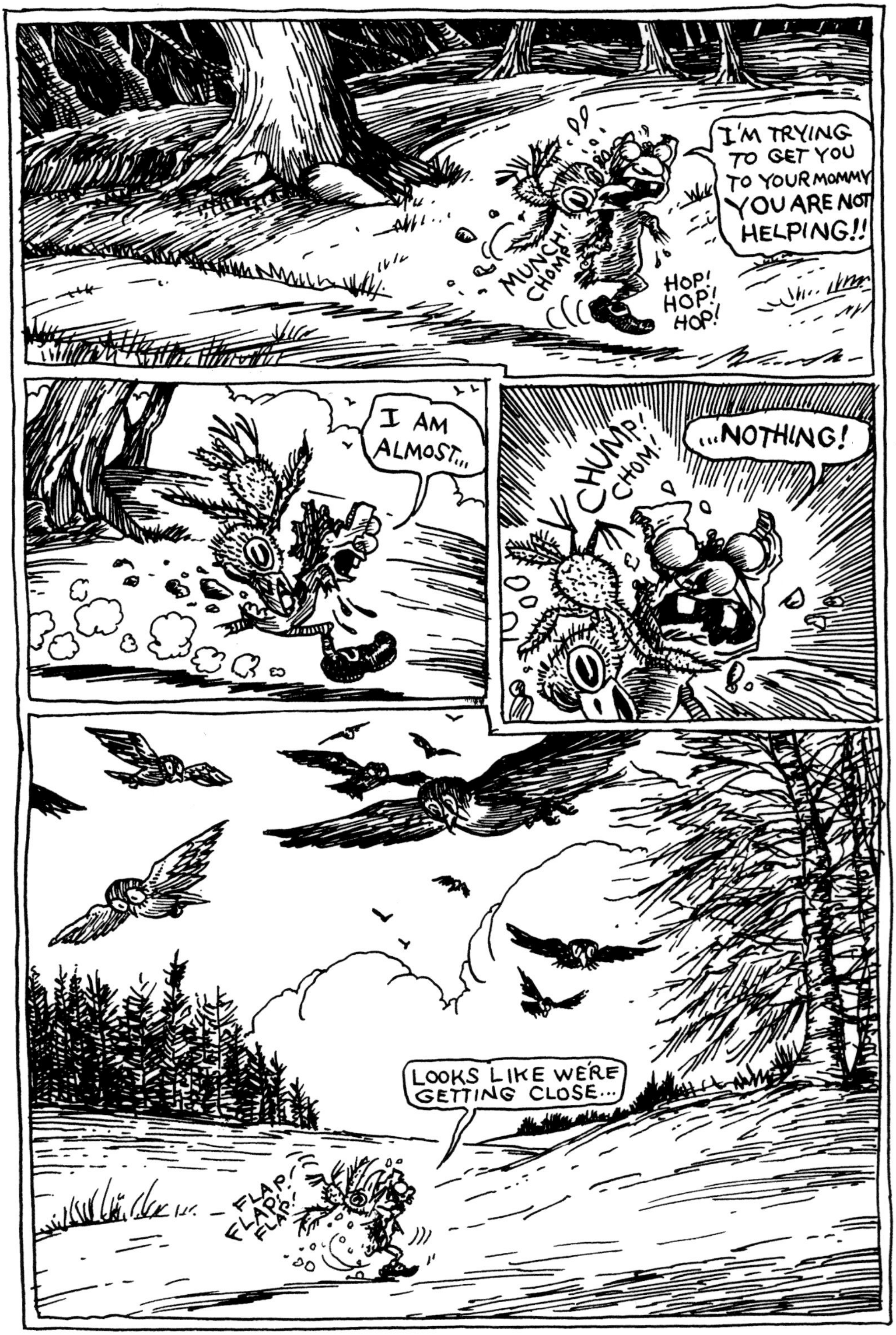
MUNCH! CHOMP!
I'M TRYING TO GET YOU TO YOUR MOMMY YOU ARE NOT HELPING!!
HOP! HOP! HOP!
I AM ALMOST...
CHUMP! CHOM!
...NOTHING!
LOOKS LIKE WE'RE GETTING CLOSE...
FLAP! FLAP! FLAP!

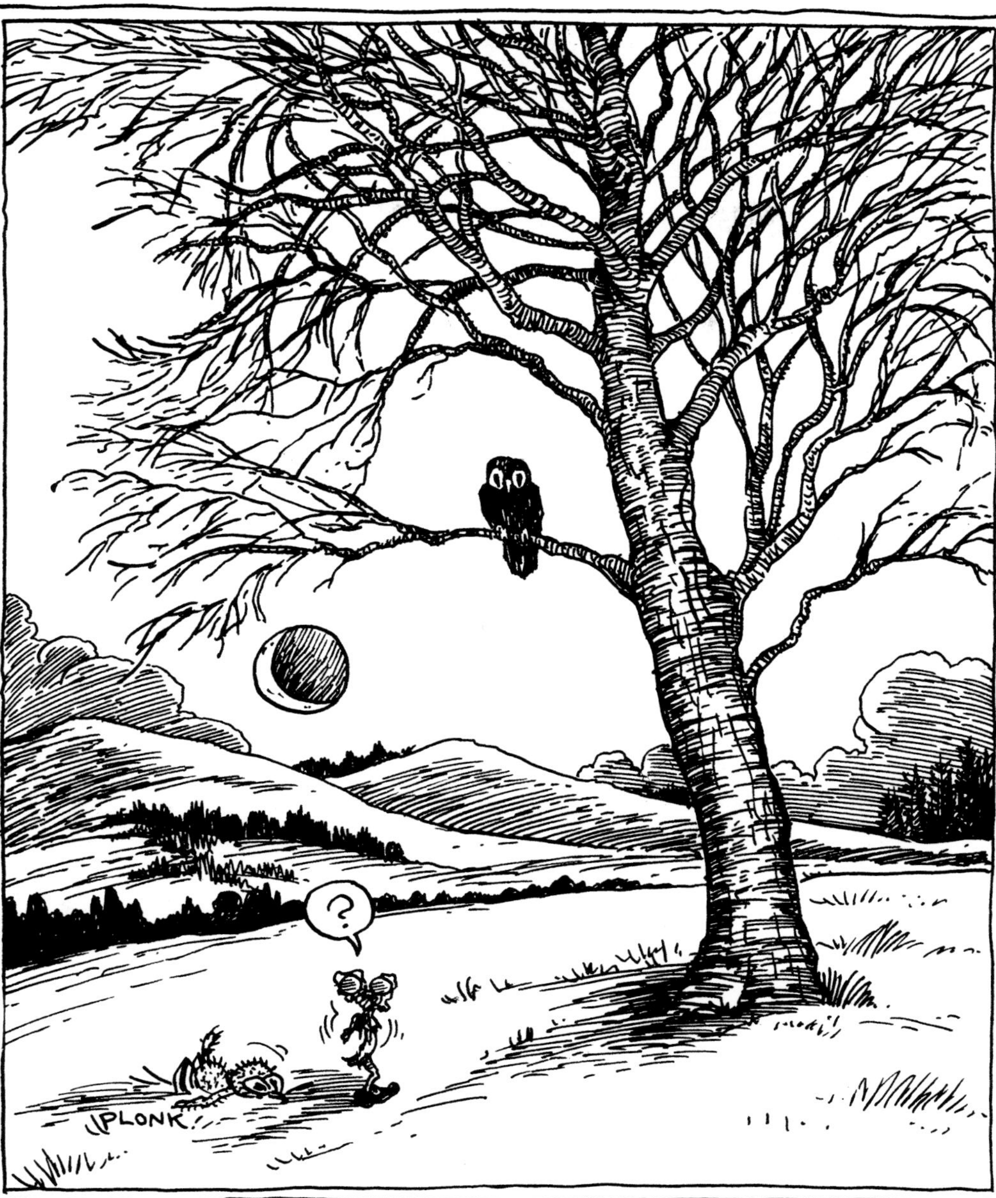
?
PLONK

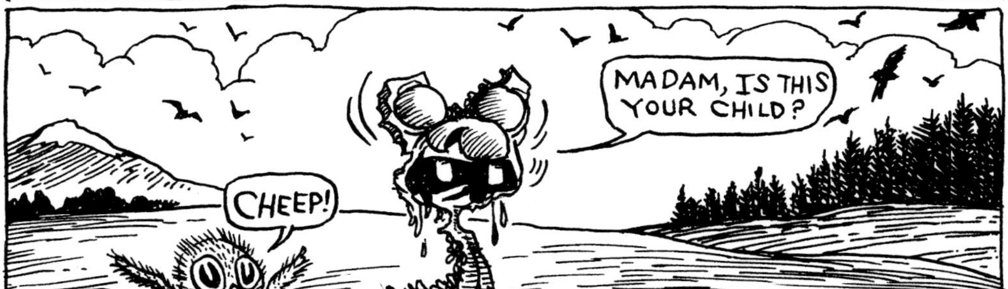
MADAM, IS THIS YOUR CHILD?
CHEEP!

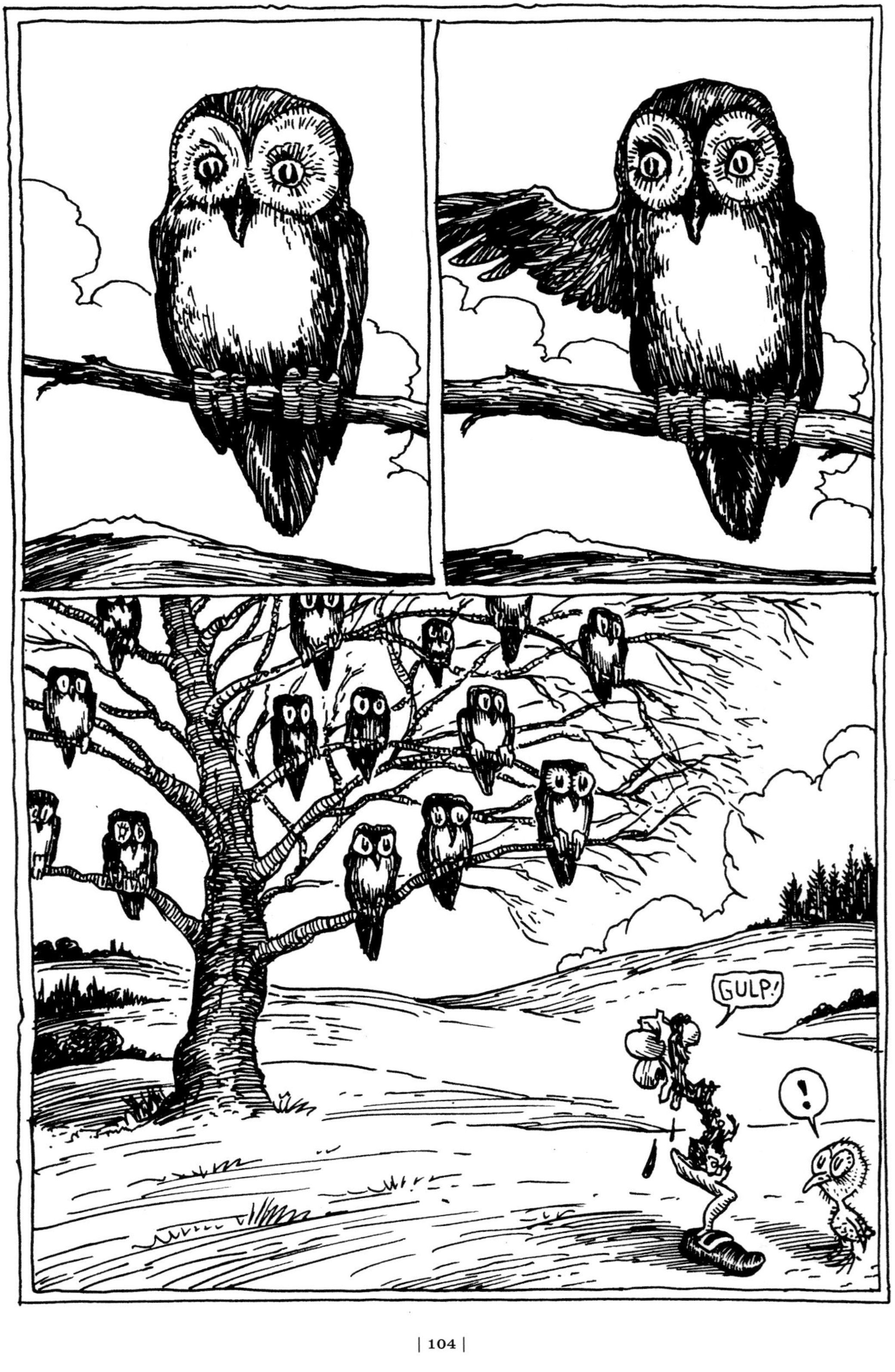
GULP!
!

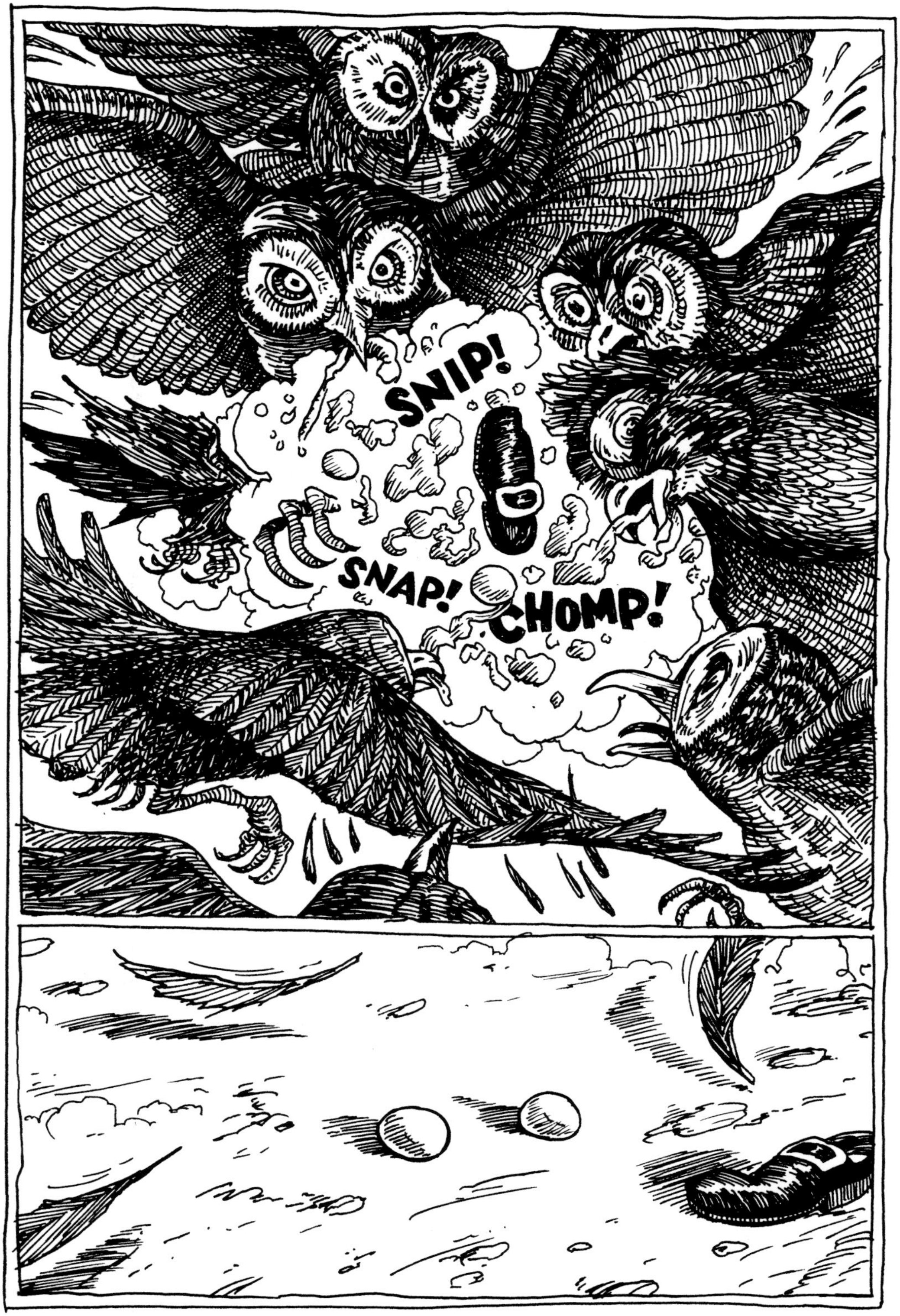
SNIP!
SNAP!
CHOMP!

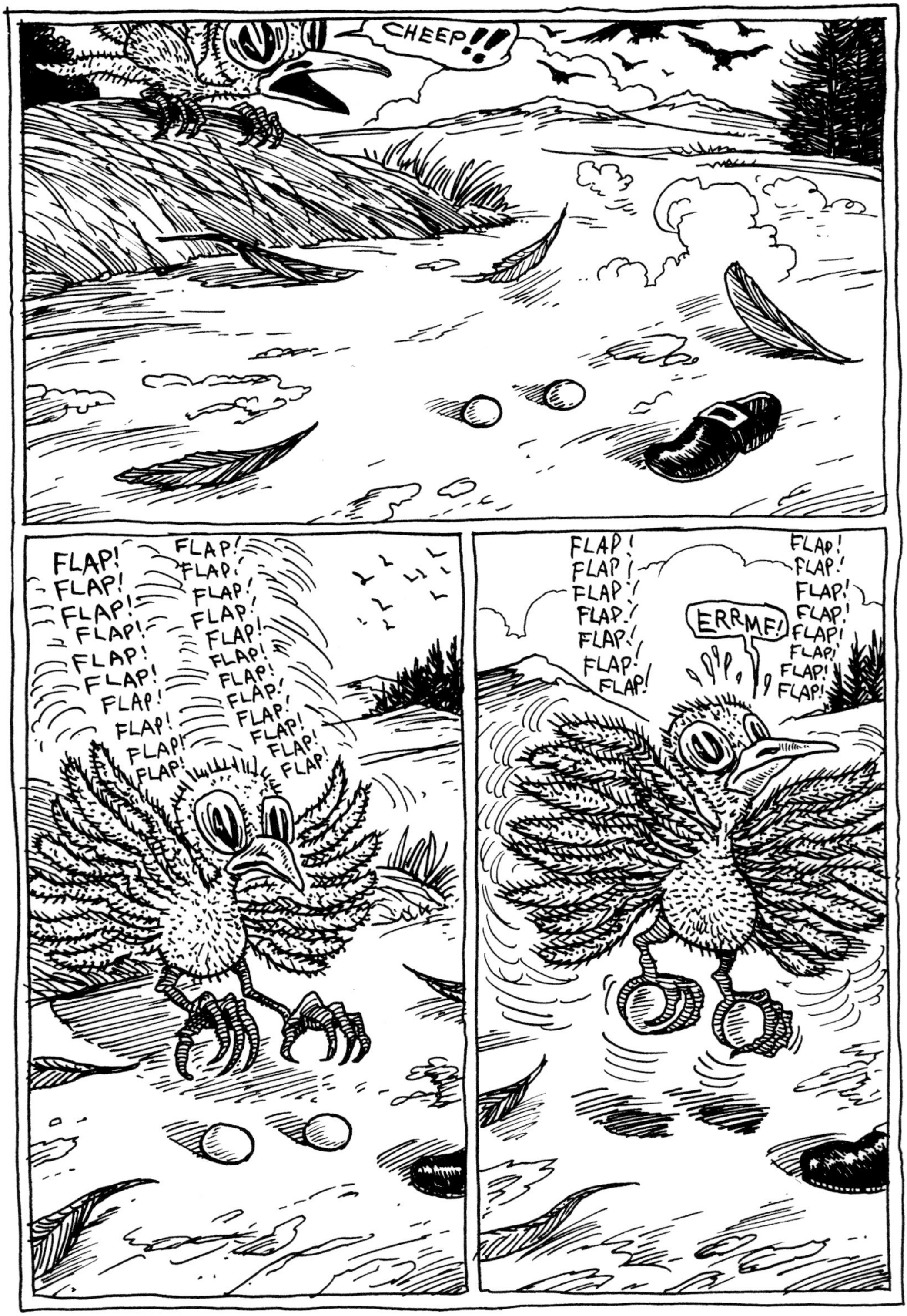
CHEEP!!
FLAP! FLAP! FLAP! FLAP! FLAP! FLAP! FLAP! FLAP! FLAP! FLAP!
FLAP! FLAP! FLAP! FLAP! FLAP! FLAP! FLAP! FLAP! FLAP! FLAP! FLAP! FLAP!
FLAP! FLAP! FLAP! FLAP! FLAP! FLAP! FLAP!
ERRMF!
FLAP! FLAP! FLAP! FLAP! FLAP! FLAP! FLAP! FLAP!

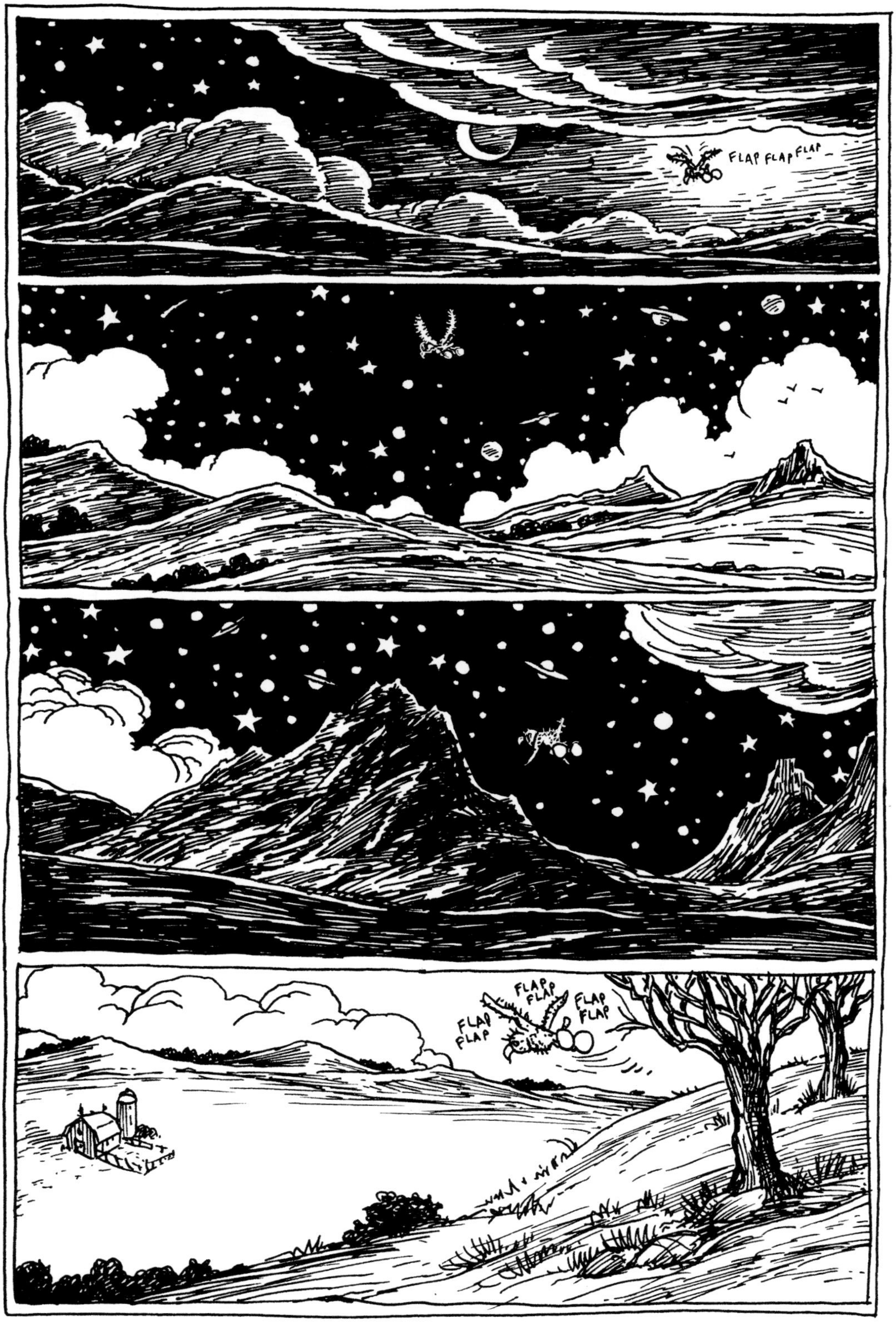
FLAP FLAP FLAP
FLAP FLAP
FLAP FLAP
FLAP FLAP

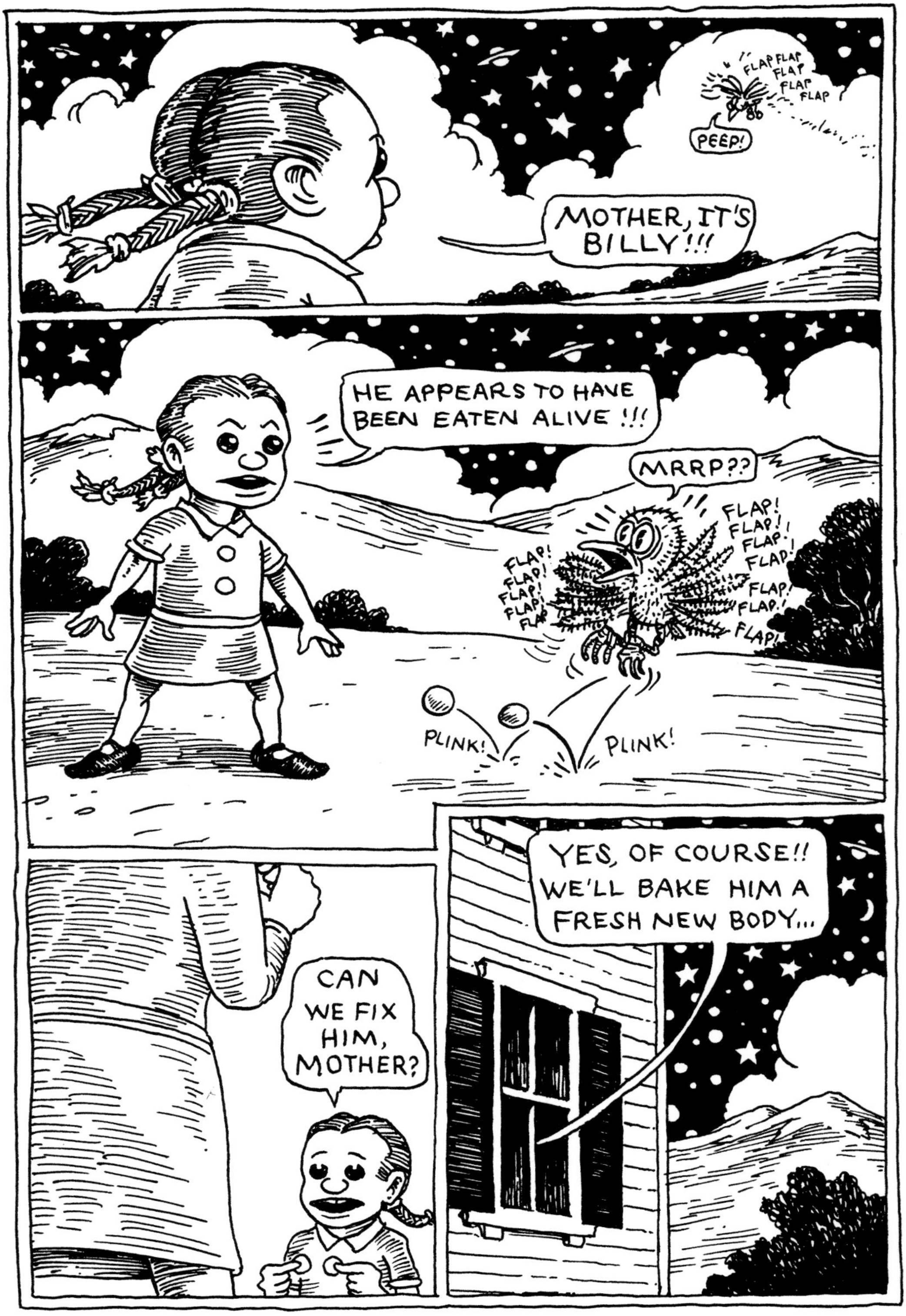
FLAP FLAP FLAP FLAP FLAP FLAP
PEEP!
MOTHER, IT'S BILLY!!!
HE APPEARS TO HAVE BEEN EATEN ALIVE!!!
MRRP??
FLAP! FLAP! FLAP! FLAP! FLAP!
FLAP! FLAP! FLAP! FLAP! FLAP! FLAP! FLAP!
PLINK!
PLINK!
CAN WE FIX HIM, MOTHER?
YES, OF COURSE!! WE'LL BAKE HIM A FRESH NEW BODY...

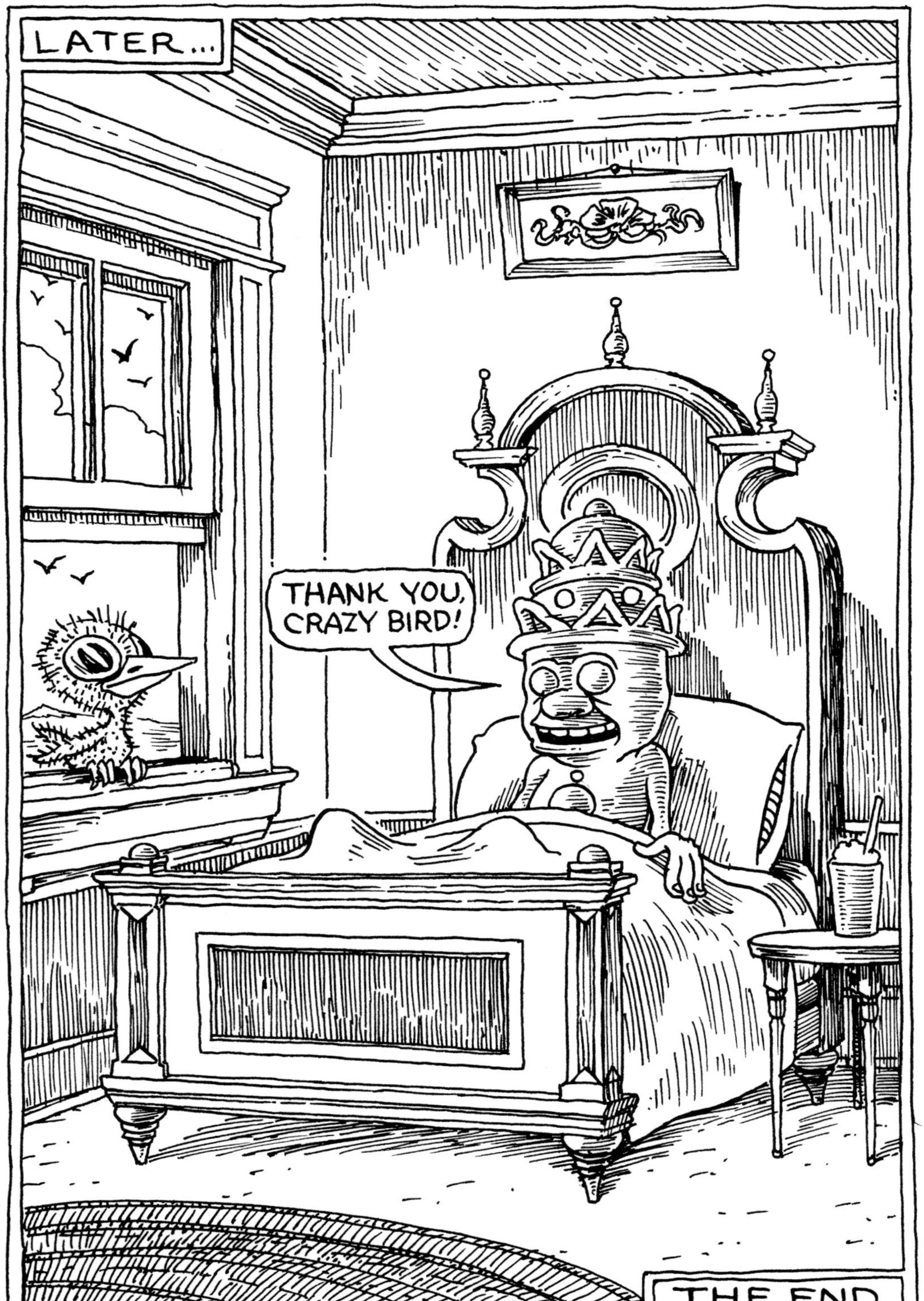
LATER...
THANK YOU, CRAZY BIRD!
THE END

☾ The End ☽

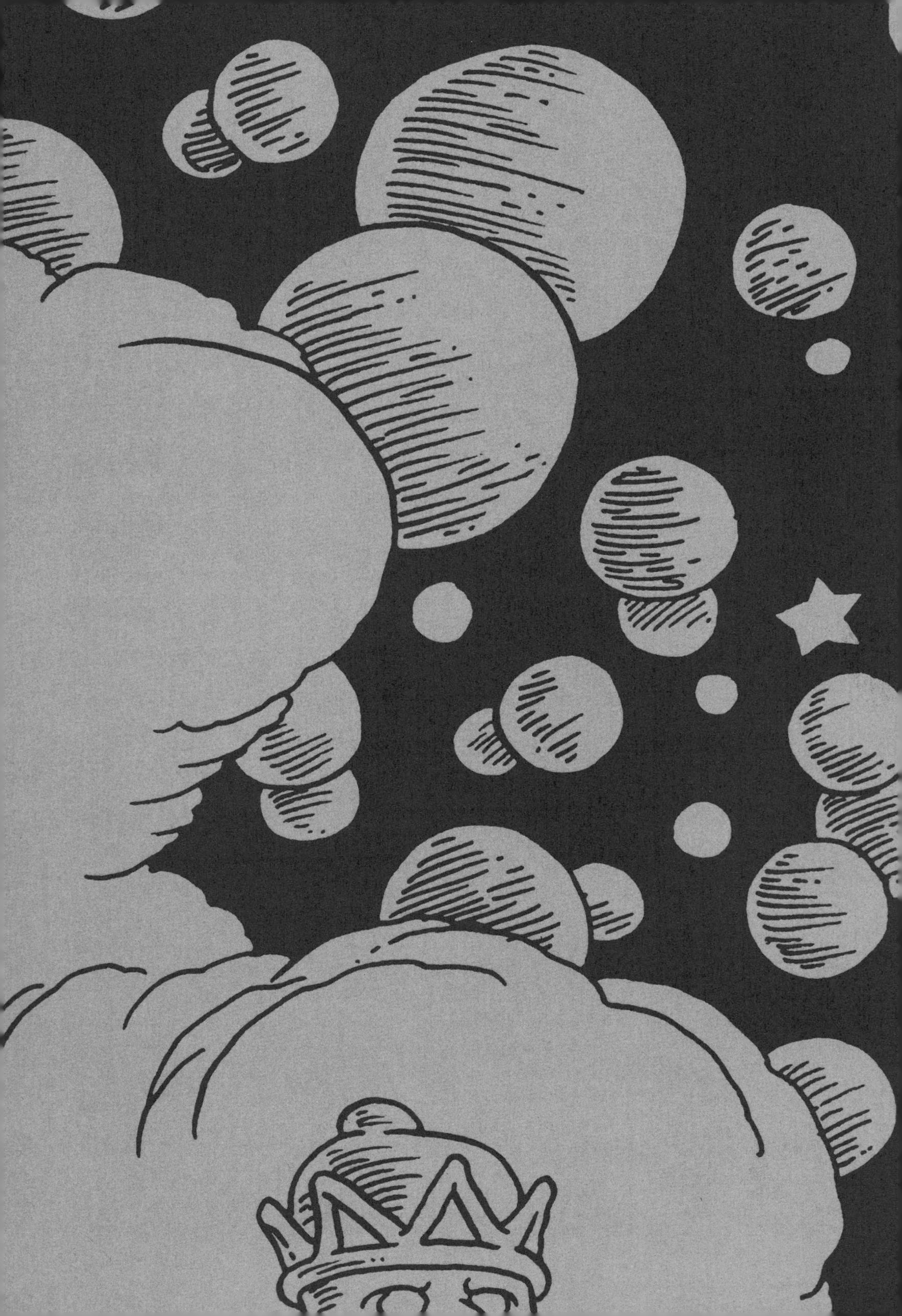